Searching the Grey Literature

MEDICAL LIBRARY ASSOCIATION BOOKS

The Medical Library Association (MLA) features books that showcase the expertise of health sciences librarians for other librarians and professionals.

MLA Books are excellent resources for librarians in hospitals, medical research practice, and other settings. These volumes will provide health care professionals and patients with accurate information that can improve outcomes and save lives.

Each book in the series has been overseen editorially since conception by the Medical Library Association Books Panel, composed of MLA members with expertise spanning the breadth of health sciences librarianship.

Medical Library Association Books Panel
Kristen L. Young, AHIP, chair
Dorothy Ogdon, AHIP, chair designate
Michel C. Atlas
Carolann Lee Curry
Kelsey Leonard, AHIP
Karen McElfresh, AHIP
JoLinda L. Thompson, AHIP
Heidi Heilemann, AHIP, board liaison

About the Medical Library Association
Founded in 1898, MLA is a 501(c)(3) nonprofit, educational organization of 3,500 individual and institutional members in the health sciences information field that provides lifelong educational opportunities, supports a knowledgebase of health information research, and works with a global network of partners to promote the importance of quality information for improved health to the health care community and the public.

Books in the Series:
The Medical Library Association Guide to Providing Consumer and Patient Health Information edited by Michele Spatz

Health Sciences Librarianship edited by M. Sandra Wood

Curriculum-Based Library Instruction: From Cultivating Faculty Relationships to Assessment edited by Amy Blevins and Megan Inman

The Small Library Manager's Handbook by Alice Graves

Mobile Technologies for Every Library by Ann Whitney Gleason

The Medical Library Association Guide to Answering Questions about the Affordable Care Act edited by Emily Vardell

Marketing for Special and Academic Libraries: A Planning and Best Practices 6. Sourcebook by Patricia Higginbottom and Valerie Gordon

Interprofessional Education and Medical Libraries: Partnering for Success edited by Mary E. Edwards

Searching the Grey Literature

A Handbook for Searching Reports, Working Papers, and Other Unpublished Research

Sarah Bonato

ROWMAN & LITTLEFIELD
Lanham • Boulder • New York • London

A wholly owned subsidiary of The Rowman & Littlefield Publishing Group, Inc.
4501 Forbes Boulevard, Suite 200, Lanham, Maryland 20706'
www.rowman.com
Published by Rowman & Littlefield

Unit A, Whitacre Mews, 26-34 Stannary Street, London SE11 4AB

British Library Cataloguing in Publication Information Available

Library of Congress Cataloging-in-Publication Data Available

ISBN 9781538100639 (cloth: alk. paper) | ISBN 9781538100646 (pbk. : alk. paper) |
ISBN 9781538100653 (electronic)

♾™ The paper used in this publication meets the minimum requirements of American
National Standard for Information Sciences—Permanence of Paper for Printed Library
Materials, ANSI/NISO Z39.48-1992.

Printed in the United States of America

Contents

Preface

Grey literature is ubiquitous. While listening to or reading the daily news, you may come across news stories about the nationwide rise of fentanyl-related drug overdoses, refugee mental health, water safety in rural communities, the presence of the alt-right on college campuses, or even a local news story on the cost of affordable housing in Los Angeles. These stories all have a common thread: they are news items originating from grey literature publications by such organizations as the Centers for Disease Control and Prevention, the World Health Organization, the Environmental Protection Agency, the Southern Poverty Law Center, and the Public Policy Institute of California. While the "white literature" of books or journal articles is indeed essential for identifying relevant research, grey literature is an indispensable source for accessing prevailing information on trending topics. One example would be the current international opiate crisis—much of the most significant and recent information is produced by local public health agencies, federal agencies, and non-governmental organizations.

Searching the Grey Literature: A Handbook for Searching Reports, Working Papers, and Other Unpublished Research is intended for librarians and information professionals who are interested in learning more about grey literature and aspire to add grey literature sources to their search methods. If you have ever been asked for a grey literature search but were unsure where to start, this book will help you tackle your search successfully. If you are an expert searcher but find that your library patrons are unfamiliar—perhaps insufferably so—with myriad grey literature sources, this book will be a constructive teaching aid. Those who are both new arrivals and established professionals in the field of librarianship may increase their knowledge about grey literature by reading this book, and perhaps acquire new searching skills and expertise. Although a wide range of librarians or information professionals working in various disciplines might find the content of this book useful, those working in the areas of health or social sciences will benefit the most from this book's content.

HOW TO USE THIS BOOK

Searching the Grey Literature is divided into eleven chapters that discuss distinct aspects of grey literature, including: an introduction to grey literature; the value of grey literature; search sources for grey literature; crafting a needs assessment before commencing a grey literature search; and resources and tips for keeping current on new developments in grey literature. Chapter 1 provides background information on grey literature, including the numerous definitions of grey literature, a short history of grey literature, and specific types of grey literature. Chapter 2 explores the often-overlooked value of grey literature, including how grey literature is a unique source of information and its specific research value in medical and health-related disciplines. Chapters 3 through 9 all discuss specific search sources for identifying relevant grey literature, including search tips and proposed decision aids to include in a search source, as well as grey literature document types in a search. Chapter 3 addresses both the strengths and weaknesses of databases as a search source for locating relevant grey literature publications and includes a list of select databases. Chapter 4 specifically discusses the grey literature document type of dissertations, including the noteworthy contribution of dissertations and a list of select search sources for identifying relevant dissertations. Chapter 5 is on unpublished clinical trials and other unpublished research studies; it also includes a list of select clinical trial registries and other sources for unpublished clinical trials and similar unpublished research. Chapter 6 is on institutional repositories as a grey literature search source and includes information on how to identify relevant repositories. Chapter 7 discusses notable characteristics of conference publications as a grey literature document type and includes a select list of resources for identifying relevant conference publications. Chapter 8 focuses on grey literature search checklists and other similar sources as a method for identifying relevant grey literature documents; it provides a brief list of select sources. Chapter 9 explores Google and other related Google-powered search tools, such as Google Scholar for grey literature searching, and makes suggestions regarding the best methods for adapting searches to identify grey literature documents. Chapter 10 builds on all of the information presented in earlier chapters in order to select the most suitable search method for a grey literature search. What types of questions should you ask before commencing a grey literature search? For example: What is the aim of the grey literature search? What grey literature document types should be included? Which search sources should be selected, and how should the search results be recorded? A short list of samples of completed grey literature searches is also included. Chapter 11 suggests resources for keeping current on what's next on the horizon for grey literature. Although it would be worthwhile to read this book from the beginning, all chapters can be read individually or consulted on an as-needed basis. For example, if you are only interested in learning about Google Scholar for grey literature searching, you can consult that individual subtopic in Chapter 9.

My motivation for writing this book is to share my knowledge and the experience I have gained with grey literature, including its worth to librarians and information professionals. When I first began working as a librarian (long before the debate of doing away with the library reference desk), I came to recognize the importance of grey literature by chance. Many of the information requests I received were not suited to simple database searches—examining the available grey literature ensured I did not come up empty handed in my searching. After I was prompted to look beyond my searches in Medline and PsycInfo, I was astounded by the wide array of information available from grey literature. Over the years, I have been responsible for providing my library patrons with grey literature searches for both systematic/scoping reviews and quick reference questions. I have also taught courses on grey literature searching and have delivered many presentations on the topic. When I have been involved with these activities, I have always discovered something unexpected about grey literature—for example, a new source or emerging search method.

Grey literature and searching for grey literature can be a formidable topic for many. A multitude of questions may come to mind: What is grey literature? How do you start a search? What types and sources should be included, and when do you stop searching? Hopefully, this book will serve as a practical guide, along with inspiring readers to recognize grey literature's unique value. As Mark Twain said, "The secret of getting ahead is getting started"; may this book aid you with any future daunting tasks.

Acknowledgments

This book would not have come to fruition without the help of many: Toni Janik, Michelle Brewer, and Michel Atlas for their interest in the topic and providing me with teaching, speaking, and writing opportunities; my employer, the CAMH Library, for supporting numerous occasions for conference attendance and enabling lifelong learning and sharing of ideas; and the Michigan Health Library Association, the Ontario Health Library Association, the Ontario Library Association, and the Medical Library Association. I also want to thank the team at Rowman & Littlefield, especially associate production editor Megan DeLancey, copy editor Shana Jones, and professional proofreader Virginia Bridges. A thank-you to my partner, John Shoesmith, for his invaluable support, and reading, reading, and *rereading* my drafts—as William Faulkner said, "Get it down. Take chances. It may be bad, but it's the only way you can do anything really good." Without John's help and encouragement, I would never have completed this book. And a most grateful thank-you to my dear mother, Margaret Miller, and to the memory of my father, Jerry Bonato.

Chapter 1

What Is Grey Literature?

> Finally, it is worth pointing out that there is a considerable resemblance between grey literature and the greyhound—a dog which everyone recognizes by certain well-defined features (it is tall, slender, with great speed and keen eyesight) but which nobody expects to have a coat which is invariably grey.—C. P. Auger

For countless librarians, information professionals, even library students, this will be a familiar research scenario:

> Search Requester: We need a search of the grey literature on [insert any of the following topics: fall prevention for seniors, bioabsorbable coronary stents, peer support for cancer survivors] for our research project.
>
> Librarian (silently shuddering, but still hopeful): Great! No problem! What grey literature document types would you like to include in your search?
>
> Search Requester: *Everything!*

Many of us have frustrating stories like this to share about being asked for a grey literature search. Grey literature can be broadly defined as everything but peer reviewed journals and academically or commercially published books (Von Hendy, 2014). The primary dilemma is that being asked for a grey lit search is not similar to being asked for other types of searches. When requesters ask for other types of searches—such as a search for a journal's impact factor, or for a Medline or Embase search on an intervention that is limited to randomized clinical trials—the requester is generally familiar with the research base. What the above scenario highlights is that it is simply impractical to include all grey literature document types in a search since the body of grey lit is vast, stretches across international borders, and recalcitrantly does not submit itself to formal means of bibliographic control. Grey literature is the behemoth of all that *other* research available that is not in book or serial format. In order to have an extensive, and productive, conversation with requesters seeking a grey lit search, librarians and information professionals must be properly equipped with knowledge of the disparate definitions of grey literature and the various document types that are classified as grey literature.

LEARNING OUTCOMES

The goal of this chapter is to provide librarians and information professionals with:

- a short history of grey literature
- an overview of the numerous definitions of grey literature
- the many and varied document types of grey literature
- traditional and untraditional grey literature publications
- the key producers of grey literature
- the main producers of grey literature in the areas of health and medicine
- quick criteria for determining if a document type can be considered grey literature

After reading this chapter, librarians and information professionals should also have basic knowledge of the complexity of the far-reaching body of grey literature output. The following introductory overview of the recent research on grey literature should also enable readers to facilitate discussions with their information users.

A SHORT HISTORY OF GREY LITERATURE

In this section, librarians and library students will be provided with a brief overview of the history of grey literature as a specific document type and the time periods that enabled grey literature to become the unique body of literature it is today. In addition, the barriers to tracing the history of grey literature will be discussed.

When was grey literature identified as a unique body of literature? Several scholarly journal articles provide a bit of historical background, along with detailing grey literature's growing importance (Auger, 1989; Rucinski, 2015; Vaska, 2010). Yet unlike the history of other literary genres—*Don Quixote*, for example, is generally recognized as the first modern novel—it is challenging to provide a chronological timeline for grey lit as there is not a multitude of research sources outlining the first grey literature publications. The history of grey literature does not lend itself to pinpointing specific dates of significance, especially when compared to other areas of scientific publishing. For example, it is quite straightforward to document the oldest continuously published medical journals (such as the *British Medical Journal* and the *New England Journal of Medicine*) and their place in the history of medical publishing. By comparison, it can be vexing to try and provide an exact outline of how and when grey literature was transformed into a body of literature that today is so worthy of research and debate.

Grey literature as a research document type does not emerge at a specific date or time, yet grey literature as a means for communicating and sharing research output is not a new format. Research scholars of grey literature have listed differing moments in time when grey literature emerged as a clearly defined type of research literature (Alberani, De Castro, & Mazza, 1990; Auger, 1989; Rucinski, 2015; Vaska, 2010), and some scholars have divided the history of grey literature into the time periods of pre-1979, 1980–1990, 1991–2000, 2001–2005, and 2006 onward (Farace & Schöpfel, 2010). There has also been discussion that as a literature format to share ideas and knowledge, grey literature is as old as the time of Socrates, if a broad and all-encompassing definition of grey literature is used (Auger, 1989; Vaska, 2010). But mostly, the history of grey literature as a format for disseminating knowledge output can be traced back to the publication of reports, such as research or technical reports. Grey literature has also been considered synonymous with the term "reports literature" (Osayande & Ukpebor, 2012).

Although there are now numerous document types that are considered to be grey literature—and we will examine these document types later in this chapter—the emergence of research and technical reports provides the main foundation for grey literature as a unique body of literature that is recognized today. Research and technical reports have been identified as key document types for communicating and sharing research findings, mostly in the scientific disciplines (Pejšová & Vaska, 2010). Early examples of research or technical reports as part of the body of grey literature date back to the early 1900s (Auger, 1989). The scientific community identified these types of research documents as unique from other types of publications as early as the 1920s (Auger, 1989). During the Second World War, research or technical reports also became a "major means of communication" (Auger, 1989), and technical reports especially became widely used to share research findings (White, 1984). Additionally, U.S. governmental funding of scientific research increased significantly during the Second World War and continued after 1945—this increased research funding lead to increased scholarly communication (Regazzi, 2015). As a result, the production of grey literature in the post-war period increased markedly (Lawrence et al., 2012).

So, while reports literature has been considered a unique type of research publication for some seventy-five years, use of the phrase "grey literature" has only been documented since the late 1970s. Sources note that the first use of the term "grey literature" originates from the York Seminar in England in 1978 (Alberani & De Castro, 2001). It was at this seminar, jointly hosted by the Commission of the European Communities and the British Library Lending Division, that grey literature was identified and accepted as a key and unique information source. The term "grey literature" specifically traces its origins to those working in the library and information science community rather than specific research disciplines like life sciences, medicine, or education (Falkingham, 2005). (Another interesting tidbit of information is that the phrase "grey literature" is also derived from the German term *graue Literatur* [Hogeweg-de Haart, Bergdahl, & Heidemann, 1985].)

Grey Literature Today

The Information Age has revolutionized the grey literature landscape. The invention of the World Wide Web in the 1990s was key to transforming the formats and dissemination of grey literature documents. Although grey literature documents were being published prior to the ability to surf and browse content on the Internet, identification and access of grey lit was complicated and limited. In short, personal computers, desktop publishing software like Adobe, and the World Wide Web have refashioned how grey literature is produced and shared (Lawrence et al., 2012). Taken together, these are the new tools and channels for producing, disseminating, and assessing scientific literature (Schöpfel, 2016). The communities and individuals embracing these new technologies have expanded quickly. One tectonic change is that even smaller organizations can now produce and post grey literature publications. As a result, grey literature is becoming an increasingly crucial component of the information landscape.

DEFINING GREY LITERATURE

Now that we have provided a snippet of historical background on grey literature, we now come to the complexities of properly defining it.

Defining the body of grey literature is problematic as there are numerous definitions of grey literature (Adams et al., 2017), and research experts on grey literature have noted that it is taxing to describe (Wood & Smith, 1993). Moreover, the available definitions in the research literature provide broad definitions of grey lit rather than providing specifics. Librarians and information professionals may find defining grey literature a herculean task—yet in order to search grey literature and provide bibliographic instruction on its sources, a pellucid outline of the body of grey literature is required. Without an understandable and unambiguous outline, there are no set parameters for *searching* grey literature, *evaluating* grey literature, or *collection development* for grey literature. Indeed, an abundant number of peer-reviewed publications mention that grey literature was searched, but often this is without providing any documentation on how the research team defined what they considered to be grey literature.

Grey literature has also often been called "fuzzy" literature (Auger, 1989; Adams, Smart, & Huff, 2017), and the rationale for this label varies immensely. Grey literature has been categorized as fuzzy because it occupies a category between academic and commercial publishing (Auger, 1989), its boundaries are not firmly defined (Soule & Ryan, 1999), and there are nebulous distinctions between grey literature documents and other open sources of information.

Grey literature has also been identified as the "fugitive" literature (Alberani, De Castro, & Mazza, 1990; Turner, Liddy, & Bradley, 2002), namely because it can be difficult to locate, it exists outside of normal peer-reviewed journal articles and scholarly books, and it is often considered part of the invisible web (Dillard, 2014). The elusive nature of grey literature means that boundaries of the definition are quite challenging to pin down and explain to others.

Grey literature's knottiness makes it an intriguing topic for scholarly discussion. As a result of grey literature being labeled both fuzzy and fugitive, and in light of how burdensome it can be to grasp, it is insuperable to define grey lit without looking at all of its numerous interrelated parts or aspects. As a result, a librarian's or informational professional's task for approaching grey literature as a research source is much more laborious. In short, in order to effectively use grey literature as a research source, librarians and information professionals should be knowledgeable of its several definitions. We will explore that next.

Definitions from the International Conference on Grey Literature

The International Conference on Grey Literature (ICGL) is the primary international source for scholarly research disseminating the topic of grey literature. The grey literature definitions that originate from the ICGL are the definitions that generally trend the most and are most often cited in scholarly research and conversation. Furthermore, these definitions are the ones most frequently used in bibliographic instruction formats, including LibGuides on grey literature. Currently, the most commonly referenced definition of grey literature is one that was debated and accepted at the 1997 ICGL in Luxemburg. This definition was expanded at the 2004 ICGL in New York and reads as follows:

> [I]nformation produced on all levels of government, academia, business and in-dustry in electronic and print formats not controlled by commercial publishing, i.e., where publishing is not the primary activity of the producing body.

At the 2010 ICGL in Prague, a new definition was proposed. The rationale given for proposing a revised definition was that prior definitions of grey literature were primarily focused on economics and failed to take into consideration the transforming research environment and emerging channels of scientific communication (Schöpfel, 2010). The proposed definition reads:

> Grey literature stands for manifold document types produced on all levels of government, academics, business and industry in print and electronic formats that are protected by intellectual property rights, of sufficient quality to be collected and preserved by libraries and institutional repositories, but not con-trolled by commercial publishers; i.e., where publishing is not the primary ac-tivity of the producing body.

Taking Apart the Puzzle of the Definition

The most straightforward approach to understanding the definitions originating from the ICGL is to examine all of the various components of the definitions. By doing so, it becomes easier to differentiate what makes grey literature distinct from other types of literature. Moreover, by understanding the various components of the definitions of grey literature from the ICGL, librarians and information professionals can confront the most ambiguous characteristic of grey literature.

Let's now take them one by one.

Information Produced on All Levels of Government, Academia, Business, and Industry

The concept of grey literature being comprised of numerous sources means that grey lit may originate from innumerable types of authors. For example, unlike several other forms of literature, grey lit publications are not limited to publications from *one* type of author focusing solely on *one* subject area. Instead, grey literature can potentially be published by a wide range of institutions—whether they be massive, medium-sized, small, or

Lilliputian—and by organizations only serving a local population or that have a broader national or international reach.

All of the specific categories of publishers mentioned are quite broad—perhaps overly broad. For example, the definition indicates that government, academia, business, and industry all publish grey literature, but even these categories contain layers and complexities that need to be understood.

Government is defined as the organization, machinery, or agency through which a political unit exercises authority and performs functions, and it is usually classified according to the distribution of power within it (*Merriam Webster*, 2016). This could be further broken down into the categories to represent the varying localities and branches of government, including federal, state/provincial, and municipal. Academia is defined as an environment or community concerned with the pursuit of research, education, and scholarship (*Merriam Webster*, 2016). Business has been defined as commercial activity, and industry has been defined as a distinct group of productive or profit-making enterprises (*Merriam Webster*, 2016).

However, the part of the definition that identifies these organizations as the producers of grey literature is somewhat problematic because there are other organizations that publish grey lit that may reside outside these communities. And the definitions originating from ICGL do not identify what types of organizations are considered part of academia, business, and industry. Moreover, there is considerable overlap between the multiple categories of grey literature.

The challenge of this component of the definition is that there are several publishers of grey literature that do not fall neatly into the categories of government, academia, business, or industry. An example would be grey literature published by authors in political parties, think tanks, non-governmental organizations (NGOs), and other professional bodies. As a result, while this part of the definition of grey literature is a convenient starting point for an information professional, potential key creators and authors of grey literature are not mentioned.

. . . In Print and Electronic Formats

This part of the definition states that grey literature cannot be defined by the available format—for example, grey literature documents are not limited to publications with print runs. As a result, the definition from the ICGL has taken into consideration the evolving formats in which information is now acquired. Also, the definition stresses that openness and inclusiveness are central components that define grey literature. As such, grey literature cannot be defined as information that takes on a specific format or is available by a specific means.

. . . Not Controlled by Commercial Publishing

Commercial publishing is undertaken by organizations or companies that operate in the open market, with profitability being the key aim. Librarians and information professionals should be mindful that there are various for-profit publishers of grey literature, including health insurance carriers such as Humana Inc. The main concern here is not that the publisher of the grey literature document is determined by commercial restraint, but rather that generating revenue and achieving a level of market success are not the main aims of a publication.

. . . Where Publishing Is Not the Primary Activity of the Producing Body

The most illuminating and most specific part of the ICGL definition of grey literature is that publishing is not the author's raison d'être for generating a publication. This is the part of the definition that is the most constructive for determining what types of documents are grey literature and which ones are not. For example, agencies such as Human Rights Watch and the Centers for Disease Control and Prevention (CDC) publish documents that are considered grey literature, but publishing is not the main mission of these organizations.

Other Key Points from the Newly Proposed Prague Definition

As previously mentioned, a new definition of grey literature was proposed at the 2010 ICGL in Prague. This definition expands on the established definition but adds the following:

Grey Literature Stands for Manifold Document Types

By indicating that grey literature documents can be represented by publications that have myriad features or forms, there is again the reminder of the diverse nature of this type of literature. Use of the term "manifold" is a reminder that definitions arising from the ICGL stress that grey literature definitions should strive to be inclusive. As a result, the definition does not specify that document types must meet a strict set of criteria in order to be classified as grey literature—a multitude of contrasting documents could potentially be categorized and considered grey literature. While this inclusiveness allows for more flexibility, there is little guidance for librarians and library users when approaching the body of grey literature. The term "manifold" also helps librarians explain to their users that grey literature cannot be labeled as one specific type of format, and that it also functions as a complete body of literature rather than as a singular source.

. . . Of Sufficient Quality to Be Collected and Preserved by Libraries and Institutional Repositories, in Print and Electronic Formats That Are Protected by Intellectual Property Rights.

This component of the expanded definition indicates the importance of merit in grey literature. It indicates that grey literature makes an imperative contribution to the research evidence on a topic. It also acknowledges the role of libraries and institutional depositories in the collection and facilitation of access to grey literature. Another intriguing component of the definition is the indication that intellectual property rights protect grey literature. Much grey literature is available from open source domains such as the U.S. government, but the definition's reference to intellectual property rights stresses that grey literature publications are truly providing a unique contribution to the body of known knowledge. Grey literature, much like other types of literature, is considered a creation of the mind.

The definitions sourced from the ICGL illustrate how formal statements on what grey literature is are wide ranging and are not fixed by a strictly outlined criteria. The key component to keep in mind is that grey literature is defined by a plenitude of characteristics.

OTHER DEFINITIONS OF GREY LITERATURE

There are many other definitions of grey literature in addition to the ones arising from the ICGL. For example, grey literature has been defined as *everything* published outside of books and journal articles (Higgins & Green, 2011; Von Hendy, 2014), publications that are not located or acquired through commercial outlets or normal channels (Schöpfel, 2010; Buchanan, Jackson, & Oberlander, 2014), and documents that are considered ephemeral (Stock & Schöpfel, 2004). It has also been suggested that documents that cannot be identified using an index or electronic database search can be considered grey literature (McKimmie & Szurmak, 2002).

While librarians and information professionals may find the sheer number of definitions nonconstructive, the multiplicity of definitions helps explain grey literature's expansiveness and the complexity of searching for it.

DOCUMENT TYPES IN GREY LITERATURE

Having addressed the history of grey literature and its multiple definitions, it is time to take a closer look at the vast array of document types that are classified as grey literature. Without knowledge of the contrasting grey literature document types, it would be exceedingly challenging to have a discussion with a researcher about designing a grey literature search strategy. This section will provide an overview of the main document types that are considered to be grey literature. Additionally, there will be a short overview of the types of documents that are considered traditional grey literature, as well as emerging untraditional grey literature document types.

Grey literature document types can vary depending on their discipline area (Sulouff et al., 2005). For example, the primary grey literature document types in the sciences may differ from grey literature document types in art history or business (Sulouff et al., 2005). Users of grey literature should not think of grey lit as the same as other traditional literature document types. In contrast to grey literature, other traditional literature document types, such as plays or short stories, have concise definitions with generally accepted set boundaries. Users of grey literature should think of grey lit not as a specific literature category, but rather as an information type that may include several types of resources (Bichteler, 1991; Tyndall, 2008). Additionally, a 2004 survey of grey literature found that users of grey literature believe that grey literature is best described by the document types it embodies (Farace, 2004).

Indeed, the document types or resources that can be classified as grey literature are remarkably broad. Several academic studies outline the assorted types of grey literature documents (Alberani, De Castro, & Mazza, 1990; Benzies et al., 2006; Mason, 2009; Myška & Šavelka, 2013; Rucinski, 2015; Schöpfel, 2010). Grey literature document types may include the following resources:

> reports (pre-prints, preliminary progress and advanced reports, technical reports, statistical reports, memoranda, state-of-the art reports, market research reports, etc.), theses, conference proceedings, technical specifications and standards, non-commercial translations, bibliographies, technical and commercial documentation, and official documents not published commercially (primarily government reports and documents). (Alberani, De Castro, & Mazza, 1990)

Like the various definitions of grey literature, the types of documents that are considered grey literature vary greatly. Some researchers have also suggested that grey literature document types may eventually evolve to include verbal material (Rothstein & Hopewell, 2009).

Traditional vs. Untraditional Grey Literature Document Types

Broadly, grey literature document types can be divided into two categories: traditional grey literature document types and untraditional, newly emerging grey literature document types. Traditional grey literature document types are publications that have been long established and classified as grey literature. Untraditional and newly emerging grey literature document types have not been customarily classified as grey literature. The following section will include a discussion of both types of grey literature documents.

GREYNET INTERNATIONAL

One of the most detailed listings of grey literature document types is available from GreyNet—the Grey Literature Network Service, an independent organization whose mission includes research, education, and raising awareness of grey literature. The benefit of using GreyNet as a guide for discussing the multifaceted nature of grey literature document types is that this list is comprised of input from the international grey literature community. Additionally, GreyNet considers external requests for either listing or delisting a document type from the grey literature document type list. GreyNet's who's who of grey literature document types also includes both traditional and untraditional grey literature document types.

GREYNET: KEY TYPES OF TRADITIONAL GREY LITERATURE DOCUMENTS

Brochures, Pamphlets, Leaflets, Fact Sheets, and Data Sheets

Brochures, pamphlets, leaflets, and fact sheets all have low page counts and contain information on specific topics. They may only be available in a paper format, but they may also be available electronically from an organization's website. Although these document types may indeed contain summaries of the available information on a topic, the content is usually intended to be introductory. Data sheets are slightly different in that they tend to contain specific technical information on a product.

Examples of Brochures, Pamphlets, Leaflets, Fact Sheets, and Data Sheets

- Brochure: U.S. Department of Health and Human Services. 2014. "Heart Truth for Women."
- Leaflet: World Health Organization. 2009. "Glove Use Information Leaflet."
- Fact Sheet: Centers for Disease Control and Prevention. 2015. "Ebola Fact Sheet."
- Data Sheet: Thomson Reuters. 2013. "Endnote X7 Guide Complete."

Textbox 1.1. Document Types in Grey Literature

Abstracts
Announcements
Annuals
Bibliographies
Blogs
Booklets
Brochures
Bulletin Boards
Bulletins
Call for Papers
Case Studies
Catalogues
Chronicles
Clinical Trial: Source Document
Codebooks
Conference Papers
Conference Posters
Conference Proceedings
Country Profiles
Course Materials
Databases
Data Papers
Datasets
Data Sheets
Deposited Papers
Directories
Discussion Papers
Dissertations
Doctoral Theses
E-Prints
E-texts
Enhanced Publications
Essays
ETD (Electronic Theses and Dissertations)
Exchange Agreements
Fact Sheets
Feasibility Studies
Flyers
Folders
Forum: Internet
Glossaries
Government Documents
Green Papers
Guidebooks
Handbooks

House Journals
Image Directories
Inaugural Lectures
Indexes
Interactive Posters
Internet Reviews
Interviews
Journals
Journals, Grey Journals, In-House
Journals, Noncommercial
Journals, Synopsis
K-blogs
Leaflets
Lectures
Legal Documents
Legislation
LibGuides
Manuals
Memoranda
Newsgroups
Newsletters
Notebooks
Orations
Off-Prints
Pamphlets
Papers: Call for Papers, Conference Papers, Deposited Papers, Discussion Papers, Green Papers, White Papers, Working Papers
Patents
Policy Documents
Policy Statements
Posters
Précis Articles
Preprints
Press Releases
Proceedings
Product Data
Programs
Project: Deliverables, Information Document (PID), Proposals, Work Packages, Work Programs
Reports: Activity Reports, Annual Reports, Bank Reports, Business Reports, Committee

Reports, Compliance Reports, Country Reports, Draft Reports, Feasibility Reports, Government Reports, Intelligence Reports, Internal Reports, Official Reports, Policy Reports, Progress Reports, Regulatory Reports, Site Reports, Stockbroker Reports, Technical Reports	Standards
	State of the Art
	Statistical Surveys
	Statistics
	Supplements
	Survey Results
	Syllabus
	Technical Documentation
	Technical Notes
Reprints	Tenders
Research Memoranda	Theses
Research Notes	Timelines
Research Proposals	Trade Directories
Research Registers	Translations
Research Reports	Treatises
Reviews	Tutorials
Risk Analyses	Web Pages
Satellite Data	Website Reviews
Scientific Protocols	Websites
Scientific Visualizations	White Books
Show cards	White Papers
Software	Working Documents
Specifications	Working Papers
Speeches	Yearbooks

GreyNet International 1992–2017, "Document Types in Grey Literature," retrieved November 20, 2017, from http://www.greynet.org/greysourceindex/documenttypes.html.

Discussion Papers

Discussion papers are print documents that address an issue in order to reach a consensus or exchange ideas (OED Online, 2016). The aim of a discussion paper is to provide a detailed overview of a topic in order to understand it more thoroughly. Discussion papers can be produced by such institutions as corporations, government agencies, think tanks, political organizations, professional associations, and non-governmental agencies.

Examples of Discussion Papers

Metroxlink. 2016. Discussion Paper for the Next Regional Transportation Plan.
University of Manchester, Centre for Growth & Business Cycle Research. 2003. The Incidence and Persistence of Corruption in Economic Development.

Green Papers

A green paper is a preliminary report of government proposals published to stimulate discussion (*Merriam Webster*, 2016). This type of publication details specific issues and then points out possible courses of action via policy and legislation. Like a discussion paper, a green paper summarizes issues on a specific topic and involves the exchange of ideas for future action.

Examples of Green Papers

United States Patent and Trademark Office. 2013. Green Paper on Copyright
    Policy, Creativity and Innovation in the Digital Economy.
Welsh Government. 2015. Our Health, Our Health Service.

Data Sets, Statistics, and Survey Results

Data sets, statistics, and survey results have been categorized as formats of grey literature and also as grey data (Gelfand & Tsang, 2015). As a grey literature document type, this kind of information may sometimes stand alone as its own source (for example, statistics available for download from the U.S. Department of Labor). These types of grey literature documents or grey data have been noted for their intertwined relationship with other grey literature documents. Some examples of common elements that bridge grey literature with grey data include: correspondence, project files, grant and ethics applications, technical reports, research reports, and signed consent forms (Gelfand & Tsang, 2015). Data sets, statistics, and survey results may also be part of a larger synthesized grey literature document or information source that is accessed individually. Data sets have been defined as collections of related data that may be accessed individually, in combination with other segments of data, or as a whole source of information (Bauder, 2014). Statistics are defined as the collection and analysis of numerical facts (*Merriam Webster*, 2016). Both data and statistics are key sources, because this "recorded factual material (is) commonly accepted in the scientific community as necessary to validate research findings."

Examples of Data Sets and Statistics

Statistics New Zealand. 2013. Urban Area Population Projections.
U.S. Department of Labor, Bureau of Labor Statistics. 2011–2014. Census of
    Fatal Occupational Injuries.

Clinical Trials

Clinical trials are research studies that explore whether a medical strategy, treatment, or device is safe and effective for humans. They are fundamental for identifying the interventions that are most effective for certain illnesses and diseases, and the types of interventions that are best for specific populations (National Heart, Lung, and Blood Institute, "What Are Clinical Trials?," retrieved from https://www.nhlbi.nih.gov/studies/clinicaltrials; Chamers, 1998). While the results of umpteen clinical trials are available in published literature, unpublished clinical trials are considered a type of grey literature (Conn et al., 2003).

Examples of Unpublished Clinical Trials

ClinicalTrials.gov [Internet]. Bethesda (MD): National Library of Medicine (US) 2015 Nov 11 Identifier NCT10756300, RENABLATE Feasibility Study CS156 (EC12-02) Study of Catheter Based Renal Denervation to Treat Resistant Hypertension. Available from https://clinicaltrials.gov/ct2/show/NCT01756300?term=hypertension&rslt=With&cond=hypertension&draw=1&rank=8.

ClinicalTrials.gov [Internet]. Bethesda (MD): National Library of Medicine (US) 2016 Sep 26 Identifier NCT00475722, Healthy Eating for Colon Cancer Prevention. Available from https://clinicaltrials.gov/ct2/show/NCT00475722?rslt=With&cond=mediterranean+diet&rank=1.

Dissertations/Theses

A dissertation or thesis is an academic document that an individual writes in order to fulfill degree requirements. They are usually submitted to obtain a doctorate (*Merriam Webster*, 2016). Primarily, they are written by students in graduate and PhD programs and generally discuss the results of original research. A dissertation/thesis must be on a topic that has not been previously researched, so these documents may be matchless sources of information when exceedingly little has been published on a topic. Examples would include research on special populations.

Examples of Dissertations/Thesis

Krugman, Paul R. 1977. "Essays on Flexible Exchange Rates."
Turing, Alan. 1938. "Systems of Logic Based on Ordinals."
Yellen, Janet. 1971. "Employment, Output and Capital Accumulation in an Open Economy: A Disequilibrium Approach."

Government Documents

Government documents are defined as official publications from government agencies. The Library of Congress defines these publications as documents issued under authority of any legislative body, executive or judicial department, ministry, bureau, agency, independent office, court, commission, or officer of any government (Library of Congress Collections Policy Statement, 2016). Legislation and legal documents are other types of grey literature that would be classified as government documents.

All levels of government produce government publications. As a result, these documents can be from federal, state, county, and land administrations or municipal sources. Examples of government documents from the federal level include publications from the U.S. federal government or the Canadian federal government. At the state or provincial level, government documents include publications from the Government of Ontario, Canada; California; and Queensland, Australia. Examples of government documents on the municipal level include documents from New York City, New York, or London, England. Government documents from counties or land administrations include publications from Oakland County, MI; Perth Public Health (Canada); or New South Wales, Australia. All levels of government collect and analyze information, and the information is mostly disseminated via grey literature documents.

The range of information produced by governments can be hugely eclectic and is not limited to specific topics. Moreover, governments also produce an exceptional output of information. For example, the U.S. federal government is among the world's most prolific producers of information (Feather & Sturges, 2003). The U.S. federal government produces publications on such topics as industry, security, statistics, energy, health, education, agriculture, international affairs, and safety.

Additionally, there are copious numbers of publications from international government sources governed by international treaties, such as the United Nations. These types of organizations are also referred to as intergovernmental organizations and would include the World Bank, World Trade Organization, International Atomic Energy, and the World Health Organization.

Government publications are an invaluable grey literature source since they offer such a wide variety of information on numerous subjects and topic areas. Often the information available will provide a synthesis of the research on a topic. A general bonus of government publications is that they are most likely open access and available for free online. Government publications may be available in a variety of formats, including PDF and HTML, or they may simply be data records from research projects.

Examples of Government Documents

City of New York. 2016. Housing New York: A Five Borough, Ten-Year Plan.
New South Wales Department of Education. 2012. Aboriginal Education in
    NSW Public Schools.
United Kingdom Ministry of Justice and National Offender Management
    Service. 2016. Prison Safety and Reform.

Newsletters

A newsletter is a small publication containing news that is chiefly of interest
to a special group. While there could be a bit of debate on whether or not
newsletters are truly considered grey literature publications, they are included
on the GreyNet International list. The cause for debate is that newsletters are
often indexed by databases that only include academic literature publications.

Examples of Newsletters

Nursing and Midwifery Board of Australia. Issue 13, September 2015. For
    Nurses and Midwifes: News.
Union Farm Newsletter. Volume 64, Issue 5, November 2016.

Policy Documents

A policy document is an all-embracing grey literature document type. While
it is difficult to locate an exact definition of policy documents, the easiest
way to think of them is as statements of the general course of action by
an organization. They will often provide a high-level plan for long-term
issues. Policy documents can be produced by a diverse range of institutions,
including governments, political organizations, professional agencies, or
other institutions.

Examples of Policy Documents

International Criminal Court. 2016. Policy Paper on Case Selection and
    Prioritization.
OECD (Organisation for Economic Co-Operation and Development). 2015.
    New Rural Policy: Linking Up for Growth.

Policy Statements

Policy statements have been defined as formal documents that outline the
means by which an organization intends to conduct its affairs, including

specific circumstances (*Collins Dictionary*, 2016). Policy statements can be documents produced by governments, professional agencies, religious organizations, hospitals, and academic institutions, along with other types of organizations.

Examples of Policy Statements

American Public Health Association. November 2015. Expanding and Coordinating Human Trafficking–Related Public Health Research, Evaluation, Education, and Prevention

Canadian Institute of Health Research, Natural Sciences and Engineering Research Council of Canada, Social Sciences of Humanities Research Council of Canada. 2005. Tri-Council Policy Statement: Ethical Conduct for Research Involving Humans.

Council on Community Pediatrics. November 2015. Promoting Food Security for All Children.

Reports

Reports are defined as official documents that provide information on a particular topic (*OED Online*, 2016). As a grey literature document type, reports are immensely broad. In fact, grey literature was once considered synonymous with reports literature (Mason, 2009), and reports dominated grey literature research output. Reports as a grey literature document type include annual reports, bank reports, business reports, government reports, intelligence reports, internal reports, progress reports, regulatory reports, stockbroker reports, and technical reports.

Annual Reports

Annual reports are comprehensive reports on a company's or organization's activities and financial standing throughout the preceding year (*Merriam Webster*, 2016). As a grey literature document type, annual reports provide merit and insight by providing data on outcome measures and specific performance indicators. Additionally, all publicly traded companies in Canada and the United States must provide the following information in their annual reports: comparison of selected financial data, balance sheets, income statement, cash flow statement, and changes in stockholders' equity. Some organizations are required by law to make their annual reports publicly available. Not-for-profit institutions also publish annual reports with the intention of providing community stakeholders with an update on the organization's activities and supplementary financial data.

Examples of Annual Reports

Costco Wholesale Corporation. 2015. Annual Report 2015.
Toronto Public Library. 2009. Our Doors Wide Open: Toronto Public Library
  Annual Report 2008.

Business Reports

Business reports are descriptions of business events and financial activities
that analyze available information (OED Online, 2016). As a grey literature document type, these reports may be freely available or strictly internal
documents. Although business reports may be considered inconsequential
for a grey literature search in the areas of health and medicine, this is a misconception. There is much overlapping information of interest in both areas,
and the importance of these reports should not be overlooked. Examples of
business reports relevant in the areas of health and medicine would be reports
by insurance agencies, reports by pharmaceutical companies, and industry
reports on health-related areas.

Examples of Business Reports

Fitzgerald Power. 2014. Retail Pharmacy Report 2014.

NGO Reports

NGOs are frequent publishers of grey literature. These types of organizations
may be focused on producing reports with a local, national, or international
focus. Examples of NGOs include Human Rights Watch, the Sierra Club,
and New Detroit—The Coalition. Although NGO publications are not specifically included in the definition of grey literature, NGOs fit the category of
organizations that do not have publishing as their primary activity. Usually
these reports are comprised of analyzed and synthesized information, or they
may contain original information completed by the NGO agency.

Examples of NGO Reports

Medecins Sans Frontieres. March 2015. Pushed to the Limit and Beyond: A
  Year into the Largest Ever Ebola Outbreak.
Save the Children. 2015. The Urban Disadvantage: State of the Worlds
  Mothers 2015.

Research Reports

A research report is a report that is often used in the sciences, technology, and engineering (Duignan, 2016). The goal of a research report is to detail the findings and disseminate the results of research and to explain the intended purpose of research findings. The difference between research reports and research published in academic publications is that reports have not been submitted to a specific publisher prior to being accepted for publication. As with other grey literature document types, there may be overlapping characteristics between research reports and other types of grey literature documents.

Example of a Research Report

San Diego Workforce Partnership. 2011. Healthcare IT Research Report.
Adams, J., King, C., & Hook, D. 2010. *Global research report—Africa.* Leeds, UK: Thomson Reuters.

Technical Reports

Technical reports are also considered grey literature publications. They are documents that describe the process, progress, or results of technical or scientific research, or they may describe the state of a technical or scientific research problem (Bobick & Berard, 2011). A technical report might also include recommendations and conclusions of research. Because of the nature of technical reports, these types of publications may also be categorized as government publications. Like many government publications, technical reports contain information that has been analyzed and synthesized. A technical report is generally a product of government-sponsored research, privately sponsored research, or research generated by academia (Bobick & Berard, 2011).

Examples of Technical Reports

Terrill, W., Paoline, E., & Ingram, J. 2012. Final technical report draft: Assessing police use of force policy and outcomes. *Unpublished report submitted to U.S. Department of Justice.* Retrieved March 6.
Canadian Institute for Health Research. 2016. Trends in Income Related Health Inequalities in Canada Technical Report.

Working Papers

Working papers as a grey literature document type are closely related to the broad grey literature document types of research reports. The main difference is that a working paper only has tentative data or analysis available (*Merriam Webster*, 2016). The aim of a working paper is to set a foundation for discussion or negation of an issue.

Examples of Working Papers

Knight, J. (2016). China's Inequality Is Important—but Which Inequality? (No. 2016-20). Centre for the Study of African Economies, University of Oxford.

Working Documents

Working documents are supporting documents related to the drafting of reports. As a grey literature document type, working documents may not always be publicly available.

Examples of Working Documents

Asian Development Bank. 2006. Poverty Handbook Analysis and Process to Support ADB Operations: A Working Document.
European Commission. 2016. Commission Staff Working Document: Review of Greening after One Year.

White Papers

White papers are defined as government reports on any topic, or detailed or authoritative reports by other types of producers on various topics. The purpose of white papers is to present solutions to particular problems (*Merriam Webster*, 2016). White papers are not restricted to publications by governmental agencies.

Examples of White Papers

Centers for Disease Control and Prevention. 2010. Establishing a Holistic Framework to Reduce Inequities in HIV, Viral Hepatitis, STDs, and Tuberculosis in the United States: An NCHHSTP White Paper on Social Determinants of Health.
Council of Europe. 2008. White Paper on Intercultural Dialogue: "Living Together as Equals in Dignity." Launched by the Council of European Ministers of Foreign Affairs at their 118th Ministerial Session (Strasbourg, 7 May 2008), Strasbourg Cedex.
Uber. 2016. Fast-Forwarding to a Future of On-Demand Urban Air Transport.

UNTRADITIONAL/NEWLY EMERGING GREY
LITERATURE DOCUMENT TYPES

With the advance of the Internet, more types of formats are being regarded as grey literature publications. This section will discuss a selection of untraditional grey literature publications. The main characteristics of these untraditional grey literature document types is that they are only available in digital form and are relativity new sources of information. The debate on whether or not the following publications could be considered grey literature is one that may change what we consider grey lit in the future. This section does not attempt to validate or invalidate untraditional publications as definite grey literature publications. Instead, the goal is to start a discussion on what untraditional publications contribute to the body of grey literature as a whole.

The challenge of these new, emerging, and untraditional formats of grey literature is that these document types are more ephemeral in nature. As a result, these formats may be more difficult to locate and thus present challenges for preserving.

Blog Posts

A blog is a website consisting of diary-like entries, or posts, in ascending order. Blogs may be from an organization or an individual. Similar to tweets (discussed below), blog posts are considered part of the new frontier of grey literature (Banks, 2009). Additionally, some serials, in addition to their print publications, will have blog posts on their web sites. For example, the *New Yorker* magazine posts original content on its site daily, but this same content will not normally appear in the print edition. Like other formats of grey literature, blog posts do not have the standard bibliographic identifiers (Banks, 2009). Like traditional grey literature formats, blog posts can also be considered fugitive or fuzzy literature because of the elusiveness of the information and susceptibility to links that eventually become unavailable (Banks, 2009).

When researching a grey literature search topic, it is possible that a blog post—for example, an NIH director's blog—could contain relevant information and thus be a significant contribution to research on a multitude of topics. These blog posts provide decidedly current information, unique content, information that may not be available elsewhere, and central organizational information. Also, blog posts do not have the time constraints of traditional publishing, like journal articles or books. The drawback to blog posts is that they lack formalized peer review, can be promotional in nature, and may not necessarily provide diverse viewpoints. In addition, bloggers themselves may have a specific motivation for the information they are posting.

Examples of Blog Posts

Centers for Disease Control and Prevention. Public Health Matters Blog: 5 Holiday Tips for a Home Safe Home. Posted on November 22, 2016. Retrieved from https://blogs.cdc.gov/publichealthmatters/2016/11/five-holiday-tips/

Peter O'Donnel. Little European Love on Show for Clinical Research. Posted on November 29, 2016. Retrieved from http://www.appliedclinicaltrialsonline.com/little-european-love-show-drug-research

PowerPoint Presentations

The electronic presentation file format of MS PowerPoint is a more recent addition to the grey literature document landscape. MS PowerPoint presentations by individual researchers or institutions are often easily available on the Internet. Although MS PowerPoint presentations are a newer document format for grey literature, they are not part of the emerging Web 2.0 sources of grey literature or grey data.

One of the main benefits of MS PowerPoint presentations is that these electronic presentations may be the only source of information on a topic. For example, an MS PowerPoint presentation may contain information that is not available in a book or journal article. PowerPoint presentations may also be a prime source of information for new research findings that will be published at a later date. There is a bit of overlap between MS PowerPoint presentations and conference publications, which are another type of grey literature document. When a paper is presented at an academic conference, the research findings will often be presented in PowerPoint, and the presentation can be identified through an Internet search. PowerPoint presentations are also ideal for finding information on a variety of topics, such as psychological tests, measurements, or scales; health statistics; research findings; special populations; and health service initiatives.

Examples of PowerPoint Presentations

Guidelines for Infection Control in Dental Health-Care Settings. 2003. Prepared by William G. Kohn, D.D.S., and Amy S. Collins, M.P.H.

Tweets and Other Web 2.0 Sources

The advance of the interactive Internet has broadened the document types that are considered grey literature. The list of grey literature document types is not as static as it has been in the past. While the addition of information sources always provides added value, it also makes defining grey literature more complicated.

Web 2.0 describes interactive Internet such as Facebook, Twitter, and Instagram. Tweets are considered one type of Web 2.0 tool. Given their limitations, tweets are not currently categorized as a key source of grey literature: namely, information in 140 characters (now 280 characters) is hardly literature (Banks, 2009). Tweets can be severely lacking in original and substantive content. Likewise, most tweets are not likely to contain original research information; instead, tweets are either part of a promotional strategy or simply direct readers to other available information. Tweets have actually been noted as a source to *share* grey literature resources (Aloia & Naughton, 2016). There has been some discussion on how tweets could be considered an emerging source of grey literature, especially if they are considered part of "grey data." As "grey data," tweets can provide pivotal information as part of a larger conversation on a topic (Banks, 2009). One example of Twitter's contribution to the grey literature or grey data landscape is the Library of Congress's announcement in 2010 of a project to archive Twitter. This type of initiative may be an indicator that searching for relevant tweets may become part of future grey literature search strategies. Yet in discussion of grey literature publication types, it might be necessary to explain to someone why tweets are not worthy for inclusion in the body of grey literature devoted to communicating research.

Examples of Tweets

NY Public Library @nypl 1 hour ago
We have hundreds of years' worth of science and medical illustrations in our collections: http://on.nypl.org/2flcgtZ.

PubMed Health @PubMedHealth Nov 17
Cohort studies: cohorts, birth cohorts—what exactly does that all mean? Check out our short explainers https://www.ncbi.nlm.nih.gov/pubmedhealth/PMHT0025833/

Websites/Pages

Websites are defined as a group of World Wide Web pages containing hyperlinks to each other and made available online by an individual, company, educational institution, government, or organization (*Merriam Webster*, 2016). There is overlap between this grey literature document type and other grey literature document types, such as blog posts. Web pages can be specific sources of information or a source for downloading grey literature documents, such as working papers or technical reports.

Examples of Websites

National Library of Medicine. 2016. *Bodulism.* Retrieved from https://medlineplus.gov/botulism.html.
Welsh Government. 2016. Health of Homeless and Specific Vulnerable Groups. Retrieved from: http://gov.wales/topics/health/nhswales/healthservice/homeless/?lang=en.

This section has helped demonstrate the diversity and vast range of grey literature document types. Having a discussion on the specific types of grey literature documents is vital. As we will examine in later chapters, it is not always possible to search for all types of grey literature, but librarians and information professionals need to be cognizant of the abundant types of grey literature in order to decide which ones to include in a search.

MAIN PRODUCERS OF GREY LITERATURE

The main producers of grey literature are research institutions; universities; international, national, and local authorities; and industrial firms (Wessels, 2010). Other producers of grey literature include:

- health care institutes
- charities
- non-governmental organizations
- corporations
- professional societies
- not-for-profit institutions

It is difficult to assess producers' overall publication output of grey literature, and the amount of grey literature varies from one subject area to another (Auger, 1989). Since grey literature is lacking in bibliographic control (Wessels, 2010), the traditional approaches of citation analysis and bibliometrics cannot be applied. As previously mentioned, the majority of grey literature documents are not indexed by databases, so the traditional research tools cannot be utilized. Grey literature is a *type* of literature—it is not subject- or discipline-focused—and it is challenging to analyze publication output, although it may be expanding three or four times faster than conventional literature (Farace, 1997).

MAIN PRODUCERS OF GREY LITERATURE DOCUMENTS IN HEALTH AND MEDICINE

There has been scant biometric research on the main producers of grey literature in the areas of health and medicine. It has been noted that life science and medicine do not produce as many grey literature documents for their research basis when compared to other subject areas such as business, education, sociology, and technology (Auger, 1989). But a great number of health and medical institutions are currently producing grey literature. These institutions include governmental agencies, charities, corporations, educational institutions, hospitals, international agencies, think tanks, NGOs, and professional associations. To track the grey literature output of all the combined types of institutions would be a perplexing task.

The grey literature output of specific organizations has also not been extensively studied. A 1990 study noted that the main producers of grey literature in the health sciences were intergovernmental agencies such as the World Health Organization. It should be noted that although the study's methodology was detailed and extensive, it does not provide an up-to-date overview of the research output in grey literature in the areas of health and science. Recent studies on grey literature in the areas of health and medicine generally focus on specific disciplines; research studies have tracked the grey literature output and the citation of grey literature sources in the areas of environmental studies, health services and health policy research, and veterinary medicine (Academy Health, 2006; Chavez, 2010; Cordes, 2013; Pelzer & Wiese, 2003).

A PROPOSED CRITERIA FOR GREY LITERATURE

When librarians and information professionals are trying to determine if a document is a grey literature publication, they may need to assess the document to see if it has any of the identifiable characteristics of grey literature. They may use the following criteria:

- Can the document be located using traditional databases, such as Web of Science or Embase?
- Does the title of the document help identify the document format?

- Does the document have an International Standard Book Number (ISBN)?
- Does the document have an International Standard Serial Number (ISSN)?
- How was the document located—in a database indexing scholarly literature, from a reference list, or from another type of search?
- Is the item indexed in a database or other bibliographic source—for example, Books in Print or Ulrich's Periodicals Directory?
- Who is the producer, publisher, or author of the document? Is there a clearly identifiable corporate author, publisher, or other individual(s) involved with the publication?

By asking the questions listed above, a librarian or information professional should be able to determine if a document is a grey literature publication. For example, consider the following two documents:

The documents listed above are both produced by the American Academy of Pediatrics. The first, *Global Child Health Advocacy: On the Front Lines*, is a book. This is determined by the bibliographic identifier of an ISBN. The second document, *Blueprint for Children: How the Next President Can Build a Foundation for a Healthy Future*, is a grey literature report from the American Academy of Pediatrics. Although this publication is from the same source, it does not have any identifying bibliographic controls such as an ISSN or ISBN. The individual report is also not indexed by databases. The exercise above helps illustrate how grey literature publications can be produced by institutions that also publish white literature, and librarians and

---

Textbox 1.2.

Document #1

Title: *Global Child Health Advocacy: On the Front Lines*
Authors: Stephen Berman MD FAAP and Judith S. Palfrey MD FAAP
Producers: Indicates that it was published by the American Academy of Pediatrics
ISSB/ISSN: 1581107803
Indexed by: Books in Print

Document #2

Title: *Blueprint for Children: How the Next President Can Build a Foundation for a Healthy Future*
Producers: American Academy of Pediatrics
Authors: No individual authors listed
Indexed by: Not indexed by the databases PubMed, Medline, Web of Science. Not listed in Books in Print

information professionals can easily identify grey literature documents by asking a series of questions.

CONCLUSION

Grey literature is a complex information source to explain. Unlike other information sources, grey literature has almost a countless number of fluctuating characteristics and has been transformed over time. There is not an uncomplicated history of grey literature and the lack of bibliographic control makes the grey literature landscape labyrinth like. The visibility of grey literature is also rapidly increasing—the quantity of research articles that either cover the topic of grey literature or mention the term grey literature has increased markedly over the past nine years (Savić, 2017). But the research cited in this chapter will hopefully help librarians and information professionals have an opening dialogue with their uses on what exactly is grey literature.

BIBLIOGRAPHY

Academy Health. (2008). Grey literature search. Retrieved from http://www.academyhealth.org/Training/ResourceDetail.cfm?ItemNumber=2351.

Adams, R. J., Smart, P., & Huff, A. S. (2017). Shades of grey: Guidelines for working with the grey literature in systematic reviews for management and organizational studies. *International Journal of Management Reviews, 19*(4), 432–454.

Alberani, V., & De Castro, P. (2001). Grey literature from the York seminar (UK) of 1978 to the year. *Inspel, 35,* 236–247.

Alberani, V., De Castro, P., & Mazza, A. M. (1990). The use of grey literature in health sciences: A preliminary survey. *Bulletin of the Medical Library Association, 78*(4), 358–363.

Aloia, D., & Naughton, R. (2016). Share# GreyLit: Using social media to communicate grey literature. *Grey Journal (TGJ), 12*(2).

Auger, C. P. (1989). *Information sources in Grey literature.* London: Bowker-Saur.

Auger, C. P. (1994). *Information sources in grey literature.* London: Bowker-Saur.

Banks, M. (2009). Blog posts and tweets: The next frontier for grey literature. *Grey Literature in Library and Information Studies.* De Gruyter.

Bauder, J. (2014). *The reference guide to data sources.* American Library Association.

Benzies, K. M., Premji, S., Hayden, K. A., & Serrett, K. (2006). State-of-the-evidence reviews: Advantages and challenges of including grey literature. *Worldviews on Evidence-Based Nursing, 3*(2), 55–61.

Bichteler, J. (1991). Geologists and gray literature: Access, use, and problems. *Science & Technology Libraries, 11*(3), 39–50.

Bobick, J. E., & Berard, G. L. (2011). *Science and technology resources: A guide for information professionals and researchers.* Libraries Unlimited.

Boekhorst, A. K., Farace, D. J., & Frantzen, J. (2005). Grey literature survey 2004: A research project tracking developments in the field of grey literature. *Grey Journal–Amsterdam, 1*(1), 41.

Buchanan, S., Jackson, R. M., & Oberlander, C. (2014). Can cooperative service solve the grey literature challenge? *OLA Quarterly, 10*(2), 5–9.

Carruthers, M. M. (2012). *Science and Technology Resources.*

Chamers. (1998). What are clinical trials? Retrieved from https://www.nhlbi.nih.gov/studies/clinicaltrials.

Chavez, T. A. (2010). Grey literature in karst research: The evolution of the karst information portal (KIP). *Grey Literature in Library and Information Studies*, 181.

Citrome, L. (2014). Beyond PubMed: Searching the "grey literature" for clinical trial results. *Innovations in Clinical Neuroscience, 11*(7–8), 42–46.

Clarke, M., Hopewell, S., & Chalmers, I. (2010). Clinical trials should begin and end with systematic reviews of relevant evidence: 12 years and waiting. *Lancet (London, England), 376*(9734), 20–21.

Conn, V. S., Valentine, J. C., Cooper, H. M., & Rantz, M. J. (2003). Grey literature in meta-analyses. *Nursing Research, 52*(4), 256–261.

Cooper, H., Hedges, L. V., & Valentine, J. C. (2009). *The handbook of research synthesis and meta-analysis.* Russell Sage Foundation.

Cordes, R. (2013). Is grey literature ever used?: Using citation analysis to measure the impact of GESAMP, an international marine scientific advisory body. *Proceedings of the Annual Conference of CAIS/Actes Du Congrès Annuel De l'ACSI,*

Dillard, D. (2014). Research guides: Meta analysis and systematic review: How to create a meta analysis and a systematic review: Grey literature sources and tools.

Discussion papers (n.d.) OED Online. March 2018. Oxford University Press. http://www.oed.com.ezproxy.torontopubliclibrary.ca/view/Entry/54109?redirectedFrom=discussion (accessed May 07, 2018).

Duignan, J. (2016). *A dictionary of business research methods.* Oxford University Press.

Falkingham, G. (2005). A whiter shade of grey: A new approach to archaeological grey literature using the XML version of the TEI guidelines. *Internet Archaeology, 17*, 14–28.

Farace, D. J. (1997). Rise of the phoenix: A review of new forms and exploitations of grey literature. *Publishing Research Quarterly, 13*(2), 69–76.

Farace, D. J. (2004). Grey literature: Grey matters in the world of networked information. *Publishing Research Quarterly, 20*(1), 3–91.

Farace, D., & Schöpfel, J. (2010). Introduction grey literature. In D. Farace and J. Schöpfel (Eds.), *Grey literature in library and information studies* (pp. 1–7). De Gruyter/Saur.

Feather, J., & Sturges, P. (2003). *International encyclopedia of information and library science.* Routledge.

Gelfand, J. M., & Tsang, D. C. (2015). Data: Is it grey, maligned or malignant? *The Grey Journal, 11*(1).

Government. (n.d.). Retrieved May 7, 2018, from https://www.merriam-webster.com/dictionary/government.

Higgins, J. P., & Green, S. (2011). *Cochrane handbook for systematic reviews of interventions*. John Wiley & Sons.

Hogeweg-de Haart, H., Bergdahl, B., & Heidemann, E. (1985). *Grey literature in social science: A concise review of literature.—B. bergdahl: Grey material-a scandinavian view.—E. heidemann: Grey literature in social sciences in the federal republic of Germany*

Jeffrey, C., Rothstein, H. R., & Hopewell, S. (2009). Grey literature. In H. Cooper, L. V. Hedges & Valentine (Eds.), *Handbook of research synthesis* (2nd ed., p. 103). Russell Sage Foundation.

Lawrence, A., Houghton, J., Thomas, J., & Weldon, P. (2012). Where is the evidence? Realising the value of grey literature for public policy and practice. Swinburne Institute for Social Research, Melbourne, Australia. Retrieved from http://apo.org.au/research/where-evidence-realising-value-grey-literature-public-policy-and-practice.

Mason, M. K. (2009). *Grey literature: History, definition, acquisition and cataloguing*. Retrieved from http://www.moyak.com/papers/grey-technical-literature.html.

McKimmie, T., & Szurmak, J. (2002). Beyond grey literature: How grey questions can drive research. *Journal of Agricultural & Food Information, 4*(2), 71–79.

Myška, M., & Šavelka, J. (2013). A model framework for publishing grey literature in open access. Retrieved from https://www.jipitec.eu/issues/jipitec-4-2-2013/3744.

Osayande, O., & Ukpebor, C. O. (2012). Grey literature acquisition and management: Challenges in academic libraries in Africa. *Grey Literature Acquisition and Management: Challenges in Academic Libraries in Africa,*

Pejšová, P., & Vaska, M. (2010). *An analysis of current grey literature document typology*. Paper presented at the Twelfth International Conference on Grey Literature: Transparency in Grey Literature, 6–7 December 2010.

Pelzer, N. L., & Wiese, W. H. (2003). Bibliometric study of grey literature in core veterinary medical journals. *Journal of the Medical Library Association: JMLA, 91*(4), 434–441.

Regazzi, J. J. (2015). *Scholarly communications: A history from content as king to content as kingmaker.*

Robinson, J. S. (1998). *Tapping the government grapevine: The user-friendly guide to US government information sources*. ABC-CLIO.

Rothstein, H. R., & Hopewell, S. (2009). Grey literature. In H. Cooper, L. V. Hedges, & J. C. Valentine (Eds.), *The handbook of research synthesis and meta-analysis* (pp. 103-125). New York: Russell Sage Foundation.

Rucinski, T. L. (2015). The elephant in the room: Toward a definition of grey legal literature. *Law Libr. J., 107*, 543.

Savić, D. (2017). *Impact of current information technology trends on the future of grey literature*. Conference on Grey Literature and Repositories, p. 6.

Schöpfel, J. (2010). *Towards a Prague definition of grey literature*. Paper presented at the Twelfth International Conference on Grey Literature: Transparency in Grey

Literature. Grey Tech Approaches to High Tech Issues. Prague, 6–7 December 2010, pp. 11–26.

Schöpfel, J. (2013). Adding value to electronic theses and dissertations in institutional repositories. *DLib Magazine, 19*(3/4).

Schöpfel, J., & Prost, H. (2016, November). Altmetrics and Grey Literature: Perspectives and Challenges. In *GL18 International Conference on Grey Literature.*

Soule, M. H., & Ryan, R. P. (1999). *Gray literature, technical briefing.* Information Technology SummIT. Retrieved from http://www.Dtic.mil/summit/tb07.html.

Stock, C., & Schöpfel, J. (2004). Grey literature in an open context: From certainty to new challenges. *GL-Conference Series*, pp. 94–105.

Sulouff, P., Bell, S., Briden, J., Frontz, S., & Marshall, A. (2005). Learning about grey literature by interviewing subject librarians: A study at the University of Rochester. *College & Research Libraries News, 66*(7), 510–515.

Third International Conference on Grey Literature: Perspectives on the Design and Transfer of Scientific and Technical Information, 13–14 November 1997, Luxembourg. Conference proceedings.

Turner, A. M., Liddy, E. D., & Bradley, J. (2002). Breathing life into digital archives: Use of natural language processing to revitalize the grey literature of public health. *Proceedings of the 2nd ACM/IEEE-CS Joint Conference on Digital Libraries*, p. 411.

Tyndall, J. (2008). How low can you go? Towards a hierarchy of grey literature. Retrieved from https://dspace.flinders.edu.au/xmlui/handle/2328/3326.

Vaska M. (2010). Introducing Grey Literature. In Vaska, M., Schöpfel, J., Fürstová, I., Polčák, R., Mach, J., Frantíková, B., ... & Dolanský, J. (Eds.), *Grey literature repositories.* VeRBuM.

Von Hendy, M. (2014). Fifty shades of scientific and technical grey literature. *Online Searcher, 38*(3), 60–65.

Wessels, R. (2010). Grey literature. In J. Feathers & P. Sturges (Eds.), *International encyclopedia of information and library science.* Abingdon, UK: Routledge.

White, H. S. (1984). *Managing the special library: Strategies for success within the larger organization.* G. K. Hall and Co.

Wood, D. N., & Smith, A. W. (1993). SIGLE: A model for international co-operation. *Interlending & Document Supply, 21*(1), 18–22.

Chapter 2

The Value of Grey Literature

> Grey literature . . . rather shabby look—defined as "grey" to differentiate it from white or open publications appearing in commercial journals and books . . . the Cinderella of literature.—Paola De Castro and Sandra Salinetti, *Grey Literature: Challenges and Responsibilities for Authors and Editors* (2016)

The story of Cinderella is a lighthearted way to begin our discussion of grey literature's value. Like Cinderella, the momentous value of grey literature may be misunderstood, misbelieved, dismissed, or overlooked. Cinderella's evil stepsisters were completely unaware of the value someone else would see in her—and they were surprised to find her treasured. Rather than just playing a less important role than books and journals, grey literature is becoming more valued in the information landscape (De Castro & Salinetti, 2006). If we examine the numerous reasons for grey literature's merit, we can discover the whole story.

But first, how do we understand value? Value is often seen through an economic lens—most definitions of value focus first and foremost on monetary worth (Jaeger et al., 2014). Value can also be simply defined as the *importance, worth, or usefulness* of something (*OED Online*, 2016). These three criteria of importance, worth, or usefulness can be applied to the body of grey literature: it is a significant information resource, it has much of merit to offer, and it is a hugely relevant source for fulfilling information requests. Still, saying that grey literature is a resource of value is not enough: we first need to be able to comprehend why grey literature is uniquely valuable, especially when it is compared to other information resources. In this chapter, we will explore the specific ways grey literature offers value.

LEARNING OUTCOMES

The goal of this chapter is to provide librarians and information professionals with an overview on:

- how to prescribe value to an information resource
- the challenges associated with measuring the value of grey literature compared to other types of information resources
- the research on the value of grey literature in the areas of health and medicine
- the reasons why grey literature is a uniquely valuable information resource
- tips for explaining to users the added value of grey literature
- the unending need for grey literature as an information source

After reading this chapter, readers should also have core knowledge of the complexity of the value offered by grey literature. By examining the varied reasons why grey literature is of value, readers will also be able to compare the merits of grey literature to other sources of information.

WHAT MAKES AN INFORMATION RESOURCE VALUABLE?

Before we explore the reasons why grey literature is a valuable information source, we first need to address what makes information resources in general valuable. The development of new technologies has enabled more information to be available to more people than at any other time in history (Feathers, 2013). Moreover, the information age has made information that much easier to locate. For example, 82 percent of Americans say they believe it is easier to locate useful information today than it was five years ago (National Opinion Research Center, 2016). Not all information resources are considered as valuable as others or have enduring value. Take, for example, the success of Google's search engine compared to the now-defunct search engines AltaVista and Excite of long ago.

Several factors influence the usefulness of an information source. An information resource can be considered of value if it does the following:

- fills in existing gaps in knowledge
- originates from a trusted source
- answers the proposed question
- has well-documented sources and references

- provides insight unavailable elsewhere
- warrants reuse and sharing
- makes a lasting contribution to the information landscape. (Fattahi & Afshar, 2006)

MEASURING VALUE

Librarians and information professionals are generally aware of the traditional methods for measuring the worth of published information sources. The value of published information sources in library or information service collections is often measured by usage statistics, journal impact factors, and an H Index. For example, the value of a library resource such as a printed book or an e-journal may be measured by how often it is circulated or downloaded. A database such as PubMed also has clear statistics on the number of searches that have been executed. An author's H Index provides information on the productivity and the citation impact of publications. These acutely specific activity-based statistics provide a clear picture of impact-based investments, and the expression of merit is seen predominantly from a purely metric perspective—value is determined by library user activity (Van Moorsel, 2005).

In comparison, the value of grey literature is remarkably problematic to measure. Grey literature's heterogeneity makes it less accessible *to* traditional forms of bibliographic data capture (Adams, Smart, & Huff, 2017). One simply cannot adapt the same traditional approaches for measuring the worth of published information resources, such as journal articles and academic books, to measuring the merit of grey literature publications and sources. For example, citation analysis searches in Thomson Reuters's Web of Science are frequently used for analyzing the use and impact of the published literature (Bar-Ilan, 2008), but they cannot be used for grey literature.

The main barrier is that grey literature, unlike traditional monographs or journals, is not a homogeneous resource. As discussed in the previous chapter, there are multifarious types of grey literature resources; measuring value is far more complicated than simply tracking bibliometric-related outcomes. For example, if a library subscribes to an electronic journal, there will generally be detailed usage statistics available. The same may not ring true for a grey literature document that is available online. Subsequently, there is an incomplete picture of how a grey literature source may be contributing to the overall information landscape (Adie, 2014).

There has been a limited amount of research on a modified approach to citations analysis for grey literature (Hutton, 2009; Sibbald et al., 2015) and the use of grey literature in select subject areas, such as marine science, veterinary medicine, and patents (Breitzman & Thomas, 2016; Cordes, 2013;

Pelzer, 2003). Other research studies have tracked the impact and notability of grey literature publications by specific organizations or in specific disciplines, such as astrology, public policy research, intergovernmental science groups, environmental protection, and public health (Hutton, 2009; Chavez et al., 2007; Lawrence et al., 2012; MacDonald, Cordes, & Wells, 2007; Revere et al., 2007; Turner, 2005; Alpi, 2005; Jacobs, Liddy, & Bradley, 2012; UK Health Forum Research & Information Services, 2013). Although the research literature on citation analysis and grey literature publications is constructive for awareness of the value of grey literature as an information resource, it is only one (particularly small) part of the wider value picture. Moreover, citation analysis is a particularly dry and pedantic way to explain the worthiness of grey literature to others. There are several other livelier reasons why grey literature is a vital contributor to one's research.

GREY LITERATURE'S UNIQUE VALUE IN MEDICINE AND HEALTH RESEARCH

Much of the research on grey literature's value and greatness focuses on the need to include grey literature results in a systematic review. In this section, will we examine the research on grey literature's potential role in a systematic review.

A systematic review is a type of literature review that collects and critically analyzes multiple research studies on a specific topic. The goal of such a review is to provide a high-level analysis of the effectiveness of health care interventions (Cochrane Consumer Network, 2017). There are systematic reviews on a wide range of health care topics, including interventions for depressive disorder, improving diabetes care among the socially disadvantaged, the effect of dance interventions on cardiovascular risk, screening for skin cancer risk in adults, and even improving handwriting (Lawlor & Hopker, 2001; Glazier et al., 2006; Rodrigues-Krause et al., 2016; Wernli et al., 2016; Hoy, Egan, & Feder, 2011).

Systematic reviews aim to identify and analyze all the relevant trials to have the most complete picture of the available evidence (Peto, 1987). Take, for example, systematic reviews on the topic of interventions to prevent stroke in patients diagnosed with atrial fibrillation. The aim is to identify all relevant studies on this topic so that all of the relevant interventions can be identified and analyzed for efficacy. It is imperative to have a wide-reaching pool of available research to analyze, which requires systematic searching (McGowan & Sampson, 2005). Narrow searches may generate a smaller number of research studies that are not truly representative of all the available information (Jadad, Moher, & Klassen, 1998). For example, if a systematic review on interventions for stroke prevention in patients with atrial fibrillation failed to identify key studies, we would not know if the systematic review's conclusion was valid. If a systematic review has an incomplete set of data or information, it will not achieve the goal of examining and evaluating all the available research on a health care intervention; including all the relevant studies on a health care intervention in a systematic review's results is crucial to having a more complete information picture (Blackhall, 2007; Hammerstrøm et al., 2010; Hopewell et al., 2007; McAuley, Tugwell, & Moher, 2000; Rothstein & Hopewell, 2009).

One way to maximize the number of results retrieved in a systematic review search is to include a search for unpublished information: in other words, results that have not been published in a journal article, and from investigators and/or organizations involved in completed or ongoing research. Including these types grey literature publications in a systematic review increases heterogeneity in the evidence base (Adams, Smart, & Huff, 2017). In our example, we aim to identify all the available studies on interventions for stroke prevention in patients diagnosed with atrial fibrillation by including studies that have yet to be published. Grey literature publications are a source of unpublished information, and its inclusion broadens the pool of available evidence.

Additionally, several agencies that sponsor or set standards for systematic reviews stress that grey literature sources should be included in reviews. Cochrane, the Campbell Collaboration, and the National Academy of Medicine all stipulate that grey literature sources should be searched by reviewers (Higgins & Green, 2011; Campbell Collaboration, 2017; Morton et al., 2011). For example, the *Cochrane Handbook for Systematic Reviews of Interventions* Version 5.1.0 notes that reviewers should include information from unpublished studies since the failure to identify trials noted in conference proceedings and other sources of grey literature might affect the conclusion of a systematic review (Hopewell et al., 2007). As the conclusion of a systematic review on the effectiveness of a health care intervention may influence future decision making by health care providers—in our example, a physician may prescribe certain drugs to reduce stroke risk associated with atrial fibrillation as a result of reading the systematic review—it is imperative that the systematic review provide the most accurate information.

Avoiding publication bias is another rationale for including grey literature sources in a systematic review. Publication bias is not the same as trying to maximize the number of search results retrieved in a systematic review search, but it is similar. Publication bias occurs when published research is systematically unrepresentative of the population of completed studies (Rothstein, Sutton, & Borenstein, 2006). By including unpublished information, or grey literature sources, in a systematic review, potential publication bias can be avoided (McDonagh et al., 2013). Including unpublished research data from such sources as clinical trials is intrinsic to obtaining a complete picture of the available research results, especially since the results of numerous clinical trials are not published (Song, 2010).

Research studies in which the reported outcomes are negative are less likely to be published (Hopewell et al., 2009). For example, say a research team recently completed a clinical trial on a new drug for controlling diabetes, and the research findings show that this new drug is ineffective. These research findings are unlikely to be published (Fanelli, 2010; Kannan & Gowri, 2014), but the information may still be available in such sources as unpublished clinical trial results available from trial registries (Becker et al., 2014). The exclusion of unpublished studies in a systematic review or meta-analysis may lead to exaggerated rates of treatment effectiveness (McAuley, Tugwell, & Moher, 2000). Failure to include grey literature sources such as unpublished studies compromises the validity and reliability of meta-analysis, especially when unpublished findings differ from published research (Dickersin, 1997; Conn et al., 2003). Systematic reviews that include sources from grey literature have been shown to have significantly less risk of bias (McAuley, Tugwell, & Moher, 2000; Hopewell et al., 2007). Even so, research has also identified that many meta-analyses do not include grey literature (Ahmed, Sutton, & Riley, 2012).

TOP TEN REASONS FOR THE VALUE
OF GREY LITERATURE

It is not uncommon to hear the Top Ten reasons listed for all sorts of things: there are the Top Ten Reasons Why Libraries Are Important, the Top Ten Wonders of the World, and the Top Ten Reasons Why Cats Are Better Pets Than Dogs (or *perhaps* vice versa). Examining the worthiness of grey literature by using a Top Ten reasons metric is useful for understanding its unique value. Thus, from the Home Office (in Wahoo, Nebraska), we propose the Top Ten reasons for grey literature's value.

1. Grey literature provides a unique global perspective.

A global perspective can be defined as having knowledge of various features of the world and how the world functions, including knowledge of people and places beyond one's own community and country, and knowledge of events and issues beyond one's local surroundings (Carr, 1993). In our current information age, knowledge is commonly shared worldwide and is more easily distributed. Grey literature publications can provide perspicacious information on issues or interventions in other countries. Often, a new intervention or initiative will commence in one community and then spread to other communities or countries. Consequently, grey literature publications can be a key source for learning about such topics as new policy initiatives that are on offer in other countries, provinces, states, or regions.

One example of this is marijuana decriminalization or legalization of medical marijuana. Recent legislative changes took place in several U.S. states, including Colorado, yet other governments enacted legislation long before elsewhere. For example, Canada legalized medical marijuana in 2001 (Canada Medical Marijuana Access Regulations), prior to states like New Jersey and Arizona, which legalized medical marijuana in 2010 (NORML, 2017). International publications on medical marijuana include grey literature such as position statements on improving regulation of medical marijuana, use and safety of medical marijuana in the workplace, and statistics on the use of medical marijuana. While information resources such as books or journal articles may sometimes be able to provide international information on medical marijuana, the volume of grey literature from international sources should not be overlooked. Also, grey literature may be a superior source for information, because an initiative that is new in few jurisdictions may not have abundant information available in published white literature.

2. Grey literature is, more often than not, free.

A simple reason for grey literature's usefulness, and one that should not be overlooked, is that grey literature is often available for free online. In other words, it is available electronically. For example, most publications from such sources as governmental agencies or non-governmental organizations (NGOs) can be downloaded at no cost. Thus, information that is available in an electronic format provides added value because of its ease of availability and dissemination (Bothma, 1996). Journal subscriptions have been increasing at a rate faster than the inflation rate for decades (Dingley, 2005), while at the same time libraries have been receiving a shrinking share of university budgets (Association of Research Libraries, 2013). This is not to say that white literature is not a worthy library investment, but cost may be a barrier for some libraries or users. Not to mention that the information available for free in a grey literature publication often may be more substantial than what is available in the white literature.

3. There may be a lack of or very little information available in published literature.

A grey literature document will often be one of the meager number of information sources available on a particular topic, especially when a search for published information does not locate multiple sources. There are several reasons why grey literature could be the sole source of information on a topic. For one, the topic might be too specific to warrant publication in white literature; the pool of potential readers may be thought to be quite small, or the topic could be a health intervention that is newly emerging and has not been widely studied.

Take the example of organic farming. Looking back in history, the term "organic farming" emerged in 1940 (Kuepper, 2010), and organic foods are now available in 73 percent of U.S. grocery stores (Callard, 2009). When organic farming began to increase in popularity in the 1980s (Brevik & Burgess, 2012), most publications providing information on this increasingly popular approach were agricultural grey literature publications (Hutchinson & Paris-Greider, 2002). Today, of course, all of that has changed, as there is now a wealth of books, along with grey literature publications, on organic farming. Another more recent example is therapeutic hypothermia for physical trauma of gunshot victims: there is much more information available in grey literature, such as unpublished clinical trials or research studies, than in published literature. In specific subject areas, some users consider grey literature publications to be unique sources of information that cannot be located elsewhere and that have content unavailable in academic journals (Lawrence et al., 2012).

4. Grey literature is a source for evidence-based practice publications.

The most often cited definition of evidence-based practice (EBP) or medicine is: "the integration of best research evidence with clinical expertise and patient values" (Sackett, 1997). While published literature—for example, a systematic review published in an academic journal—is a source for evidenced-based practice information, there are also evidenced-based practice documents that can be classified as grey literature.

EBP sources such as evidence briefs, rapid reviews, clinical pathways, guidelines, and good practice documents may not be available in published white literature. EBP documents may be published as both stand-alone documents on a website and as journal articles: for example, the American Academy of Pediatrics guidelines are published on the organization's website and in the journal *Pediatrics*. However, EBP sources are often only available as grey literature publications, especially if the EBP document is from a governmental agency or professional organization such as the Registered Nurses' Association of Ontario. Other examples include publications from the following agencies: Agency for Health Care Research and Quality, National Institute for Health Care and Excellence, National Cancer Institute, Campbell Collaboration, and Canadian Agency for Drugs and Technology in Health. These agencies' publications are not indexed by databases and would be missed if grey literature sources were not searched.

5. Grey literature sources can complement sources located in published literature.

A literature search is an organized search for all the research on a specific topic. Users have varied motivations for requesting or completing a literature search: for example, they may want to understand a topic in more detail or identify new areas for research. Grey literature can help provide structure to a traditional literature search that has focused on sources located in published literature, and grey literature can often fill in gaps in the academic literature (Garengo, Biazzo, & Bititci, 2005). Users will often ask a librarian or other information professional for assistance with a literature search—and just as often, the literature search request will be lacking in clarity, or it will be too narrow or too broad to be successfully searched.

Grey literature documents on a topic can provide users with preceptive background information to frame their research question and may even help them figure out what topics they *want* to search and what topics they *don't* want information on. Take, for example, a user requesting a search on mobile phone interventions for health. The requested search terms are a little vague. For instance, how is health defined? Does the user require information on mobile phone interventions for specific populations, such as adolescents, or perhaps on specific disorders, such as diabetes? Sometimes a grey literature publication can be a useful guide for answering such questions. Using our example, there is a grey literature publication from the World Health Organization titled *mHealth: New Horizons for Health Through Mobile Technologies*. This 112-page document has information on mobile phone interventions such as appointment reminders and raising awareness, and it could be a uniquely informative source for determining the scope of a literature search. Furthermore, a grey literature publication can be an exceptional source for identifying search terms to be used in a literature search.

6. Grey literature sources may provide a more detailed information picture.

The average word count of scientific journal articles is 2,000 to 3,000 words (*New England Journal of Medicine*, 2017). The discussion of results and the conclusion of many of these articles may not have particularly detailed information. Publishers cannot be faulted for word-count restrictions; after all, scientific journal articles are intended to be short, concise communication vehicles that outline new discoveries or synthesize current research on a specific topic. In short, scientific journal articles are not intended to provide detailed background information on a topic. Information from grey literature publications may provide more detailed content, especially when compared to the content available in a book chapter or journal article. Unpublished studies may also provide readers with detailed information on such topics as process or implementation, which could be absent from a scientific research paper (Fountain, 2002).

Since the majority of grey lit publications are produced by organizations whose primary purpose is not publishing per se, there is no publisher-enforced word-count limit. Grey literature publications may also be sources of detailed qualitative data, since there often are no page-count restrictions (Finfgeld-Connett & Johnson, 2013). As result, there is much more freedom to provide greater coverage of varying issues related to a topic, including not only a brief discussion of a new initiative or intervention, but also in-depth discussions of potential action.

Grey literature may also provide detailed data that is not available in academic research (Albino et al., 2011). Take, for example, a research request on how to build community partnerships. While research literature will analyze and address the outcomes of community partnerships on such topics as HIV/AIDS prevention or nursing education, the information does not provide much guidance for specific steps, such as how to initiate community partnerships. There also are only are a few books on this topic. But grey literature publications on this topic are numerous, both from larger governmental agencies and NGOs, as well as from smaller organizations that have published toolkits on starting community partnerships. For example, the supremely well-known and well-regarded Centers for Disease Control and Prevention (CDC) has published a guide, called *Partnership Evaluation*, about evaluating community partnerships, and the somewhat less-known National Association of County & City Health Officials has also published a guide, called *Mobilizing Community Partnerships in Rural Communities*, on the topic.

7. Grey literature publications can be accessible and relevant to a wider range of readers.

There is a wealth of grey literature written specifically for such professionals as librarians, child protection workers, first responders, policy makers, community organizers, public defenders, parolee officers, clinicians, and nurses. For example, police and other law enforcement agencies produce a sizeable amount of grey literature (Sturges & Cooke, 2007). Publications are often produced as grey literature because their topics may only be of interest to a limited number of readers (Wessels, 2003), and commercial publications need to have a wider readership to be successful. Generating revenue is generally not the motivation for publishing grey literature: rather, impact over profit has been pointed to as a key factor of grey literature–producing organizations (Wessels, 2003). Thus, grey literature–producing organizations can choose to write publications for their chosen target audience. Grey literature publications are prized sources for practitioners and decisions makers in numerous disciplines since grey lit sources such as clinical practice guidelines, program evaluation reports, and research reports often contain information relevant to specific disciplines (Godin et al., 2015). For example, numerous online toolkits are available for social workers, and these toolkits are published by governmental agencies and other organizations, such as charities. One example is the publication *Solution Focused Practice: A Tool Kit for Working with Children and Young People*, published by the UK organization National Society for the Prevention of Cruelty to Children.

Academic research in books or journal articles is also generally intended for a decidedly narrow and specific audience. Moreover, there has been much debate around how often—or, better stated, how little—academic papers are read. A 2007 study noted that up to 50 percent of academic papers are never read by anyone other than their authors, referees, and journal editors (Meho, 2007). Of course, readership of academic publications, including journal articles, can vary across professions. For example, although physicians read academic journal articles, they read less than other professionals working in areas such as engineering, astronomy, and social sciences (Tenopir et al., 2007). Also, academic research is often written for other academics and may not be accessible to practitioners and policy makers because of the format and language used (Kelly, 2015). For example, academic social scientists have been criticized for using language in an imprecise way (Billig, 2013), while grey literature publications are often specifically intended for practitioners (Adams, Smart, & Huff, 2017; Albino et al., 2011). In short, grey literature publications can often provide straightforward, intelligible, and *useful* information on how to do something. Academic research is just one part of many in the evidence base, and other sources provide further information and contextual knowledge (Nutley, Walter, & Davies, 2007).

Grey literature publications have also been identified as being more relevant to specific readers, such as professionals working in the areas of policy development and public health (UK Health Forum Research & Information Services, 2013; Grey Lit Strategies). Likewise, while scientific evidence is vital for the evidence base, other sources of evidence are often used to support decision making. For example, professionals in public health use a number of other sources besides scientific research articles. Research into the use of evidence by public health practitioners and policy makers found that they also use sources such as websites, evidence about best practices from local and provincial organizations, and information from charities or community organizations (Orton et al., 2011).

8. Grey literature may be the most current source of information.

It takes time for research results to be published in scholarly literature. In the publishing cycle, the dissemination of new information must complete the arduous journey from submission to publication. Because of this delay, the most up-to-date information may not be available in books or journal articles. Grey literature has been noted for its ability to be more contemporaneous (Fountain, 2002) and may provide up-to-date information that is not available in published academic research literature (Adams, 2012; Albino et al., 2011; Martin & Assenov, 2012; Adams, Smart, & Huff, 2017). Grey literature is also an essential channel for communication because information can become available at an earlier date than in published literature (Soule & Ryan, 1999). Grey literature publication types such as conference papers and technical reports have been noted for containing more current scientific information than books or journal articles (Robinson, 1988; Drott, 1995). Additionally, some research organizations may choose to make their findings available in grey literature to avoid the delay that is associated with publishing in academic research literature (Wessel, 2003).

Clinical trial sources are one type of grey literature publication that contains more up-to-date information than white literature. The delay between research and publication of new research from clinical trials does not allow for real-time examination of new interventions. The median time between the submission of a manuscript to an academic journal and acceptance for publication is 100 days (Himmelstein, 2015). On average, it takes eight and a half years to study and test an experimental drug before it becomes available to the general patient population (FDA, 2015). The average time span for clinical trial results to be published after the completion of the clinical trial is two years (Ross et al., 2013). As a result, relying solely on clinical trial information from published literature (i.e., clinical trial results published in a journal article) means that the most recent information on an intervention may be overlooked. The unavailability of timely information from clinical trials in published literature is a barrier to evaluating new interventions (Citrome, 2014).

9. Grey literature is a major source for knowledge dissemination.

Knowledge dissemination has been defined as an "active process to communicate results to potential users by targeting, tailoring and packaging the message for a particular target audience" (Straus, Tetroe, & Graham, 2009). Grey literature has been a key resource for disseminating new research for a number of decades (Hutton, 2009), and grey literature publications can comprise the primary publishing output of many organizations (O'Dell et al., 2004; MacDonald, Cordes, & Wells, 2004). The exigency of communicating research results using multifaceted venues is recognized as a best practice by many national and international institutions (De Castro & Salinetti, 2013).

Indeed, many organizations may actively decide not to publish in academic literature and make the results available in the grey literature instead (Wessel, 2003). Grey literature publications can also be the key component of an organization's knowledge dissemination strategy. The main aim is to convey the research findings as quickly and effortlessly as possible rather than publish for commercial gain (Wessel, 2003).

Many organizations that produce grey literature seek to impact current practice and policy, and this is the rationale for producing grey literature publications in the first place (Lawrence et al., 2012). As a result, grey literature publications can be a key modus operandi for communication (Lawrence et al., 2012) and for adding to the evidence base.

10. Grey literature offers diverse sources of information.

Reason number ten is, in many ways, a composite of all of the other reasons for valuing grey literature. We have examined a number of reasons for grey literature's merit, but overall, grey literature offers sources of information that arise from countless voices. Grey literature is characterized by its diversity and heterogeneity (Adams, Smart, & Huff, 2017): a variety of information is available from grey literature sources, and divergent groups of information users may benefit from grey literature. Additionally, grey literature publications are produced by various types of authors and organizations; for example, grey literature is produced by large organizations as well as small ones, by organizations that have an international mandate, and by organizations that only have a localized mission. Grey literature's diversity is also evident in the multitude of readers grey lit publications are written for. As previously mentioned, grey literature publications can be written for very specific populations, including first responders, engineers, midwives, patient educators, psychiatric nurses, psychologists, public health workers, school principals, and urban planners, to name but a few.

EXPLAINING VALUE

Explaining the worthiness of grey literature to library patrons may be an onerous task. The value of things like good news will always be evident (Harmon, 2003), but the value of other things may be unrecognized or unknown. Warren Buffet has said, "Price is what you pay; value is what you get." Value has also been defined as whether or not the invested resources warrant the outcome (Ramsey & Schickedanz, 2010). An intervention in cancer care can be described as having value if patients, their families, physicians, and health insurers all agree that benefits afforded by the intervention are sufficient to support the total sum of resources expended for its use (Ramsey & Schickedanz, 2010).

The best approach for explaining to users the merit of grey literature is to point out what grey literature has to offer them since it is not always evident or obvious. Moreover, librarians and other information professionals may also need to recognize that grey literature will serve the needs of users differently. For example, the information needs of a public health nurse may vary from the information needs of a research coordinator for a clinical trial. Also, distinct types of grey literature publications may offer more value to some than to others—those in one discipline may value conference publications over grey literature publications from organizations such as think thanks (Sulouff et al., 2005). The next section will provide tips for explaining the value of grey literature to information services and library users.

TIPS FOR EXPLAINING THE VALUE
OF GREY LITERATURE

Tip 1

Ask: "Do you know that grey literature is valued by many institutions?"

Users may assume that a search for grey literature publications is unnecessary and that literature searches for published research in databases such as Embase, Medline, and PsycInfo are considered far more essential and key to obtaining information. Moreover, authors can be shamefully instructed by peer-reviewed journals to avoid references to grey literature sources (Instructions to Authors, International Journal for Quality in Healthcare). Still some information users may not be cognizant that several evidence-based research institutions, such as Cochrane, the Campbell Collaboration, and the Joanna Briggs Institute, all require their reviewers to search grey literature, so grey literature publications can be included in a review. Additionally, agencies that fund systematic review projects, such as the Canadian Institute for Health Research (CHIR), may want to see the intent to search grey literature on a grant application.

Tip 2

Suggestion: "Don't let the peer reviewers surprise you."

It is easier to include grey literature from the beginning of the search process rather than as an afterthought. Once a systematic review manuscript has been submitted to a journal and begins the peer review process, referees may criticize or reject the manuscript for not including grey literature sources. While there has been a wealth of research on the worthiness of the inclusion of grey literature, there has been exceedingly little on the rationale for excluding grey literature from a systematic review. Revising a search strategy is hardly a minor revision, especially since the data extraction process will have to be re-executed to include any new citations.

Revising a search strategy to include grey literature sources is an even more convoluted process—the entire search scope, types of sources included, and search strategy will need to be reexamined and reassessed. If users do not want to include grey literature sources in a search, they should be advised that they may need to provide a clear rationale and may suffer the consequences for doing so. It may be wiser to simply search a subset of grey literature—for example, conference proceedings or clinical trials with available results—than to exclude grey literature altogether. Also, including a grey literature search from the beginning may make the manuscript more likely to be accepted for publication.

Tip 3

Remind: "Grey literature is a peer-reviewed source."

Although grey literature is considered its own separate category from peer-reviewed resources (Adams et al., 2016; Benzies et al., 2006), grey literature is often produced by prominent experts and practitioners (Coad, Hardicre, & Devitt, 2006). Grey literature will often undergo multiple forms of peer review; for example, grey literature reports may go through several levels of internal and agency review (Seymour, 2010; Lawrence et al., 2012). It has also been suggested that grey literature publications that involve interagency collaboration are subjected to more peer review than manuscripts submitted to journals.

Tip 4

Inquire: "Are you focusing on evidence-based practice information?"

As mentioned in value reason number four, grey literature is often a source of evidence-based practice publications, such as guidelines, evidence briefs, clinical pathways, and rapid reviews. If grey literature sources are excluded from a search, key evidence-based practice documents will be missed. For example, publications from such evidence-based practice organizations as National Institute for Health and Care Excellence (NICE) and Substance Abuse and Mental Health Services Administration (SAMHSA) will be missed if a search does not include grey literature sources. Finally, syntheses of grey literature help researchers and practitioners understand what types of interventions exist for a particular problem, the full range of evaluations that may have been conducted, and whether more intervention development and evaluation are needed (Adams et al., 2016).

Also, if a user is seeking health services information, the majority of policy documents that discuss topics such as overall plans and merits of future action are often located in grey literature–producing organizations such as think tanks, NGOs, and governmental agencies. These types of documents may be excluded if grey literature sources are not used.

Tip 5

Inquire: "What level of detail do you need?"

This is also known as the "lost time is never found again" pointer. Who doesn't want to save time by not having to read through numerous search hits from a database search if it is not necessary? Numerous grey literature publications provide in-depth summaries and synthesized information. Examples of these types of grey literature publications include publications from sources such as the Agency for Healthcare Research and Quality (AHRQ), the Canadian Agency for Drugs and Technologies in Health (CADTH), the Department of Veterans Affairs, and the Institute for Quality and Efficiency in Health Care (IQWIG). Grey literature publications that summarize and combine information will include research from multiple sources and will identify, assess, and amalgamate the research findings. A grey literature publication may help a user become more information-efficient as someone else has completed all of the needed analysis. Of course, this does not preclude a highly focused and traditional literature review; rather, a grey literature publication can always be used as a complement and supplement.

CONCLUSION

Grey literature offers a worthy body of knowledge. Moreover, several varying estimates and metrics can be used to determine and demonstrate its worth. Grey literature has been identified as a paramount source of information in every field of knowledge (De Castro & Salinetti, 2013), and there are various elements to the value of grey literature. Grey literature has also been called *grey* because "the grey in grey literature refers to the brain's grey matter since so much of it is highly intellectual, and is significant for research and development in many subject areas" (Mason, 2009). The key takeaway point is that grey literature occupies its own distinguished position in the body of research literature.

BIBLIOGRAPHY

Adam, T., Hsu, J., De Savigny, D., Lavis, J. N., Røttingen, J. A., & Bennett, S. (2012). Evaluating health systems strengthening interventions in low-income and middle-income countries: are we asking the right questions?. *Health policy and planning, 27*(suppl_4), iv9-iv19.

Adams, J., Hillier-Brown, F. C., Moore, H. J., Lake, A. A., Araujo-Soares, V., White, M., et al. (2016). Searching and synthesising "grey literature" and "grey information" in public health: Critical reflections on three case studies. *Systematic Reviews, 5*(1), 164.

Adams, R. J., Smart, P., & Huff, A. S. (2017). Shades of grey: Guidelines for working with the grey literature in systematic reviews for management and organizational studies. *International Journal of Management Reviews, 19*(4), 432–454.

Adie, E. (2014). The grey literature from an altmetrics perspective—opportunity and challenges. *Research Trends, 37*, 23–25.

Ahmed, I., Sutton, A. J., & Riley, R. D. (2012). Assessment of publication bias, selection bias, and unavailable data in meta-analyses using individual participant data: a database survey. *Bmj, 344*, d7762.

Albino, V., Dangelico, R. M., Natalicchio, A., & Yazan, D. M. (2011). Alternative energy sources in cement manufacturing. Network for Business Sustainability, Richard Ivey School of Business of Western Ontario.

Alpi, K. M. (2005). Expert searching in public health. *Journal of the Medical Library Association: JMLA, 93*(1), 97–103.

Association of Research Libraries. (n.d.) Monographs & Serials Costs in ARL Libraries, 1986-2013. Retrieved from http://www.arl.org/storage/documents/monograph-serial-costs.pdf.

Bar-Ilan, J. (2008). Which h-index? A comparison of WoS, scopus and google scholar. *Scientometrics, 74*(2), 257–271.

Becker, J. E., Krumholz, H. M., Ben-Josef, G., & Ross, J. S. (2014). Reporting of results in ClinicalTrials.gov and high-impact journals. *JAMA, 311*(10), 1063–1065.

Benzies, K. M., Premji, S., Hayden, K. A., & Serrett, K. (2006). State-of-the-evidence reviews: Advantages and challenges of including grey literature. *Worldviews on Evidence-Based Nursing, 3*(2), 55–61.

Bergman, M. K. (2001). White paper: The Deep Web: Surfacing hidden value. *Journal of Electronic Publishing, 7*(1).

Billig, M. (2013). *Learn to write badly: How to succeed in the social sciences.* Cambridge University Press.

Blackhall, K. & Ker, K. (2007). Finding studies for inclusion in systematic reviews of interventions for injury prevention–the importance of grey and unpublished literature. *Injury prevention, 13*(5), 359–359.

Borenstein, M., Rothstein, H., & Sutton, A. (2005). *Publication bias in meta-analysis: Prevention, assessment and adjustments.* Wiley.

Bothma, T. J. (1996). Added Value in Electronic Publications.

Breitzman, A., & Thomas, P. (2016). An analysis of references from US patents to NIST-supported technical outputs.

Breitzman Sr, A., & Thomas, P. (2016). An Analysis of References from US Patents to NIST-Supported Technical Outputs.

Brevik, E. C., & Burgess, L. C. (2012). *Soils and human health.* CRC Press.

Callard, A. (2009). A decade in food trends. *Smithsonian.com.* Retrieved from https://www.smithsonianmag.com/arts-culture/a-decade-in-food-trends-76395204/

Carr, C. (1993). Global, national and resource-based strategies: An examination of strategic choice and performance in the vehicle components industry. *Strategic Management Journal, 14*(7), 551–567.

Chavez, T. A., Perrault, A. H., Reehling, P., & Crummett, C. (2007). The impact of grey literature in advancing global karst research: An information needs assessment for a globally distributed interdisciplinary community. *Publishing Research Quarterly, 23*(1), 3–18.

Citrome, L. (2014). Beyond PubMed: searching the "Grey Literature" for clinical trial results. *Innovations in clinical neuroscience, 11*(7–8), 42.

Coad, J., Hardicre, J., & Devitt, P. (2006). How to search for and use "grey literature" in research. *Nursing Times, 102*(50), 35–36.

Cochrane Consumer Network (n.d.) Retrieved from http://consumers.cochrane.org/what-systematic-review.

Conn, V. S., Valentine, J. C., Cooper, H. M., & Rantz, M. J. (2003). Grey literature in meta-analyses. *Nursing Research, 52*(4), 256–261.

Cordes, R. (2013). *Is grey literature ever used? Using citation analysis to measure the impact of GESAMP, an international marine scientific advisory body.* Proceedings of the Annual Conference of CAIS/Actes Du Congrès Annuel De l'ACSI.

De Castro, P., & Salinetti, S. (2006). "Uniform requirements" for grey literature: A proposal for the adoption of "Nancy style." *Publishing Research Quarterly*, *22*(1), 12–17.

De Castro, P., & Salinetti, S. (2013). "6.4: Grey Literature: Challenges and Responsibilities for Authors and Editors." In P. Smart, H. Maisonneuve, & A. Polderman (eds.), Science Editors' Handbook European Association of Science Editors.

De Castro, P., & Salinetti, S. (2013). Grey literature: A growing need for good practice. *European Science Editing*, *39*(3).

De Castro, P., Salinetti, S., & Banks, M. (2006). Awareness and empowerment in document production and distribution as a "must" for open access: Experiences from the "Nancy style" to guarantee quality.

Dickersin, K. (1997). How important is publication bias? A synthesis of available data. *AIDS education and prevention*, *9*, 15–21.

Dingley, B. (2005). US periodical price Index–2004.

Drott, M. C. (1995). Reexamining the role of conference papers in scholarly communication. *Journal of the American Society for Information Science*, *46*(4), 299.

Fanelli, D. (2010). Do pressures to publish increase scientists' bias? An empirical support from US States Data. *PloS one*, *5*(4), e10271.

Fattahi, R., & Afshar, E. (2006). Added value of information and information systems: A conceptual approach. *Library Review*, *55*(2), 132–147.

Feathers, J. (2013). *The information society: A study of continuity and change* (6th ed.). Facet Publishing.

Finfgeld-Connett, D., & Johnson, E. D. (2013). Literature search strategies for conducting knowledge-building and theory-generating qualitative systematic reviews. *Journal of Advanced Nursing*, *69*(1), 194–204.

Food and Drug Administration. (2015). How Drugs are Developed and Approved. Retrieved from https://www.fda.gov/Drugs/DevelopmentApprovalProcess/HowDrugsareDevelopedandApproved/default.htm.

Fountain J. (2002). Grey matter: Unpublished research report. *Social Work in Europe*, *9*, 65.

Garengo, P., Biazzo, S., & Bititci, U. S. (2005). Performance measurement systems in SMEs: A review for a research agenda. *International Journal of Management Reviews*, *7*(1), 25–47.

Glazier, R. H., Bajcar, J., Kennie, N. R., & Willson, K. (2006). A systematic review of interventions to improve diabetes care in socially disadvantaged populations. *Diabetes Care*, *29*(7), 1675–1688.

Godin, K., Stapleton, J., Kirkpatrick, S. I., Hanning, R. M., & Leatherdale, S. T. (2015). Applying systematic review search methods to the grey literature: A case study examining guidelines for school-based breakfast programs in Canada. *Systematic Reviews*, *4*(1), 138.

Goodman, M. (2015). *Future crimes: Everything is connected, everyone is vulnerable and what we can do about it*. Anchor.

Hammerstrøm, K., Wade, A., Jørgensen, A. K., & Hammerstrøm, K. (2010). Searching for studies. *Education*, *54*, 11.3.

Harmon, R. (2003). Marketing information systems. *Encyclopedia of information systems, 3*(1), 137–151.

Higgins, J. P., & Green, S. (2011). *Cochrane handbook for systematic reviews of interventions*. John Wiley & Sons.

Himmelstein, D. (2015). Publication delays at PLOS and 3,475 other journals. *Satoshi Village 9*(1).

Hopewell, S., Loudon, K., Clarke, M. J., Oxman, A. D., & Dickersin, K. (2009). Publication bias in clinical trials due to statistical significance or direction of trial results. *Cochrane Database of Systematic Reviews* 2009, Issue 1. Art. No.: MR000006. DOI: 10.1002/14651858.MR000006.pub3.

Hopewell, S., McDonald, S., Clarke, M. J., & Egger, M. (2007). Grey literature in meta-analyses of randomized trials of health care interventions. *Cochrane Database of Systematic Reviews* 2007, Issue 2. Art. No.: MR000010. DOI: 10.1002/14651858. MR000010.pub3.

Hoy, M. M., Egan, M. Y., & Feder, K. P. (2011). A systematic review of interventions to improve handwriting. *Canadian Journal of Occupational Therapy, 78*(1), 13–25.

Hutchinson, B. S., & Paris-Greider, A. (2002). *Using the agricultural, environmental, and food literature.* CRC Press.

Hutton, G. R. (2009). *Scientific grey literature in a digital age: Measuring its use and influence in an evolving information economy.* Proceedings of the 2009 Canadian Association of Information Science Conference, Ottawa, Ontario, pp. 1–15.

Jacobs, J. A., Jones, E., Gabella, B. A., Spring, B., & Brownson, R. C. (2012). Peer reviewed: Tools for implementing an evidence-based approach in public health practice. *Preventing Chronic Disease, 9.*

Jadad, A. R., Moher, D., & Klassen, T. P. (1998). Guides for reading and interpreting systematic reviews: II. How did the authors find the studies and assess their quality? *Archives of Pediatrics & Adolescent Medicine, 152*(8), 812–817.

Jaeger, P. T., Gorham, U., Bertot, J. C., & Sarin, L. C. (2014). *Public libraries, public policies, and political processes: Serving and transforming communities in times of economic and political constraint.* Rowman & Littlefield.

Kannan, S., & Gowri, S. (2014). Contradicting/negative results in clinical research: Why (do we get these)? Why not (get these published)? Where (to publish)? *Perspectives in Clinical Research, 5*(4), 151–153.

Kay, M., Santos, J., & Takane, M. (2011). mHealth: New horizons for health through mobile technologies. *World Health Organization, 64*(7), 66–71.

Kelly, W. R. (2015). *Criminal justice at the crossroads: Transforming crime and punishment.* Columbia University Press.

Kuepper, G. (2010). A brief overview of the history and philosophy of organic agriculture. Poteau, OK: Kerr Center for Sustainable Agriculture.

Kugley, S., Wade, A., Thomas, J., Mahood, Q., Jørgensen, A. K., Hammerstrøm, K., et al. (2016). Searching for studies: A guide to information retrieval for Campbell Systematic Reviews. Campbell Methods Guides 2016: 1. DOI: 10.4073/ cmg.2016.1.

Lawlor, D. A., & Hopker, S. W. (2001). The effectiveness of exercise as an intervention in the management of depression: Systematic review and meta-regression analysis of randomised controlled trials. *BMJ (Clinical Research Ed.), 322*(7289), 763–767.

Lawrence, A., Houghton, J., Thomas, J., & Weldon, P. (2012). Where is the evidence? Realising the value of grey literature for public policy and practice. Swinburne Institute for Social Research, Melbourne, Australia. Retrieved from http://apo.org.au/research/where-evidence-realising-value-grey-literature-public-policy-and-practice.

MacDonald, B. H., Cordes, R. E., & Wells, P. G. (2004). Grey literature in the life of GESAMP, an international marine scientific advisory body. *Publishing Research Quarterly, 20*(1), 25–41.

MacDonald, B. H., Cordes, R. E., & Wells, P. G. (2007). Assessing the diffusion and impact of grey literature published by international intergovernmental scientific groups: The case of the gulf of Maine council on the marine environment. *Publishing Research Quarterly, 23*(1), 30–46.

Martin, S. A., & Assenov, I. (2012). The genesis of a new body of sport tourism literature: A systematic review of surf tourism research (1997–2011). *Journal of Sport & Tourism, 17*(4), 257–287.

McAuley, L., Tugwell, P., & Moher, D. (2000). Does the inclusion of grey literature influence estimates of intervention effectiveness reported in meta-analyses? *The Lancet, 356*(9237), 1228–1231.

McDonagh, M., Peterson, K., Raina, P., Chang, S., & Shekelle, P. (2013). *Avoiding bias in selecting studies: Methods guide for effectiveness and comparative effectiveness reviews.* Agency for Healthcare Research and Quality.

McGowan, J., & Sampson, M. (2005). Systematic reviews need systematic searchers. *Journal of the Medical Library Association: JMLA, 93*(1), 74–80.

McKenna, C., Burch, J., Suekarran, S., Walker, S., Bakhai, A., Witte, K., et al. (2010). A systematic review and economic evaluation of the clinical effectiveness and cost-effectiveness of aldosterone antagonists for postmyocardial infarction heart failure. *Health Technology Assessment (Winchester, England), 14*(24), 1–162.

Meho, L. I. (2007). The rise and rise of citation analysis. *Physics World, 20*(1), 32.

Morton, S., Berg, A., Levit, L., & Eden, J. (2011). *Finding what works in health care: Standards for systematic reviews.* National Academies Press.

National Opinion Research Center (NORC). (2016). *Investigating how Americans navigate the modern information environment.* NORC at the University of Chicago.

NEJM frequently asked questions. (n.d.). Retrieved January 11, 2017, from http://www.nejm.org.myaccess.library.utoronto.ca/page/author-center/frequently-asked-questions.

NORMAL. (n.d.). State Info. Retrieved from https://norml.org/states.

Nutley, S., Jung, T., & Walter, I. (2008). The many forms of research-informed practice: A framework for mapping diversity. *Cambridge Journal of Education, 38*(1), 53–71.

Nutley, S. M., Walter, I., & Davies, H. T. (2007). *Using evidence: How research can inform public services.* Policy Press.

O'Dell, C., Dallman, D., Vesely, M., & Vigen, J. (2004). Fifty years of experience in making grey literature available: Matching the expectations of the particle physics community. *Publishing Research Quarterly 20*(1), 84–91.

Orton, L., Lloyd-Williams, F., Taylor-Robinson, D., O'Flaherty, M., & Capewell, S. (2011). The use of research evidence in public health decision making processes: Systematic review. *PloS One, 6*(7), e21704.

Peto, R. (1987). Why do we need systematic overviews of randomized trials? (Transcript of an oral presentation, modified by the editors). *Statistics in medicine, 6*(3), 233–240.

Pelzer, N. L., & Wiese, W. H. (2003). Bibliometric study of grey literature in core veterinary medical journals. *Journal of the Medical Library Association: JMLA, 91*(4), 434–441.

Ramsey, S., & Schickedanz, A. (2010). How should we define value in cancer care? *The Oncologist, 15 Suppl* 1, 1–4.

Revere, D., Turner, A. M., Madhavan, A., Rambo, N., Bugni, P. F., Kimball, A., et al. (2007). Understanding the information needs of public health practitioners: A literature review to inform design of an interactive digital knowledge management system. *Journal of Biomedical Informatics, 40*(4), 410–421.

Rodrigues-Krause, J., Farinha, J. B., Krause, M., & Reischak-Oliveira, Á. (2016). Effects of dance interventions on cardiovascular risk with ageing: Systematic review and meta-analysis. *Complementary Therapies in Medicine, 29,* 16–28.

Ross, J. S., Mocanu, M., Lampropulos, J. F., Tse, T., & Krumholz, H. M. (2013). Time to publication among completed clinical trials. *JAMA Internal Medicine, 173*(9), 825–828.

Rothstein, H. R., & Hopewell, S. (2009). Grey literature. In H. Cooper, L. V. Hedges, & J. C. Valentine (Eds.), The handbook of research synthesis and meta-analysis (pp. 103–25). New York: Russell Sage Foundation.

Rothstein, H. R., Sutton, A. J., & Borenstein, M. (2006). *Publication bias in meta-analysis: Prevention, assessment and adjustments.* John Wiley & Sons.

Sackett, D. L. (1997). *Evidence-based medicine: How to practice and teach EBM.* WB Saunders Company.

Schöpfel, J. (2013). Adding value to electronic theses and dissertations in institutional repositories. *DLib Magazine, 19*(3/4).

Schopfel, J., & Stock, C. (2008). Grey foundations in information landscape: A report on the 9th international conference on grey literature, Antwerp, 10–11 December 2007. *Interlending & Document Supply, 36*(2).

Seymour, D. J. (2010). *In the trenches around the ivory tower: Introduction to black-and-white issues about the grey literature.*

Sibbald, S. L., MacGregor, J. C., Surmacz, M., & Wathen, C. N. (2015). Into the gray: A modified approach to citation analysis to better understand research impact. *Journal of the Medical Library Association: JMLA, 103*(1), 49–54.

Song, F., Parekh, S., Hooper, L., Loke, Y. K., Ryder, J., Sutton, A. J., ... & Harvey, I. (2010). Dissemination and publication of research findings: an updated review of related biases. *Health Technol Assess, 14*(8), 1–193.

Soule, M. H., & Ryan, R. P. (1999). Gray literature, technical briefing. *Information Technology summIT.* Retrieved from http://www.Dtic.mil/summit/tb07.Html.

Straus, S. E., Tetroe, J., & Graham, I. (2009). Defining knowledge translation. *CMAJ: Canadian Medical Association Journal = Journal De l'Association Medicale Canadienne, 181*(3–4), 165–168.

Sturges, P., & Cooke, L. (2007). Finding the grey in the blue: Transparency and disclosure in teaching. The Grey Journal: An International Journal on Grey Literature, 4(1), pp. 21–28.

Sulouff, P., Bell, S., Briden, J., Frontz, S., & Marshall, A. (2005). Learning about grey literature by interviewing subject librarians: A study at the university of Rochester. *College & Research Libraries News, 66*(7), 510–515.

Tenopir, C., King, D. W., Clarke, M. T., Na, K., & Zhou, X. (2007). Journal reading patterns and preferences of pediatricians. *Journal of the Medical Library Association: JMLA, 95*(1), 56–63.

Turner, A. M., Liddy, E. D., & Bradley, J. (2002). *Breathing life into digital archives: Use of natural language processing to revitalize the grey literature of public health.* Proceedings of the 2nd ACM/IEEE-CS Joint Conference on Digital Libraries, p. 411.

UK Health Forum Research & Information Services. (2013). *Discussion paper: Grey literature in public health: Valuable evidence?*

Van Moorsel, G. (2005). Client value models provide a framework for rational library planning (or, phrasing the answer in the form of a question). *Medical Reference Services Quarterly, 24*(2), 25–40.

Wernli, K. J., Henrikson, N. B., Morrison, C. C., Nguyen, M., Pocobelli, G., & Blasi, P. R. (2016). Screening for skin cancer in adults: Updated evidence report and systematic review for the US preventive services task force. *JAMA, 316*(4), 436–447.

Wessels, R. (2003). Grey literature. *International Encyclopedia of Information and Library Science*. Routledge.

Chapter 3

Databases for Grey Literature

A bibliographic database is defined as:

> a computer file consisting of records, each containing a uniform description of
> a specific document or bibliographic item, usually retrievable by author, title,
> subject heading (descriptor) or keyword(s). Many bibliographic databases are
> general in scope and coverage; others provide access to literature of a specific
> discipline or a group of disciplines. (Reitz, 2004)

Select bibliographic databases can be a key research source for searching
grey literature. Some databases contain both published and unpublished literature, while other databases may only include grey literature publications.

LEARNING OUTCOMES

The goal of this chapter is to provide librarians, information professionals,
and library students with:

- a proposed working definition for bibliographic databases containing grey
  literature content
- an explanation of the difference between searching a bibliographic database and searching a website for grey literature
- bibliographic databases' strengths as research tools for locating grey literature publications
- bibliographic databases' weaknesses as research tools for locating grey
  literature publications
- tips for searching bibliographic databases for grey literature

- a list of select bibliographic databases that include grey literature publications, including:
  - producer of the database
  - temporal coverage
  - cost
  - scope of database and grey literature content
- the main bibliographic databases for health and medicine
- a proposed decision-making aid for adding bibliographic databases to a grey literature search

After reading this chapter, the reader should have a basic knowledge of using bibliographic databases for a grey literature search. The following introductory overview of bibliographic databases for grey literature should also enable librarians and information professionals to facilitate discussions with their information users on using these databases for searching grey literature.

BIBLIOGRAPHIC DATABASES INDEXING GREY LITERATURE PUBLICATIONS

Bibliographic databases are well-known research tools for searching published literature. For example, most systematic reviews in journal articles will have a search methodology section mentioning the bibliographic databases that have been searched. Most bibliographic databases primarily index published literature, such as journal articles. However, there are bibliographic databases that either include grey literature content with published literature or that focus specifically on grey literature.

What Is the Difference between a Bibliographic Database and a Website?

Long gone are the days of the print Indexus Medicus or PsycLit on CD-ROM or—*gasp*—Current Contents on diskettes. Currently, bibliographic databases are primarily accessed and searched online. The main difference between searching a bibliographic database and searching a website is that when you search a bibliographic database, you are searching across a spectrum of records all at once, and the records have a uniform description. Those collections of records also have specific criteria for inclusion that are set by the creator of the bibliographic database—this is generally defined as the scope of the bibliographic database. The scope of a database lists the type of material that is indexed in the database, so searchers can have an expectation of the types of sources and topics that will be retrieved by a search. For example, the scope of Embase indicates that it is a biomedical bibliographic database of published literature and that the database is produced by Elsevier B.V. Databases containing grey literature content function in the same way—their records have been selected for inclusion because they meet specific selection criteria.

A WORKING DEFINITION OF BIBLIOGRAPHIC DATABASES CONTAINING GREY LITERATURE PUBLICATIONS

Librarians and information professionals are quite familiar with bibliographic databases such as Academic OneFile, Medline, Embase, Scopus, and CINAHL. The navigation screens of these databases have such features as searches by author, title, keywords in the abstract, and subject headings, as well as the ability to limit publications by year, document type, and language; navigation screens of these databases also support the use of Boolean operators. A large number of the bibliographic databases available for locating grey literature publications are not commercially produced or mighty bibliographic databases; rather, these bibliographic databases are available for free online and index less content. Databases that index grey literature documents may not have numerous familiar search features, and the bibliographic databases that can be used to locate grey literature publications will often look remarkably different from the bibliographic databases used to search published literature. In this chapter, the term "bibliographic databases" will be applied to:

- online research sources that can be used to search across numerous records at once to identify records meeting set criteria; and
- online research tools that have been specifically created to direct users to publications.

ADVANTAGES OF USING BIBLIOGRAPHIC DATABASES FOR LOCATING GREY LITERATURE PUBLICATIONS

There are numerous advantages to using bibliographic databases for locating grey literature publications. Again, let's use a Top Ten framework to examine both the benefits and drawbacks of using bibliographic databases as a grey literature research resource.

1. It is straightforward to document the search process.

Bibliographic databases are tremendously handy resources if the documentation of a grey literature search is required for a systematic review or guideline. A librarian or information professional can provide the list of search terms and titles of the bibliographic databases that have been searched. It is also easy to provide a clear rationale on why a specific database was selected for a search.

2. You will receive a set number of search results meeting set criteria.

A bibliographic database search will provide a clear number of total search results meeting a set search criterion. Unlike using Internet search engines such as Google, there will be a definitive number of search results retrieved. For example, a search for the term "gun safety" as a textword in the database SafetyLIT lists that there are 101 hits.

3. Searches in bibliographic databases are reproducible.

Unlike general Internet searches, bibliographic databases will deliver the same search results for a set search criterion. The results will not change because of the searcher's geographic search location or previous searches in the database. So, for example, if a librarian in the Weequahic neighborhood in Newark, New Jersey, does a search in the grey literature database PsycExtra, and another librarian in Allen Cove, Hancock County, Maine, uses the same search terms in the database PsycExtra, they will both receive the exact same search results.

4. Bibliographic databases often provide a clear scope of the included content.

Most bibliographic databases generally provide users with a clear outline of the subjects and specific types of documents indexed by the databases. Thus, searchers have a clearer picture of the content that their search results will retrieve. For example, Centre for Agriculture and Bioscience International (CABI), the producer of the database Global Health, clearly states that Global Health is a bibliographic database for locating research on public health from journal articles, books, and reports.

5. Bibliographic databases include content from numerous sources.

A bibliographic database search identifies search results from numerous sources. For example, a PubMed search on liver transplantation complications will identify search results from research published in such journals as *Clinical Transplantation*, *American Journal of Transplantation*, and *Pediatric Transplantation*. This saves users from having to search each journal website individually or having to guess which journals have published relevant content on a topic. Bibliographic databases containing grey literature content have the identical advantage: searchers may not need to search individual sources or guess at which sources contain relevant content. By searching a bibliographic database, sources from numerous grey literature publishers are searched simultaneously. Databases are also knowledge discovery tools, so search results in a database may direct users to additional information sources that were not previously familiar to them.

6. Bibliographic databases are an *almost* painless-to-use source to suggest to users.

Librarians and information professionals are often required to provide a search consultation, so that patrons can then proceed with executing a search themselves. If a librarian or information professional needs to refer users to sources for searching grey literature, bibliographic databases are an ideal resource. Explaining how to search for grey literature sources can be complicated and tedious, especially if a patron is unfamiliar with searching or is newly acquainted with a search topic. Yet it does not require much effort to direct a user to a bibliographic database and provide directions on how to execute a simple search. Basically, databases are hassle-free to suggest on the grey literature search journey. This option avoids overly complicated explanations on advanced Internet search techniques and referring users to multiple sources or specific websites.

7. Wide ranges of bibliographic databases are available.

As will be discussed in greater detail later in this chapter, a wide range of bibliographic databases are available. For instance, there are databases with grey literature content on economics, education, public policy, and transportation. As a result, librarians and information professionals can select from a large range of bibliographic databases that can be utilized for a grey literature search. As we will see, there are so many smaller subject-specific bibliographic databases that it can be easy to select and search only the ones that are the most relevant to a search topic.

8. Users can often select and export search results.

Unlike Internet search engines or institutional repositories, many bibliographic databases allow users to select specific search results and/or export search results. If a librarian or information professional is executing a search for a systematic review, being able to export search results may be especially convenient.

9. Most databases allow users to search select search fields.

Bibliographic databases generally allow users to search for specific authors or specific search terms occurring in the title or text. Librarians and information professionals have the option of designing a search strategy that is either very sensitive or specific. A bonus is that a librarian or information professional has the option of explaining the search strategy to patrons.

10. They are a much-needed time saver.

Bibliographic databases may save searchers time. A grey literature search can be limited to database searches instead of searching several sources. This can be a much-needed shortcut that replaces the need to identify and search a long list of sources.

WEAKNESSES OF BIBLIOGRAPHIC DATABASES AS A RESEARCH TOOL FOR LOCATING GREY LITERATURE PUBLICATIONS

1. A bibliographic database might not include the most current research.

Larger and more popular bibliographic databases are frequently updated. For example, new and updated citations are added to the PubMed database seven days a week (U.S. National Library of Medicine, National Institutes of Health, "Daily Medline/PubMed Updates," May 28, 2014, retrieved from https://www.nlm.nih.gov/pubs/techbull/mj14/mj14_daily_medline_pubmed_updates.html). The little-sister-like databases that can be used to locate grey literature publications often do not have information updates as frequently as larger databases. As a result, it may be challenging to ascertain whether the latest available research is included. A tip: searchers should always try judging a database's currency by performing a quick search and scanning the publication years of the search hits.

2. How much grey literature content does that database *really* include?

Most bibliographic databases used for research focus on indexing published literature. Although there are several bibliographic databases that claim to include grey literature content, it can be challenging to determine how much grey literature content is truly included. For example, a database producer may provide insightful information on the number of citations in a database, but there will not be any information on what percentage of those citations are from grey literature. A case study of this is the excellent bibliographic database NIOSH-2. The NIOSH-2 database is an excellent resource for searching occupational safety and health publications. It includes over 57,000 citations. While grey literature publications from the National Institute for Occupational Safety and Health such as "NIOSH Alerts" and "Current Intelligence Bulletins" are included in the NIOSH-2 database, it is uncertain what percentage of the database content is devoted to grey literature. Many bibliographic databases containing grey literature content will also contain content from published literature—such as NIOSH-2—and sometimes a database search for grey literature publications will regretfully deliver very few hits from grey literature sources.

3. Bibliographic databases containing grey literature have few bells and whistles.

All bibliographic databases are not created equal. Certain databases provide a Cadillac-worthy array of search features; others may invoke the days of the Chrysler K-Car or even the Ford Model-T. The numerous search features available in such databases as PubMed or Web of Science may not be available in the smaller bibliographic databases that index grey literature publications. For example, database users may not be able to limit their results by publication type, and sometimes Boolean searching is not available. The bibliographic databases that index grey literature are still highly valuable resources, but librarians and information professionals should be aware of potential database limitations.

4. Users may be unable to determine how comprehensive a database is.

Larger databases such as PubMed or Scopus will provide estimates on the number of citations in the database, or they will indicate which journals they have indexed. Smaller databases providing grey literature content sometimes do not provide detailed information on the number of citations included in the database. For example, the free database National Criminal Justice Abstracts Database is an excellent source for accessing research on such topics as corrections, courts, drugs, law enforcement, and juvenile justice, but it is difficult to determine the number of records the database contains.

5. You might have to guess a database's selection criteria.

This is another content-unknown factor. Compared to databases indexing published literature, many bibliographic databases that index grey literature may not provide detailed selection criteria. PubMed provides detailed information on whether a journal is indexed completely or just selectively, while many bibliographic databases that index grey literature content are not as forthright. For example, if a database indexes grey literature publications from an organization, there may be some ambiguity about whether all of the organization's publications are selected for inclusion or whether they are selectively indexed. The excellent bibliographic database Native Health Database provides a case study in this quandary: while the database does index grey literature publications from the Indian Health Service, it is unclear if all of the governmental agency's publications are included in the database or just select ones.

6. Databases all have some degree of bias.

All bibliographic databases have some level of bias; for example, a bibliographic database may be biased to English-language-only publications or have a North American publication focus rather than a European one. Bibliographic databases indexing grey literature publications are just as vulnerable to bias. For example, when using bibliographic databases for searching grey literature, librarians and information professionals should try to determine if the database is biased toward only including grey literature publications from larger organizations or if it has a specific geographical focus.

7. Databases can cease publication.

This is also known as the dreaded 404 error, or the "now you see me, now you don't" problem. Large databases such as PubMed, Embase, and Web of Science are extremely well-established bibliographic resources that have been indexing publications for many years, and they will mostly likely continue to do so far into the future. *Index Medicus*, which has coverage as far back as 1879, is another example of a well-established resource. Unfortunately, it is not uncommon for smaller bibliographic databases that contain grey literature content to cease publication. An unfortunate example of a database ceasing publication includes the VIOLIT: Violence Database from the Center for the Study and Prevention and Violence in Boulder, Colorado.

8. Databases can cease updating.

Unfortunately, it is not uncommon for producers of smaller bibliographic databases that contain grey literature to cease updating the databases, and new citations are not added after a specific date. Two examples of this are the Grey Literature Report from the New York Academy of Medicine and the ETOH database. New citations ceased to be added to the Grey Literature Report in 2017. The ETOH database was once a matchless source for identifying grey literature publications in the discipline of alcohol studies, but the National Institute on Alcohol and Alcoholism ceased providing support for ETOH in 2003. Although the database is still available in an archived version, it cannot be searched for recent grey literature publications.

9. A database search may not direct you to all of the grey literature content available.

Searches for systematic reviews include numerous database searches in order to identify all of the relevant results. The steps for using databases for a grey literature search is similar: numerous databases may need to be searched in order to capture all of relevant grey literature on a given topic. Obtaining a comprehensive selection of references can involve searching several databases, because the topic content and publication coverage may vary between each database. For example, there is no grey literature database that provides access to all government publications from the myriad layers of municipal, state, and federal agencies and departments.

10. But are databases better than Google?

Google has become the first—and sometimes one-stop—source for locating relevant research and sources on a topic. The strength of Google for quickly identifying relevant and recent information on a topic is unmatched. Users may also wonder why they should bother with a database search for grey literature publications when a Google search quickly delivers the needed search results. However, database searches provide a means to identify Deep Web content, while a Google search may not identify more than 16 percent of the surface web content available (Bergman, 2001). Database searches are a vital search tool for Deep Web searching.

BIBLIOGRAPHIC DATABASES

Most databases indexing grey literature publications are subject-specific and focus on providing coverage only on a defined field. This section will provide information on select databases that index grey literature, including the database producer, temporal coverage, access, cost, database scope, and grey literature content. If a database is only available by paid subscription, alternative free sources will be suggested. The majority of the databases listed are subject-based rather than multidisciplinary and therefore will not be relevant for all search topics. Additionally, databases providing access to grey literature content are available in all shapes and sizes—some sources resemble bibliographic databases that index published literature and other sources may use more of a web portal search interface. The following list only includes databases that provide access to multiple types of grey literature publications. Database sources for identifying dissertations and conference proceedings/papers will be discussed in Chapter 4.

Select Databases for Identifying Grey Literature Publications

- **AccessUN**
  Producer: Readex: A Division of Newsbank
  Access: http://www.readex.com/content/access-un
  Temporal Coverage: 1945–Present
  Cost: Subscription
  Database Scope and Grey Literature Content: United Nations publications; includes more than 500,000 current and archived United Nations documents. Also provides access to the full text or links to the full text.
  Free Alternatives: United Nations Online Document System, https://documents.un.org; United Nations Document Center, http://www.un.org/

en/documents/index.html; United Nations Bibliographic Information Systems (UBISNET), http://unbisnet.un.org/; and United Nations Treaty Collection, https://treaties.un.org/.

- **African Index Medicus**
  Producer: World Health Organization & the Association for Health Libraries in Africa
  Access: http://indexmedicus.afro.who.int/
  Temporal Coverage: 2000–Present
  Cost: Free
  Database Scope and Grey Literature Content: Index for health literature published in Africa or about Africa. Grey literature content includes research reports, technical reports, and dissertations, along with journal articles.

- **Africa Portal Digital Library**
  Producer: Centre for International Governance Innovation (CIGI) and the South African Institute of International Affairs (SAIIA)
  Access: https://www.africaportal.org/library
  Temporal Coverage: N/A
  Cost: Free
  Database Scope and Grey Literature Content: Online resource for policy issues related to Africa. Grey literature content includes research reports, occasional papers, and policy briefs, along with journal articles and books.

- **AGRICultural OnLine Access (AGRICOL)**
  Producer: United States Department of Agriculture, National Agriculture Library
  Access: agricola.nal.usda.gov/
  Temporal Coverage: 17th Century–Present
  Cost: Free
  Database Scope and Grey Literature Content: Index for the collections of the U.S. Department of Agriculture on publications relevant to agriculture, veterinary sciences, entomology, plant sciences, forestry, aquaculture and fisheries, agricultural economics, extension and education, nutrition, and environmental sciences. Grey literature content includes reports, journal articles, books, and book chapters.

- **ANROWS Resources Databases**
  Producer: Australia's National Research Organisation for Women's Safety Limited (ANROWS)
  Access: http://www.accessitsoftware.com.au/AST01/#!dashboard
  Temporal Coverage: N/A
  Cost: Free

Database Scope and Grey Literature Content: Source for Australian resources on reducing the incidence and impact of violence against women and their children. Grey literature content includes reports and conference presentations, along with journal articles, books, and book chapters.

- **Arctic Science and Technology Information System (ASTIS)**
  Producer: Arctic Institute of North America at the University of Calgary
  Access: www.aina.ucalgary.ca/astis/
  Temporal Coverage: N/A
  Cost: Free

  Database Scope and Grey Literature Content: The Arctic Science and Technology Information System (ASTIS) database contains 82,000 records describing publications and research projects about northern Canada. This database contains citations from both the published peer reviewed literature and grey literature documents such as government publications. The subject content of this database also includes publications on indigenous populations.

- **AQUASTAT**
  Producer: Food and Agriculture Organization of the United Nations
  Access: http://www.fao.org/nr/water/aquastat/data/query/index. html?lang=en
  Temporal Coverage: 1958–Present
  Cost: Free

  Database Scope and Grey Literature Content: Information on water and agriculture, including information from specific countries or regions. The content of this database is primarily grey literature or grey data content.

- **AusPat**
  Producer: IP Australia
  Access: https://www.ipaustralia.gov.au/search/gss
  Temporal Coverage: 1904–Present
  Cost: Free

  Database Scope and Grey Literature Content: Source for Australian patents. Database content is exclusively patents.

- **Australian Government Publications**
  Database Producer: Australian Government
  Access: https://www.australia.gov.au/about-government/publications
  Temporal Coverage: N/A
  Cost: Free

  Database Scope and Grey Literature Content: Grey literature content focuses on governmental reports.While a source for identifying recent publications, but not a one stop search source. Searching the websites of individual agencies is also advisable

- **Australian Indigenous Health*InfoNet***
  Producer: Australian Indigenous Health*InfoNet*
  Access: http://www.healthinfonet.ecu.edu.au/
  Temporal Coverage: N/A
  Cost: Free
  Database Scope and Grey Literature Content: Source for research on Aboriginal and Torres Strait Islander health. Grey literature content includes research reports and dissertations, as well as journal articles.

- **BIAB Online: British and Irish Archaeological Bibliography**
  Producer: Council for British Archaeology
  Access: www.biab.ac.uk
  Temporal Coverage: 1940–Present
  Cost: Free
  Database Scope and Grey Literature Content: Online bibliography for British and Irish archaeology contains over 150,000 references from the year 1695 onward. Online and hard-copy publications; local, regional, national, and international publications; books, articles, conference proceedings, and grey literature.

- **Bibliography of Nordic Criminology**
  Producer: Scandinavian Research Council of Criminology and Criminal Justice of Denmark
  Access: http://www.nsfk.org/BIBLIOGRAPHY
  Temporal Coverage: N/A
  Cost: Free
  Database Scope and Grey Literature Content: Criminological research literature published in Nordic countries or by authors from Nordic countries that have been published elsewhere. Grey literature publications include research reports, as well as books and journal articles. This database stopped being updated in 2008.

- **Black Studies Center**
  Producer: ProQuest
  Access: http://www.proquest.com/products-services/bsc.html
  Temporal Coverage: N/A
  Cost: Subscription
  Database Scope and Grey Literature Content: Includes scholarly essays, recent periodicals, historical newspaper articles, and reference books. Grey literature content includes oral history videos.

- **Campbell Systematic Reviews**
  Producer: The Campbell Collaboration
  Access: https://www.campbellcollaboration.org/campbell-library.html

Temporal Coverage: 2000–Present

Cost: Free

Database Scope and Grey Literature Content: The Campbell Collaboration produces reviews in the areas of crime and justice, education, international development, and social welfare.

Campbell Systematic Reviews is one of three series available from the Campbell Library—a Campbell Methods Series and Campbell Policies and Guidelines are also available. Campbell Systematic reviews focus on the effects of interventions in the social and behavioral sciences.

- **Canadian Electronic Library—Health Research Collection and Public Policy Collection**

  Producer: desLibris

  Access: http://www.canadianelectroniclibrary.ca/Default.aspx

  Temporal Coverage: 2003–Present

  Cost: Subscription only

  Database Scope and Grey Literature Content: Source for Canadian-specific public policy and health content. Grey literature content includes research papers, reports, studies, policy papers and briefs, discussion papers, numbered series, working papers, political party platforms, evidence reviews, systematic reviews, economic evaluations, and environmental scans, as well as books and journal articles.

  Free Alternatives: The majority of documents indexed by the Canadian Electronic Library can be easily located for free online by either structured Google searches or by searching Government of Canada Publications (http://www.publications.gc.ca/site/eng/home.html#) and websites of Canadian provinces and territories.

- **Canadian Patent Database**

  Producer: Canadian Intellectual Property Office, Government of Canada

  Access: http://www.ic.gc.ca/opic-cipo/cpd/eng/introduction.html

  Temporal Coverage: 1869–Present

  Cost: Free

  Database Scope and Grey Literature Content: Database includes 148 years of patent descriptions and images; 2,280,000 patent documents are included.

- **Canadian Research Index**

  Producer: ProQuest

  Access: http://www.proquest.com/products-services/canadian_research.html

  Temporal Coverage: 1982–Present

  Cost: Subscription

  Database Scope and Grey Literature Content: Includes Statistic Canada monographs and serials, as well as Canadian federal, provincial, and municipal documents. French content is also included. Database content is primarily grey literature documents.

Free Alternatives: Government of Canada Publications (http://www. publications.gc.ca/site/eng/home.html) and websites of individual Canadian provinces and territories.

- **CareSearch Grey Literature**
  Producer: CareSearch
  Access: https://www.caresearch.com.au/caresearch/tabid/523/Default.aspx
  Temporal Coverage: N/A
  Cost: Free
  Database Scope and Grey Literature Content: Database for palliative care information and evidence. Grey literature content includes conference abstracts and government publications, along with articles from journals that are not indexed by Medline, Embase, CINAHL, and PsycInfo

- **Catalog of U.S. Government Publications**
  Producer: U.S. federal government
  Access: http://catalog.gpo.gov
  Temporal Coverage: 1976–Present
  Cost: Free
  Database Scope and Grey Literature Content: Index to U.S. government publications. Includes descriptive information for current and historical publications. Content is almost exclusively grey literature publications. Finding aid for identifying electronic and print publications from the legislative, executive, and judicial branches of the U.S. federal government.

- **CDC WONDER (Wide-Ranging Online Data for Epidemiologic Research)**
  Producer: U.S. Centers for Disease Control and Prevention
  Access: https://wonder.cdc.gov/
  Temporal Coverage: N/A
  Cost: Free
  Database Scope and Grey Literature Content: Data sets about mortality, cancer incidence, hospital discharges, AIDS, behavioral risk factors, and diabetes, along with other health-related topics. Grey literature content includes reports, recommendations and guidelines, statistical research data, and journal articles.

- **Central and Eastern European Online Library (CEEOL)**
  Producer: CEEOL
  Access: www.ceeol.com
  Temporal Coverage: N/A
  Cost: Can be searched for free, but full text of citations must be purchased

Database Scope and Grey Literature Content: Multipurpose database, including general reference, economy, jurisprudence, social science, and history, with a focus on Central and Eastern Europe. Database content mostly includes books, book chapters, and journal articles, but some grey literature documents are included.

- **CHBD: Circumpolar Health Bibliographic Database**
  Producer: Canadian Institutes of Health Research (CIHR) Team in Circumpolar Health Research
  Access: www.aina.ucalgary.ca/chbd
  Temporal Coverage: 1920–Present
  Cost: Free
  Database Scope and Grey Literature Content: Database indexing research on human health in the circumpolar region. Grey literature content includes conference papers, governmental reports, and other grey literature content. Also indexes books, book chapters, and journal articles.

- **Child Welfare Information Gateway**
  Producer: U.S. Department of Health & Human Services Administration for Children & Families
  Access: https://library.childwelfare.gov/cwig/ws/library/docs/gateway/SimpleSearchForm
  Temporal Coverage: 1910–Present
  Cost: Free
  Database Scope and Grey Literature Content: Information on child welfare issues. Grey literature content includes research reports, program evaluations, best practice guidelines from both U.S. and international agencies, and journal articles. This resource replaces the former *Child Abuse, Child Welfare & Adoption Database.*

- **CHI Navigator**
  Producer: U.S. Centers for Disease Control and Prevention
  Access: https://wwwn.cdc.gov/chidatabase
  Temporal Coverage: N/A
  Cost: Free
  Database Scope and Grey Literature Content: Source for interventions in community health. This database is intended for frontline workers in hospitals and health systems, public health agencies, community health centers, and community action agencies. Content on four action areas is included: socioeconomic factors, physical environment, health behaviors, and clinical care. Grey literature content focuses on evaluation and outcome data.

- **CIA Electronic Reading Room**
  Producer: Central Intelligence Agency
  Access: https://www.cia.gov/library/readingroom/home

Temporal Coverage: N/A

Cost: Free

Database Scope and Grey Literature Content: Source for documents released through the Freedom of Information Act and other CIA release programs. Database content is primarily grey literature content.

- **Clearinghouse on Abuse and Neglect of the Elderly (CANE)**
  Producer: University of Delaware
  Access: http://www.cane.udel.edu/
  Temporal Coverage: 1980–Present
  Cost: Free
  Database Scope and Grey Literature Content: Index for literature on elder abuse. Grey literature content includes agency reports, hearing transcripts, and memoranda of understanding, as well as journal articles and books.

- **CMA Infobase: Clinical Practice Guidelines Database**
  Producer: Canadian Medical Association
  Access: https://www.cma.ca/En/Pages/clinical-practice-guidelines.aspx
  Temporal Coverage: N/A
  Cost: Free
  Database Scope and Grey Literature Content: Database of Canadian evidence-based clinical practice guidelines. Grey literature content includes guidelines published by governmental agencies, as well as guidelines published in journals.

- **Cochrane Library**
  Producer: Cochrane
  Access: http://www.cochranelibrary.com/
  Temporal Coverage: 1992–
  Cost: Subscription. Users can search the databases free of charge and access abstracts.
  Database Scope and Grey Literature Content: Database collection includes the Cochrane Central Register of Controlled Trials, Cochrane Database of Methodology Reviews, Cochrane Database of Systematic Reviews, Cochrane Methodology Register, Database of Abstracts of Reviews of Effects, Health Technology Assessment Database, and NHS Economic Evaluation Database. Health-related topics are covered; the focus is on effectiveness and appropriateness of interventions.

- **Columbia International Affairs Online (CIAO)**
  Producer: Columbia University Press
  Access: http://www.ciaonet.org/
  Temporal Coverage: N/A
  Cost: Subscription. Users can search the databases free of charge and access abstracts.

Database Scope and Grey Literature Content: Resource for documents and
   articles devoted to research, analysis, and scholarship on international
   politics and related fields, including security studies, global finance,
   diplomatic practice, humanitarian law, global governance, development
   studies, and environmental studies. Primary content is journal articles
   and books, but select working papers, policy briefs, and special reports
   are included.

- **CORDIS**
   Producer: European Commission
   Access: http://cordis.europa.eu/home_en.html
   Temporal coverage: N/A
   Cost: Free

   Database Scope and Grey Literature Content: Source for European
      Commission's EU-funded research projects. Grey literature primarily
      focuses on reports, but other content types also include booklets, project
      details, and the research* eu magazine. Also includes content previously
      searched via the CORDIS Library.

- **CrimDoc (Criminology Library Grey Literature)**
   Producer: Centre of Criminology Library, University of Toronto
   Access: http://link.library.utoronto.ca/criminology/crimdoc/index.cfm
   Temporal Coverage: N/A
   Cost: Free

   Database Scope and Grey Literature Content: Source for research on crim-
      inology, including criminal justice, penology and corrections, juvenile
      delinquency/young offenders, and law enforcement. Content is entirely
      grey literature publications, including government publications, unpub-
      lished papers, working papers, and research reports.

- **Database of Promoting Health Effectiveness Reviews (DOPHER)**
   Producer: EPPI-Centre at the UCL Institute of Education, London
   Access: https://eppi.ioe.ac.uk/webdatabases4/Intro.aspx?ID=9
   Temporal Coverage: N/A
   Cost: Free

   Database Scope and Grey Literature Content: Provides coverage of sys-
      tematic and non-systematic reviews of effectiveness in health promotion
      and public health.

- **Declassified Documents Reference System (DDRS)**
   Producer: Gale
   Access: www.gale.com/us-declassified-documents-online
   Temporal Coverage: 1900–2008
   Cost: Subscription only

   Database Scope and Grey Literature Content: Includes full text access to
      U.S. State Department political analyses, White House confidential file

materials, National Security Council policy statements, and CIA intelligence memoranda.

Free Alternatives: Search the websites of the CIA Electronic Reading Room; FBI Records: The Vault; Federation of American Scientists: Project on Government Security; National Security Archive; and U.S. Department of State Virtual Reading Room.

- **Defense Technical Information Center Technical Reports Collection**
  Producer: Defense Technical Information Center
  Access: http://www.dtic.mil/dtic/
  Temporal Coverage: N/A
  Cost: Free
  Database Scope and Grey Literature Content: More than one million final reports on U.S. Department of Defense–funded research, development, test, and evaluation activities. All content is grey literature.

- **Digital Library for International Research (DLIR)**
  Producer: Council of American Overseas Research Centers (CAORC)
  Access: http://www.dlir.org/
  Temporal Coverage: N/A
  Cost: Free
  Database Scope and Grey Literature Content: Database is primarily a union catalog, including books, journals, and reports. Grey literature content includes research reports published by CAORC member centers.

- **Disaster Lit**
  Producer: National Library of Medicine
  Access: https://projectreporter.nih.gov/reporter.cfm
  Temporal Coverage: N/A
  Cost: Free
  Database Scope and Grey Literature Content: Database covering freely available documents on disaster medicine and public health. Database content is primarily grey literature publications, including expert guidelines, research reports, conference proceedings, training classes, and fact sheets.

- **DORIS: Database of Research into Stroke**
  Producer: Cochrane Stroke Group
  Access: http://www.askdoris.org/doris2017/doris17_main.asp?opt=2709
  Temporal Coverage: N/A
  Cost: Free, but users must register
  Database Scope and Grey Literature Content: Information on guidelines, evidence, and systematic reviews in stroke care. Grey literature content includes guidelines as well journal articles.

- **EconLit**
  Producer: American Economic Association

Access: https://www.aeaweb.org/econlit/

Temporal Coverage: 1886–Present

Cost: Subscription

Database Scope and Grey Literature Content: Database for scholarly economic literature. Grey literature content includes working papers, conference proceedings, and dissertations, as well as journal articles and books.

Free Alternatives: Google Scholar, Google searches for working papers from economic institutions

- **Education Resource Information Center: ERIC**

Producer: National Library of Education (United States)

Access: https://eric.ed.gov/

Temporal Coverage: 1966–Present

Cost: Free, but paid subscriptions available from such library vendors as Ovid and ProQuest

Database Scope and Grey Literature Content: Bibliographic index to education-related literature. Grey literature content includes grey literature publications produced or funded by the U.S. Department and other U.S. federal governmental departments; grey literature publications produced by state or local agencies; research from non-profit, professional policy, and international organizations.

- **eHRAF World Cultures**

Producer: Human Relations Area Files, Inc. at Yale University

Access: http://ehrafworldcultures.yale.edu/ehrafe/

Temporal Coverage: N/A

Cost: Subscription

Database Scope and Grey Literature Content: Cross-cultural and ethnographic database that contains historical and recent information on all aspects of cultural and social life; includes books and monographs. Grey literature and grey data content includes dissertations and photo collections.

Free Alternative: Google Scholar

- **Environmental Sciences and Pollution Management (ESPM)**

Producer: ProQuest

Access: http://proquest.libguides.com/espm

Cost: Subscription

Database Scope and Grey Literature Content: Multidisciplinary database providing comprehensive coverage of environmental science. Grey literature content includes reports as well as journal articles and books.

Free Alternatives: Google Scholar, websites of individual governmental agencies and environmental NGOs

- **Espacenet**
  Producer: European Patent Office
  Access: https://worldwide.espacenet.com/
  Temporal Coverage: N/A
  Cost: Free
  Database Scope and Grey Literature Content: Patents published world-
    wide, including patents from European Patent Office, WIPO, and
    Japanese Patent Office. Only the grey literature publication types of
    patents are included.
- **ETOH Database**
  Producer: National Institute on Alcohol and Alcoholism
  Access: http://www.hazelden.org/websearch/etohsearch
  Temporal Coverage: 1960–2003
  Cost: Free
  Database Scope and Grey Literature Content: Bibliographic resource on
    alcohol-related topics. Database is now hosted by Hazelden Betty Ford
    Foundation and only contains records prior to 2004. Grey literature con-
    tent includes research reports, working papers, and conference proceed-
    ings, as well as journal articles, books, and book chapters.
- **EU Bookshop**
  Producer: European Union
  Access: https://bookshop.europa.eu/en/home/
  Temporal Coverage: N/A
  Cost: Free
  Database Scope and Grey Literature Content: Source for European Union
    publications. Database grey literature content includes research reports,
    as well as e-books and paper books published by the European Union.
- **FBI Records: The Vault**
  Producer: Federal Bureau of Investigation
  Access: https://vault.fbi.gov/
  Temporal Coverage: N/A
  Cost: Free
  Database Scope and Grey Literature Content: Source for documents from
    the FBI released through the Freedom of Information Act. Database con-
    tent is primarily grey literature.
- **Forced Migration Online: Digital Library**
  Producer: Refugees Studies Centre, University of Oxford
  Access: http://www.forcedmigration.org/digital-library
  Temporal Coverage: N/A
  Cost: Free
  Database Scope and Grey Literature Content: Includes more than 5,700
    full-text documents on forced migration. Grey literature publications

include working papers and policy briefs; also includes articles from select journals.

- **Foundation Directory Online (FDO)**
  Producer: Foundation Center
  Access: https://fconline.foundationcenter.org/
  Temporal Coverage: N/A
  Cost: Subscription
  Database Scope and Grey Literature Content: Content focuses on information regarding funding opportunities, but this database can be used to identified unpublished research studies that have received funding; the results are not available in the published literature.
- **FreePatentsOnline**
  Producer: FPO
  Access: http://www.freepatentsonline.com/search.html
  Temporal Coverage: N/A
  Cost: Free, but subscription option available that provides Advanced Search features
  Database Scope and Grey Literature Content: U.S. patents and patent applications, European patents and patent applications, and Patent Abstracts of Japan.
- **GambLIB database**
  Producer: International Gambling Research Institute
  Access: http://www.gamblib.org/
  Temporal Coverage: 1680–Present
  Cost: Free
  Database Scope and Grey Literature Content: Database on gambling research. Grey literature content includes annual reports, research reports, dissertations, working papers, and background papers, along with journal articles, book chapters, and books.
- **Global Development Finance (GDF)**
  Producer: The World Bank
  Access: http://data.worldbank.org/data-catalog/global-financial-development
  Temporal Coverage: 1960–2014
  Cost: Free
  Database Scope and Grey Literature Content: Financial indicators for developing countries, including GDF focuses on financial flows, trends in external debt, major economic aggregates, key debt ratios, average terms of new commitments, currency composition of long-term debt, debt restructuring, scheduled debt service projections, and other major financial indicators for developing countries.
- **Global Health**

Producer: CAB International

Access: http://www.cabi.org/publishing-products/online-information-resources/global-health/

Temporal Coverage: 1910–Present

Cost: Subscription

Database Scope and Grey Literature Content: Bibliographic index on global health, including community health, refugee and migrant health, public health practice and policy, health promotion, health policy and planning, epidemiology, nutrition and rural health. Forty percent of the material contained in Global Health is unique to the database. Grey literature content includes reports as well as journal articles, books, and book chapters.

Free Alternatives: Google Scholar; individual sites of international health NGOs

- **Global Health and Human Rights Database**

Producer: Lawyers Collective and O'Neill Institute for National and Global Health Law at Georgetown University

Access: http://www.globalhealthrights.org/

Temporal Coverage: N/A

Cost: Free

Database Scope and Grey Literature Content: Database for legislation from around the world relating to health and human rights. Grey literature content includes judgments, instruments, and constitutions involving health and human rights.

- **Google Scholar**

Producer: Google

Access: https://scholar.google.ca/

Temporal Coverage: N/A

Cost: Free

Database Scope and Grey Literature Content: Contains academic journals and books, conference papers, theses and dissertations, preprints, abstracts, technical reports, court opinions, and patents. Scope is multidisciplinary. Grey literature content includes government reports, technical reports, white papers, and dissertations.

Note: please see Chapter 9 for more detailed information on Google Scholar.

- **Government Publications Canada**

Database Producer: Government of Canada

Access: http://publications.gc.ca/site/eng/ourCatalogue.html

Temporal Coverage: N/A

Cost: Free

Database Scope and Grey Literature Content: Central point of access to
publications authored by the federal Government of Canada.

- **Grants Online Database (Formally AHRQ GOLD)**
  Producer: Agency for Healthcare Research and Quality (AHRQ)
  Access: https://gold.ahrq.gov/projectsearch/
  Temporal Coverage: N/A
  Cost: Free
  Database Scope and Grey Literature Content: A searchable database of
  more than six thousand grants funded by AHRQ. Can be used to identify
  research that has been funded but not published.

- **GreenFILE**
  Producer: EBSCO
  Access: GreenInfoOnline.com
  Temporal Coverage:
  Cost: Free
  Database Scope and Grey Literature Content: Index to publications on
  global climate change, green building, pollution, sustainable agricul-
  ture, renewable energy, and recycling. Includes such grey literature
  publications as pamphlets, governmental reports, and environmental
  organization, along with journal articles.

- **Healthcare Management Information Consortium (HMIC)**
  Producer: U.K. Department of Health, Nuffield Institute for Health (Leeds
  University Library), King's Fund Library
  Access: http://www.ovid.com/site/catalog/databases/99.jsp
  Temporal Coverage: 1983–Present
  Cost: Subscription
  Database Scope and Grey Literature Content: Index to publications on the
  British National Health Service, the quality of health services, health
  administration, health systems and services, management, and occupa-
  tional medicine. Includes grey literature content such as reports from
  the Department of Health in England and the King's Fund, as well as
  journal articles.
  Free Alternatives: The websites of the Department of Health (DH)
  in England and the King's Fun can be searched for grey literature
  publications.

- **Health Library for Disasters**
  Producer: World Health Organization (WHO) and the Pan American
  Health Organization (PAHO)
  Access: http://helid.digicollection.org/en/
  Temporal Coverage: N/A
  Cost: Free

Database Scope and Grey Literature Content: Source for public health information on emergency preparedness and response. Database content consists primarily of grey literature publications such as guidelines, field guides, manuals, newsletters, and other training materials.

- **HSRProj (Health Services Research Projects in Progress)**

  Producer: National Library of Medicine

  Access: https://wwwcf.nlm.nih.gov/hsr_project/home_proj.cfm

  Database Scope and Grey Literature Content: Information on in-progress research projects receiving governmental and foundation funding. International in scope and can be searched for the names of performing and sponsoring agencies; names and addresses of principal investigators; beginning and ending years of projects; and information about study design and methodology, including demographic characteristics of the study group, number of subjects in the study population, population base of the study sample, and source of the project data. This source focuses more on unpublished health services research than on unpublished clinical trial data.

- **HSTAT: Health Services/Technology Assessment Text**

  Producer: National Library of Medicine (United States)

  Access: www.ncbi.nlm.nih.gov/books/NBK16710

  Temporal Coverage: N/A

  Cost: Free

  Database Scope and Grey Literature Content: Includes evidence reports and technology assessments from the Agency for Healthcare Research and Quality (AHRQ), treatment guidelines from the National Institutes of Health (NIH) Consensus Conference Reports and Technology Assessment Reports, HIV/AIDS Treatment Information Service (ATIS), Treatment Improvement Protocols and Prevention Enhancement Protocols System Substance Abuse from the Mental Health Services Administration Treatment Improvement Protocols (TIP) and the Substance Abuse and Mental Health Services Administration's Center for Substance Abuse Treatment (SAMHSA/CSAT), U.S. Preventive Services Task Force's Guide to Clinical Preventive Services, Reports of the Surgeon General, and health technology evaluations from the Health Technology Advisory Committee (HTAC) of the Minnesota Health Care Commission (MHCC). Database content consists of primarily grey literature publications.

- **HUD USER Database**

  Producer: U.S. Department of Housing and Urban Development

  Access: https://www.huduser.gov/portal/home.html

  Temporal Coverage: 1970–Present

  Cost: Free

Database Scope and Grey Literature Content: Web portal on housing, community development, and urban planning. Grey literature and grey data content includes research briefs, research reports, working papers, and data sets, as well as HUD periodicals such as *Cityscape*, *Evidence Matters*, *The Edge*, and *Insights*.

- **IDEAS**

  Producer: Co-operative project, but run by Christian Zimmermann at the Research Division of the Federal Reserve Bank of St. Louis

  Access: https://ideas.repec.org/

  Temporal Coverage: N/A

  Cost: Free

  Database Scope and Grey Literature Content: Bibliographic database on economics and finance research. Grey literature content includes working papers and conference papers, as well as journal articles, books, and book chapters.

- **IDP Database of Research on International Education**

  Producer: Australian Council for Educational Research (ACER)

  Access: http://opac.acer.edu.au/IDP_drie/

  Temporal Coverage: 1990–Present

  Cost: Free

  Database Scope and Grey Literature Content: Database on international education. Grey literature content includes research reports, policy statements, discussion papers, government publications, and dissertations, along with journal articles, books, and book chapters.

- **Indigenous Studies Portal**

  Producer: University of Saskatchewan

  Access: iportal.usask.ca

  Temporal Coverage: N/A

  Cost: Free

  Database Scope and Grey Literature Content: Database of full-text electronic resources such as books, articles, theses, and documents, as well as digitized materials such as photographs, archival resources, and maps. Focus is primarily on First Nations and Aboriginals of Canada. Grey literature content includes data tables, field notes, oral histories, and dissertations.

- **LILACS**

  Producer: Latin American and Caribbean Center on Health Sciences Information, or BIREME

  Access: lilacs.bvsalud.org/en

  Temporal Coverage: N/A

  Cost: Free

Database Scope and Grey Literature Content: LILACS is an index of scientific and technical literature of Latin America and the Caribbean. Grey literature content includes dissertations and reports, along with journal articles and monographs.

- **Maternal and Child Health Digital Library**
  Producer: Welch Medical Library at the Johns Hopkins University
  Access: http://mchlibrary.jhmi.edu/
  Temporal Coverage: 1910–Present
  Cost: Free
  Database Scope and Grey Literature Content: Source for current and historical evidence on maternal and child health. Grey literature content includes reports and brochures/pamphlets, along with journal articles and books.

- **MetaLib**
  Database Producer: U.S. federal government
  Access: https://metalib.gpo.gov
  Temporal Coverage: N/A
  Cost: Free
  Database Scope and Grey Literature Content: A federated search engine from the U.S. Government Publishing Office. Can be used to search across multiple U.S. federal government databases. Grey literature documents such as governmental reports are included, along with published research.

- **Minority Health and Health Equity Archive**
  Producer: Center for Health Equity, University of Maryland; hosted by the University Library System, University of Pittsburgh
  Access: http://minority-health.pitt.edu/
  Temporal Coverage: 1882–Present
  Cost: Free
  Database Scope and Grey Literature Content: Information on minority health and health disparities research and policy. Grey literature content includes reports, dissertations, and conference papers, along with journal articles and books.

- **NASA Technological Reports Server**
  Producer: National Aeronautics and Space Administration (NASA)
  Access: http://www.library.ucsb.edu/node/2561
  Temporal Coverage: 1916–Present
  Cost: Free
  Database Scope and Grey Literature Content: Current and historical technical and engineering literature produced by the National Advisory Committee for Aeronautics (NACA) and the National Aeronautics and Space Administration (NASA). Database content includes grey literature

publications such as conference papers, meeting papers, patents, and research reports. Journal articles, images, and technical videos are also included.

- **National Center for Farmworker Health Digital Library**
  Producer: National Center for Farmworker Health
  Access: http://lib.ncfh.org/?pid=30
  Temporal Coverage: 1930–Present
  Cost: Free
  Database Scope and Grey Literature Content: Information on migrant and farmworker health. Grey literature content includes research reports, along with journal articles and books.
- **National Guideline Clearinghouse**
  Producer: Agency for Healthcare Research and Quality
  Access: https://www.guideline.gov/
  Temporal Coverage: 1998–Present
  Cost: Free
  Database Scope and Grey Literature Content: Source for clinical practice evidence-based guidelines from both U.S. and international organizations and societies. Includes guideline summaries, guideline syntheses, and expert commentaries on a wide variety of health-related topics. Grey literature content includes guidelines from organizations or societies that have not been published in academic journals, as well as guidelines from published sources.
- **Native Health Database**
  Producer: University of New Mexico
  Access: hscssl.unm.edu/nhd
  Temporal Coverage: N/A
  Cost: Free
  Database Scope and Grey Literature Content: The Native Health Database contains bibliographic information on research related to the health and healthcare of American Indians, Alaska Natives, and Canadian First Nations. Grey literature content includes reports, community engagement projects, policy documents, guidelines, and manuals, as well as articles and books.
- **NCBI Bookshelf**
  Producer: National Center for Biotechnology Information
  Access: https://www.ncbi.nlm.nih.gov/books/
  Temporal Coverage: 1900–Present
  Cost: Free
  Database Scope and Grey Literature Content: Searchable collection of books, reports, databases, and other scholarly literature in life sciences and health. Grey literature content includes reports from both U.S. and

international governmental agencies and organizations, along with open access e-books.

- **NCJRS Abstracts Database**

  Producer: National Criminal Justice Reference Service (NCJRS), U.S. Department of Justice

  Access: https://www.ncjrs.gov/App/AbstractDB/AbstractDBSearch.aspx

  Temporal Coverage: 1971–present

  Cost: Free

  Database Scope and Grey Literature Content: Contains citations on law enforcement, crime prevention and security, criminal justice, and juvenile justice. Grey literature content includes government reports, research reports, and unpublished research; journal articles and books are also included.

- **NIH RePORTER**

  Producer: National Institutes of Health

  Access: https://projectreporter.nih.gov/reporter.cfm

  Temporal Coverage: N/A

  Cost: Free

  Database Scope and Grey Literature Content: Tool for searching NIH-funded research projects and accessing publications and patents supported by NIH funding. Database content includes links to studies published in journal articles. NIH RePorter can also be used to identify unpublished research results.

- **NIOSH-2**

  Producer: National Institute for Occupational Safety and Health (NIOSH)

  Access: https://www2a.cdc.gov/nioshtic-2/n2help.asp

  Temporal Coverage: 1930–present

  Cost: Free

  Database Scope and Grey Literature Content: NIOSH-2 is a bibliographic database of occupational safety and health publications. Grey literature content includes documents, grant reports, and other communication products supported in whole or in part by NIOSH.

- **NTIS Bibliographic Database**

  Producer: NTIS, U.S. Chamber of Commerce

  Access: https://classic.ntis.gov/

  Temporal Coverage: 1964–Present

  Cost: Free version available at https://classic.ntis.gov/. A subscription version with more powerful search features is available.

  Database Scope and Grey Literature Content: Contains U.S. government–sponsored research and publications from federal agencies. Grey literature and grey data content includes conference proceedings, technical research reports, data files, computer programs, and audio-visual products, as well as journal articles.

- **Open Grey (Formerly OpenSIGLE)**
  Producer: INIST-CNRS
  Access: www.opengrey.eu
  Temporal Coverage: 1980–Present
  Cost: Free
  Database Scope and Grey Literature Content: Access to 700,000 bibliographical references of grey literature produced in Europe. Database content is multidisciplinary, covering science, technology, biomedical science, economics, social science, and humanities. Grey literature document types include technical or research reports, doctoral dissertations, conference papers, official publications, and other types of grey literature.

- **Ovid HealthStar**
  Producer: Wolters Kluwer
  Access: http://ospguides.ovid.com/OSPguides/hstrdb.html
  Temporal Coverage: 1966-Present
  Cost: subscription
  Database Scope and Grey Literature Content: Source for research on health care delivery. Primarily focuses on the published literature, but also *according* to the database scope notes includes the grey literature document types of technical reports and government documents. Free alternatives would include *NTIS Bibliographic Database.*

- **PAIS International**
  Producer: CSA
  Access: www.csa.com/factsheets/pais-set-c.php
  Temporal Coverage: 1914–Present
  Cost: Subscription
  Database Scope and Grey Literature Content: Index for public policy, social policy, and the social sciences. Grey literature content includes government documents, statistical compilations, committee reports, and research reports, as well as journal articles and books
  Free Alternative: Google Scholar

- **PDQ (Pretty Darn Quick)**
  Producer: FP7 Seventh Framework Programme, European Union, and Norwegian Agency for Development Cooperation (NORAD). Hosted by Evidence-Based Medicine Unit, Pontificia Universidad Católica de Chile.
  Access: https://www.pdq-evidence.org/
  Temporal Coverage: 1948–Present
  Cost: Free

Database Scope and Grey Literature Content: Focus on best available evidence for decision support in health systems. Grey literature content includes evidence briefs from governmental agencies, along with systematic reviews and primary research published in scholarly journal research.

- **PILOTS Database (Published International Literature on Traumatic Stress)**

  Producer: National Center for PTSD (U.S.)

  Access: www.ptsd.va.gov/professional/pilots-database

  Temporal Coverage: N/A

  Cost: Free

  Database Scope and Grey Literature Content: Electronic index to the worldwide literature on PTSD and other mental health consequences of exposure to traumatic events. Grey literature content includes dissertations and reports, as well as journal articles and books.

- **Policy File**

  Producer: ProQuest

  Access: http://www.proquest.com/products-services/policyfile.html

  Temporal Coverage: N/A

  Cost: Free

  Database Scope and Grey Literature Content: Index for policy topics, including both foreign and domestic policy. Grey literature content includes research reports from think tanks, non-governmental organizations, research institutes, university centers, and advocacy groups.

- **Policy File Index**

  Producer: ProQuest

  Access: http://www.proquest.com/products-services/policyfile.html

  Temporal Coverage: 1990–Present

  Cost: Subscription

  Database Scope and Grey Literature Content: Index for policy topics, including both foreign and domestic policy. Grey literature content includes research reports from think tanks, non-governmental organizations, research institutes, university centers, and advocacy groups.

  Free Alternatives: Google Scholar; searching individual websites of think tanks or NGOs

- **POPLINE**

  Producer: Knowledge for Health (K4Health) Project

  Access: www.popline.org

  Temporal Coverage: 1970–Present; selected citations dating back to 1827

  Cost: Free

Database Scope and Grey Literature Content: Citations and abstracts on population and family planning, specifically research in contraceptive methods, family planning services, human fertility, maternal and child health, HIV/AIDS in developing countries, program operations and evaluation, demography, and other related health, law, and policy issues. Grey literature content includes conference papers, governmental reports, intergovernmental agency reports, and NGO publications. Database also indexes peer-reviewed literature from journal articles.

- **Project Research Online**
  Producer: Agency for Health Care Research and Quality (AHRQ)
  Access: https://gold.ahq.gov/
  Temporal Coverage: N/A
  Cost: Free
  Database Scope and Grey Literature Content:

- **PsycExtra**
  Producer: American Psychological Association
  Access: http://www.apa.org/pubs/databases/psycextra/
  Temporal Coverage: N/A
  Cost: Subscription
  Database Scope and Grey Literature Content: Psychology and behavioral health–related content. Grey literature content includes conference proceedings, newsletters, reports, patient-oriented fact sheets, brochures, and guidelines. There is no overlapping content between PsycInfo and PsycExtra. Content is entirely grey literature.
  Free Alternatives: Grey literature report; structured Google searches

- **Publications New Zealand**
  Database Producer: National Library New Zealand
  Access: https://natlib.govt.nz/collections/a-z/publications-new-zealand
  Temporal Coverage: N/A
  Cost: Free
  Database Scope and Grey Literature Content: Source foridentifying publications from or about New Zealand. Grey literature content includes reports, along with published sources. Searching the websites of individual agencies is also advisable

- **Publications UK**
  Database Producer: UK government
  Access: https://www.gov.uk/government/publications
  Temporal Coverage: N/A
  Cost: Free
  Database Scope and Grey Literature Content: Use to searchfor UK governmental department publication. Grey literature content focuses on

governmental reports. Searching the websites of individual agencies is also advisable.

- **REHABDATA**

  Producer: National Rehabilitation Center

  Access: http://www.naric.com/?q=en/REHABDATA

  Temporal Coverage: 1956–Present

  Cost: Free

  Database Scope and Grey Literature Content: Database on disability and rehabilitation, including physical, mental, and psychiatric disabilities, independent living, vocational rehabilitation, special education, assistive technology, law, and employment. Grey literature content includes reports, as well as journal articles and books.

- **SafetyLit**

  Producer: SafetyLit Foundation

  Access: www.safetylit.org

  Temporal Coverage: Mid-17th Century–Present

  Cost: Free

  Database Scope and Grey Literature Content: SafetyLit indexes research on preventing unintentional injuries, violence, and self-harm. Grey literature content includes dissertations, conference papers, and reports from government agencies and other institutions. SafetyLit also includes journal articles, books, and book chapters.

- **Science.gov**

  Producer: Interagency Science.gov Alliance

  Access: https://www.science.gov/

  Temporal Coverage: 1900–Present

  Cost: Free

  Database Scope and Grey Literature Content: Gateway for publications and research by U.S. government science agencies. Search over 60 databases and more than 2,200 websites from 15 federal agencies, compiling 200 million pages of U.S. government science research and development results. Grey literature content includes reports along with journal articles.

- **SciTech Connect (formerly the Information Bridge)**

  Producer: U.S. Department of Energy

  Access: https://www.osti.gov/scitech/

  Temporal Coverage: 1997–Present

  Cost: Free

  Database Scope and Grey Literature Content: Access to research from the U.S. Department of Energy. Grey literature content includes reports, conference publications, and patents, along with select journal articles and monographs.

- **SciTech Connect**
  Producer: U.S. Department of Energy, Office of Science and Technical Information
  Access: www.osti.gov/scitech
  Temporal Coverage: N/A
  Cost: Free
  Database Scope and Grey Literature Content: SciTech provides access to science, technology, and engineering research information from the U.S. Department of Energy. Grey literature content includes conference papers, program documents, technical reports, and dissertations.
- **Scottish Government Publications**
  Database Producer: Scottish Government
  Access: http://www.gov.scot/Publications/
  Temporal Coverage: N/A
  Cost: Free
  Database Scope and Grey Literature Content: Use to search for Scottish governmental department publication. Grey literature content focuses on governmental reports. Searching the websites of individual agencies is also advisable.
- **Social Care Online**
  Database Producer: Social Care Institute for Excellence (SCIE)
  Access: https://www.scie-socialcareonline.org.uk/
  Temporal Coverage: 1980s–Present
  Cost: Free
  Database Scope and Grey Literature Content: Source forresearch on all aspects of social work and social care. Grey literature content includes publications from think tanks, research organizations, charities, and government departments, as well as journal articles and book chapters.
- **Social Science Research Network (SSRN)**
  Producer: Elsevier
  Access: https://www.ssrn.com/en/
  Temporal Coverage: N/A
  Cost: Database can be searched for free, but downloading content requires a subscription
  Database Scope and Grey Literature Content: Information on accounting, economics, financial economics, legal scholarship, and management from specialized research networks. Grey literature content includes working papers as well as journal articles.
- **Technical Report Archive & Image Library (TRAIL)**
  Producer: University of Washington Libraries
  Access: http://www.technicalreports.org/trail/search/
  Temporal Coverage: 1940–1975

Cost: Free

Database Scope and Grey Literature Content: Scientific, agricultural, or engineering U.S. government technical reports. Database content consists primarily of grey literature document technical reports.

- **TRIP Database**

  Producer: Trip Database Ltd.

  Access: https://www.tripdatabase.com/index.htmlindex.html

  Temporal Coverage: N/A

  Cost: Free. Subscription required for TRIPPro.

  Database Scope and Grey Literature Content: TRIP is promoted as a clinical search engine for evidence-based medicine rather than as a traditional bibliographic database. Grey literature content in TRIP includes blogs, evidence-based synopses, systematic reviews not published in journal literature, guidelines, patient information leaflets, regulatory guidance, and active clinical trials.

- **TRIS Online**

  Producer: The National Academies of Science, Engineering, Medicine

  Access: https://trid.trb.org/

  Temporal Coverage: 1970–present (with selected prior coverage)

  Cost: Free

  Database Scope and Grey Literature Content: Database on transportation-related research worldwide, including aviation, construction, pedestrians and bicyclists, pipelines, public transportation, and policy. Grey literature content includes conference papers, reports, and project summaries; journal articles and books are also included.

- **Truth Tobacco Industry Documents**

  Producer: University of California, San Francisco (UCSF) and the Truth Initiative

  Access: https://www.industrydocumentslibrary.ucsf.edu/tobacco/

  Temporal Coverage: 1950–Present (with selected prior coverage)

  Cost: Free

  Database Scope and Grey Literature Content: Formerly the Legacy Tobacco Documents Library. Source for information on advertising, manufacturing, marketing, sales, and scientific research of tobacco products. Also includes tobacco industry internal corporate documents produced during litigation between U.S. states and the seven major tobacco industry organizations. Grey literature content includes research reports as well as journal articles.

- **UNESCO Database**

  Producer: United Nations Educational, Scientific and Cultural Organization (UNESCO)

  Access: http://www.unesco.org/new/en/unesdoc-database/

Temporal Coverage: N/A

Cost: Free

Database Scope and Grey Literature Content: Bibliographic database of UNESCO documents as well as non-UNESCO publications. Grey literature content includes mission reports, documents of UNESCO institutes and regional offices, as well as journal articles.

• **USAID Development Experience Clearinghouse**

Producer: U.S. Agency for International Development

Access: dec.usaid.gov/dec

Temporal Coverage: 1975–

Cost: Free

Database Scope and Grey Literature Content: Records in USAID Development Experience Clearinghouse are entirely grey literature and include oral histories of retired USAID staff, program planning documents from USAID, and descriptions of past USAID-sponsored projects.

• **U.S. Department of State Virtual Reading Room**

Producer: U.S. Department of State

Access: https://foia.state.gov/Search/Search.aspx

Temporal Coverage: N/A

Cost: Free

Database Scope and Grey Literature Content: Source for documents from the U.S. Department of State through the Freedom of Information Act. Database content is primarily grey literature.

• **WorldWideScience.org**

Producer: WorldWideScience Alliance, developed and maintained by the U.S. Office of Science and Technical Information

Access: https://worldwidescience.org/

Temporal Coverage:

Cost: Free

Database Scope and Grey Literature Content: Research from over seventy countries on such topics as energy, medicine, agriculture, environmental studies, and basic science. Includes grey literature content, along with journal articles. Advanced Search provides the most options for limiting search results to grey literature.

SEARCH TIPS FOR GREY LITERATURE DATABASES

Look for an Advanced Search Option

Also known as the "Avoid the 'Where's Waldo?' Conundrum" tip. Using the Advanced Search option in a database will allow you to execute a more targeted search by selecting specific fields, document types, or year ranges. Searching specific fields will help you determined why a database search retrieves particular search results.

Do a General Search First

Also known as the "Dress Rehearsal" tip. Start each database search by executing a general search. This will help you see the range of content on the search topic that the database provides. Performing a general search will also help you decide if you need to narrow or broaden your search topic, as well as whether searching a particular database is a worthy investment of time.

Adapt Your Search Strategy

Also known as the "KISS—Keep It Simple, Searcher" tip. Librarians and other information professionals are likely to be familiar with complicated Medline, PubMed, and Embase search strategies that use numerous subject headings, keywords, and search filters. Yet the search interface of most grey literature databases does not provide the same level of detailed searching. As a result, simple search strategies in grey literature databases are more likely to retrieve the optimal search results than overly complicated detailed search strategies.

Look for a Specific Grey Literature Publication by Title

Also known as the "Usual Suspects" tip. Are you familiar with a key grey literature publication on your search topic? One way to ascertain the grey literature coverage of a database is to see if the needed content will be included. This can be accomplished by searching for a known grey literature publication. If the database search does not retrieve the publication, then you will know that the grey literature content in the database may be lacking, allowing you to move on to other sources. Struggling to find relevant content in a database should not be akin to hunting for the elusive Keyser Söze.

Check for Recent Content

Also known as the "Somewhere in Time" or "A Connecticut Yankee in King Arthur's Court" tip. Librarians and information professionals are often trusted to direct users to the most recent information on a topic. Many of the databases containing grey literature content may not be frequently updated, and search results may be outdated. Search results should include current grey literature publications rather than a retro snapshot of grey literature publications from ten years ago. Confirming the currency of the content in a database is an indispensable step, otherwise much relevant content may be missed.

GREY LITERATURE DATABASES RECOMMENDED BY KNOWLEDGE SYNTHESIS—CREATING HEALTH CARE AGENCIES AND ORGANIZATIONS

Several health care agencies and organizations that support the development of evidence-based practice publications will list recommended grey literature databases. These recommendations are generally included in their guidelines on information retrieval. The following is an overview of grey literature databases that are recommended by select agencies producing knowledge synthesis. As we will see, the list of recommended databases for searching grey literature is quite limited, but the available documentation can be used as a starting point to select which databases should be used for a grey literature search.

Cochrane

Cochrane (previously known as the Cochrane Collaboration) is an independent, global, not-for-profit, NGO comprised of Cochrane contributors from over 130 countries. Cochrane's goals include producing up-to-date systematic reviews and other knowledge synthesis, and to make this evidence available and accessible to a worldwide population (Cochrane, "About Us," 2017, retrieved from http://www.cochrane.org/about-us). Cochrane produces the *Cochrane Handbook for Systematic Reviews of Interventions* Version 5.1.0, which is a guide on the process of preparing and updating Cochrane systematic reviews. Section 6.2.1.8 of the handbook provides a brief overview of bibliographic databases for identifying grey literature publications, and the following databases are recommended:

• Healthcare Management Information Consortium (HMIC)

- OpenSIGLE
- National Technical Information Service (NTIS)
- PsycExtra

The Campbell Collaboration

The Campbell Collaboration is an international, not-for-profit, NGO and "aims to help people make well-informed decisions about the effects of interventions in the social, behavioral, and educational arenas" (The Campbell Collaboration: Better Evidence for a Better World. Retrieved from https://www.campbellcollaboration.org/). The Campbell Collaboration produces and disseminates systematic reviews on social and behavioral interventions, with the aim of helping the policymakers, practitioners, researchers, and members of the general public identify what interventions work. The Campbell Collaboration Information Retrieval Group has published a guide on information retrieval methods for systematic reviews: *Searching for Studies: A Guide to Information Retrieval for Campbell Systematic Reviews*. The searching guidelines mention that their list of recommended databases may contain both published and unpublished document types and Appendix II of the guide provides a detailed list of grey literature search sources, including databases with grey literature content. The following databases with grey literature content are included in the recommendations:

- Healthcare Management Information Consortium (HMIC)
- ISI Index to Social Sciences and Humanities Proceedings (discussed in Chapter 7)
- ISI Index to Scientific and Technical Proceedings (discussed in Chapter 7)
- Ovid HealthSTAR
- PAIS International
- PolicyFile
- PsycEXTRA
- Bibliography of Nordic Criminology
- Child Welfare Information Gateway
- Child Abuse, Child Welfare, and Adoption Database (now included in the Child Welfare Information Gateway)
- CORDIS Library (now CORDIS)
- HUD USER Database
- National Technical Information Service
- NCJRS Abstracts Database
- OpenSIGLE (now OpenGrey)
- Social Care Online
- Social Science Research Network (SSRN) eLibrary

- TRIS Online

The Health and Medicine Division (HMD) of the National Academies of Sciences, Engineering, and Medicine

The HMD of the National Academies of Sciences, Engineering, and Medicine (formerly the Institute of Medicine) is a private U.S. not-for-profit institution with the aim of providing "independent, objective analysis and advice to the nation and conduct[ing] other activities to solve complex problems and inform public policy decisions related to science, technology, and medicine" (National Academies of Sciences, Engineering, and Medicine—HMD, "About HMD," September 2016, retrieved from http://www.nationalacademies.org/hmd/About-HMD.aspx). HMD has published recommended standards for conducting systematic reviews, and its publication *Finding What Works in Health Care: Standards for Systematic Reviews* outlines twenty-one standards for developing high-quality systematic reviews on comparative effectiveness research. Grey literature databases are listed as a search source in Standard 3.2.1, which also indicates that researchers should consult grey literature databases as they are an indispensable tool for reducing publication and language bias. The following grey literature databases are recommended:

- New York Academy of Medicine Grey Literature Report (note: this source is no longer being updated)
- OAIster (note: see Chapter 6 for more information on this resource)
- ProQuest Dissertations & Theses Database (note: see Chapter 5 for more information on this resource)
- OpenSIGLE System for Information on Grey Literature (note: OpenSIGLE is now Open Grey)

The Agency for Health Care Research and Quality (AHRQ)

The AHRQ is a U.S. governmental agency that is part of the U.S. Department of Health and Human Services. AHRQ's mission is "to produce evidence to make health care safer, higher quality, more accessible, equitable, and affordable, and to work within the U.S. Department of Health and Human Services and with other partners to make sure that the evidence is understood and used." The AHRQ Effective Health Care Program has published the *Methods Guide for Effectiveness and Comparative Effectiveness Reviews*, and the chapter "Finding Grey Literature Evidence and Assessing for Outcome and Analysis Reporting Biases When Comparing Medical Interventions: AHRQ and the Effective Health Care Program" recommends sources for identifying grey literature on conventional drugs and devices. Grant databases are specifically recommended:

- NIH RePORTER
- Foundation Directory Online
- HSRProj
- AHRQ GOLD (now the Project Research Online Database)

The chapter "Finding Evidence for Comparing Medical Interventions" also has a list of recommended specialized databases to be considered as search sources, but the listed databases are not specifically advised as sources for locating grey literature publications.

National Institute for Health and Care Excellence (NICE)

The NICE is a nondepartmental public body (NDPB) that is accountable to its sponsor department, the Department of Health, United Kingdom. NICE's mission is to improve outcomes for people using the National Health Service and other public health and social services. NICE produces evidence guidance and advice, including NICE guidelines and other evidence summaries. The publication *Developing NICE Guidelines: The Manual* mentions that searching sources for identifying grey literature publications may be principal for certain reviews. Appendix G, "Sources for Evidence Reviews," contains a list of recommended specialized databases, but the database sources are not specifically identified as sources to search for locating grey literature publications.

A DECISION AID FOR SELECTING DATABASES FOR A GREY LITERATURE SEARCH

Unfortunately, there is not a one-stop database source for grey literature publications. Alas, there is not even an equivalent of an NHL Original Six team–inspired list of top databases for identifying grey literature. As discussed earlier in this chapter, there are numerous available databases for identifying grey literature publications; still, it is neither feasible nor fruitful to search all the available databases for grey literature publications.

Textbox 3.1. A Proposed Decision Aid for Selecting Grey Literature Databases to Search

---

1. Is there a subject-specific database available that matches your search topic?

Subject specific databases such as CINAHL or Embase are used to identify journal articles in specific disciplines; databases with grey literature content can also be utilized to identify topic-specific publications. If a user is hoping to identify grey literature publications on criminology-related topics, for example, a subject-appropriate database such as NCJRS Abstracts Database should be searched. Additionally, if there is a subject-specific database that is available for your search topic, the chances increase that a peer reviewer may expect to see it listed on the sources searched.

2. Do you need to identify a specific grey literature publication type?

Just as database searches in Medline or PsycInfo can be limited to review articles, a grey literature database search can be used to locate specific types of grey literature publications. For example, if the aim of a grey literature database is to locate U.S. federal government publications, then the search can be limited to such sources as Catalog of U.S. Government Publications or the NTIS Bibliographic Database.

3. Do you need to follow recommended search guidelines?

Often, a librarian or information professional may be using published searching guidelines to select search sources. If your overall search plan requires following published searching guidelines, check to see if the searching guidelines recommend specific grey literature databases. For example, the *Cochrane Handbook for Systematic Reviews of Interventions* Version 5.1.0 does recommend specific databases for identifying grey literature publications. This way, if need be, you can provide supporting references for your selection of specific databases in your grey literature search.

CONCLUSION

Databases can be used to identify grey literature publications and a plentitude of database sources are available. A searcher can use databases containing grey literature content as part of a systematic approach to identify relevant grey literature publications, as well as for more focused and quick searches. Databases may also be pertinent sources for identifying specific types of government publications, such as governmental reports or working papers. There are a great number of free subject-specific databases available, but searchers must take extra steps to determine the quality, percentage of grey literature content and temporal coverage of databases. Still, unlike journal articles and books, there is little bibliographic control of grey literature (Schöpfel & Farace, 2010) and databases are not a one-stop source for locating relevant grey literature documents. A comprehensive grey literature search requires taking additional search steps beyond just searching databases.

BIBLIOGRAPHY

Adams, J., Hillier-Brown, F. C., Moore, H. J., Lake, A. A., Araujo-Soares, V., White, M., et al. (2016). Searching and synthesising "grey literature" and "grey information" in public health: Critical reflections on three case studies. *Systematic Reviews*, *5*(1), 164.

Adams, R. J., Smart, P., & Huff, A. S. (2017). Shades of grey: Guidelines for working with the grey literature in systematic reviews for management and organizational studies. *International Journal of Management Reviews*, *19*(4), 432–454.

Adie, E. (2014). The grey literature from an altmetrics perspective—opportunity and challenges. *Research Trends*, *37*, 23–25.

Albino, V., Dangelico, R. M., Natalicchio, A., & Yazan, D. M. (2011). Alternative energy sources in cement manufacturing. Network for Business Sustainability, Richard Ivey School of Business of Western Ontario.

Alpi, K. M. (2005). Expert searching in public health. *Journal of the Medical Library Association: JMLA*, *93*(1), 97–103.

Bar-Ilan, J. (2008). Which h-index? A comparison of WoS, scopus and google scholar. *Scientometrics*, *74*(2), 257–271.

Becker, J. E., Krumholz, H. M., Ben-Josef, G., & Ross, J. S. (2014). Reporting of results in ClinicalTrials.gov and high-impact journals. *JAMA*, *311*(10), 1063–1065.

Benzies, K. M., Premji, S., Hayden, K. A., & Serrett, K. (2006). State-of-the-evidence reviews: Advantages and challenges of including grey literature. *Worldviews on Evidence-Based Nursing*, *3*(2), 55–61.

Bergman, M. K. (2001). White paper: The Deep Web: Surfacing hidden value. *Journal of Electronic Publishing*, *7*(1).

Billig, M. (2013). *Learn to write badly: How to succeed in the social sciences.* Cambridge University Press.

Borenstein, M., Rothstein, H., & Sutton, A. (2005). *Publication bias in meta-analysis: Prevention, assessment and adjustments.* Wiley.

Breitzman, A., & Thomas, P. (2016). An analysis of references from U.S. patents to NIST-supported technical outputs.

Brevik, E. C., & Burgess, L. C. (2012). *Soils and human health.* CRC Press.

Callard, A. (2009). A decade in food trends. *Smithsonian.com*. Retrieved from https://www.smithsonianmag.com/arts-culture/a-decade-in-food-trends-76395204/

Carr, C. (1993). Global, national and resource-based strategies: An examination of strategic choice and performance in the vehicle components industry. *Strategic Management Journal*, *14*(7), 551–567.

Chavez, T. A., Perrault, A. H., Reehling, P., & Crummett, C. (2007). The impact of grey literature in advancing global karst research: An information needs assessment for a globally distributed interdisciplinary community. *Publishing Research Quarterly, 23*(1), 3–18.

Coad, J., Hardicre, J., & Devitt, P. (2006). How to search for and use "grey literature" in research. *Nursing Times, 102*(50), 35–36.

Conn, V. S., Valentine, J. C., Cooper, H. M., & Rantz, M. J. (2003). Grey literature in meta-analyses. *Nursing Research, 52*(4), 256–261.

Cordes, R. (2013). *Is grey literature ever used? Using citation analysis to measure the impact of GESAMP, an international marine scientific advisory body.* Proceedings of the Annual Conference of CAIS/Actes Du Congrès Annuel De l'ACSI.

De Castro, P., & Salinetti, S. (2006). "Uniform requirements" for grey literature: A proposal for the adoption of "Nancy style." *Publishing Research Quarterly, 22*(1), 12–17.

De Castro, P., & Salinetti, S. (2013). "6.4: Grey Literature: Challenges and Responsibilities for Authors and Editors." In P. Smart, H. Maisonneuve, & A. Polderman (eds.), Science Editors' Handbook European Association of Science Editors.

De Castro, P., & Salinetti, S. (2013). Grey literature: A growing need for good practice. *European Science Editing, 39*(3).

De Castro, P., Salinetti, S., & Banks, M. (2006). Awareness and empowerment in document production and distribution as a "must" for open access: Experiences from the "Nancy style" to guarantee quality.

Dingley, B. (2005). US periodical price Index–2004.

Drott, M. C. (1995). Reexamining the role of conference papers in scholarly communication. *Journal of the American Society for Information Science, 46*(4), 299.

Fattahi, R., & Afshar, E. (2006). Added value of information and information systems: A conceptual approach. *Library Review, 55*(2), 132–147.

Feathers, J. (2013). *The information society: A study of continuity and change* (6th ed.). Facet Publishing.

Finfgeld-Connett, D., & Johnson, E. D. (2013). Literature search strategies for conducting knowledge-building and theory-generating qualitative systematic reviews. *Journal of Advanced Nursing, 69*(1), 194–204.

Fountain J. (202). Grey matter: Unpublished research report. *Social Work in Europe, 9*, 65.

Garengo, P., Biazzo, S., & Bititci, U. S. (2005). Performance measurement systems in SMEs: A review for a research agenda. *International Journal of Management Reviews, 7*(1), 25–47.

Glazier, R. H., Bajcar, J., Kennie, N. R., & Willson, K. (2006). A systematic review of interventions to improve diabetes care in socially disadvantaged populations. *Diabetes Care, 29*(7), 1675–1688.

Godin, K., Stapleton, J., Kirkpatrick, S. I., Hanning, R. M., & Leatherdale, S. T. (2015). Applying systematic review search methods to the grey literature: A case study examining guidelines for school-based breakfast programs in Canada. *Systematic Reviews, 4*(1), 138.

Goodman, M. (2015). *Future crimes: Everything is connected, everyone is vulnerable and what we can do about it.* Anchor.

Hammerstrøm, K., Wade, A., Jørgensen, A. K., & Hammerstrøm, K. (2010). Searching for studies. *Education, 54,* 11.3.

Higgins, J. P., & Green, S. (2011). *Cochrane handbook for systematic reviews of interventions.* John Wiley & Sons.

Himmelstein, D. (2015). Publication delays at PLOS and 3,475 other journals. *Satoshi Village 9*(1).

Hopewell, S., Loudon, K., Clarke, M. J., Oxman, A. D., & Dickersin, K. (2009). Publication bias in clinical trials due to statistical significance or direction of trial results. Cochrane Database of Systematic Reviews 2009, Issue 1. Art. No.: MR000006. DOI: 10.1002/14651858.MR000006.pub3.

Hopewell, S., McDonald, S., Clarke, M. J., & Egger, M. (2007). Grey literature in meta-analyses of randomized trials of health care interventions. Cochrane Database of Systematic Reviews 2007, Issue 2. Art. No.: MR000010. DOI: 10.1002/14651858. MR000010.pub3.

Hoy, M. M., Egan, M. Y., & Feder, K. P. (2011). A systematic review of interventions to improve handwriting. *Canadian Journal of Occupational Therapy, 78*(1), 13–25.

Hutchinson, B. S., & Paris-Greider, A. (2002). *Using the agricultural, environmental, and food literature.* CRC Press.

Hutton, G. R. (2009). *Scientific grey literature in a digital age: Measuring its use and influence in an evolving information economy.* Proceedings of the 2009 Canadian Association of Information Science Conference, Ottawa, Ontario, pp. 1–15.

Jacobs, J. A., Jones, E., Gabella, B. A., Spring, B., & Brownson, R. C. (2012). Peer reviewed: tools for implementing an evidence-based approach in public health practice. *Preventing chronic disease, 9.*

Jadad, A. R., Moher, D., & Klassen, T. P. (1998). Guides for reading and interpreting systematic reviews: II. How did the authors find the studies and assess their quality? *Archives of Pediatrics & Adolescent Medicine, 152*(8), 812–817.

Jaeger, P. T., Gorham, U., Bertot, J. C., & Sarin, L. C. (2014). *Public libraries, public policies, and political processes: Serving and transforming communities in times of economic and political constraint.* Rowman & Littlefield.

Kannan, S., & Gowri, S. (2014). Contradicting/negative results in clinical research: Why (do we get these)? Why not (get these published)? Where (to publish)? *Perspectives in Clinical Research, 5*(4), 151–153.

Kay, M., Santos, J., & Takane, M. (2011). mHealth: New horizons for health through mobile technologies. *World Health Organization, 64*(7), 66–71.

Kelly, W. R. (2015). *Criminal justice at the crossroads: Transforming crime and punishment.* Columbia University Press.

Kuepper, G. (2010). A brief overview of the history and philosophy of organic agriculture. *Poteau, OK: Kerr Center for Sustainable Agriculture.*

Kugley, S., Wade, A., Thomas, J., Mahood, Q., Jørgensen, A. K., Hammerstrøm, K., et al. (2016). Searching for studies: A guide to information retrieval for Campbell Systematic Reviews. Campbell Methods Guides 2016: 1. DOI: 10.4073/ cmg.2016.1.

Lawlor, D. A., & Hopker, S. W. (2001). The effectiveness of exercise as an intervention in the management of depression: Systematic review and meta-regression analysis of randomised controlled trials. *BMJ (Clinical Research Ed.)*, *322*(7289), 763–767.

Lawrence, A., Houghton, J., Thomas, J., & Weldon, P. (2012). Where is the evidence? Realising the value of grey literature for public policy and practice.

MacDonald, B. H., Cordes, R. E., & Wells, P. G. (2004). Grey literature in the life of GESAMP, an international marine scientific advisory body. *Publishing Research Quarterly*, *20*(1), 25–41.

MacDonald, B. H., Cordes, R. E., & Wells, P. G. (2007). Assessing the diffusion and impact of grey literature published by international intergovernmental scientific groups: The case of the Gulf of Maine council on the marine environment. *Publishing Research Quarterly*, *23*(1), 30–46.

Martin, S. A., & Assenov, I. (2012). The genesis of a new body of sport tourism literature: A systematic review of surf tourism research (1997–2011). *Journal of Sport & Tourism*, *17*(4), 257–287.

McAuley, L., Tugwell, P., & Moher, D. (2000). Does the inclusion of grey literature influence estimates of intervention effectiveness reported in meta-analyses? *The Lancet*, *356*(9237), 1228–1231.

McDonagh, M., Peterson, K., Raina, P., Chang, S., & Shekelle, P. (2013). *Avoiding bias in selecting studies: Methods guide for effectiveness and comparative effectiveness reviews*. Agency for Healthcare Research and Quality.

McGowan, J., & Sampson, M. (2005). Systematic reviews need systematic searchers. *Journal of the Medical Library Association: JMLA*, *93*(1), 74–80.

McKenna, C., Burch, J., Suekarran, S., Walker, S., Bakhai, A., Witte, K., et al. (2010). A systematic review and economic evaluation of the clinical effectiveness and cost-effectiveness of aldosterone antagonists for postmyocardial infarction heart failure. *Health Technology Assessment (Winchester, England)*, *14*(24), 1–162.

Meho, L. I. (2007). The rise and rise of citation analysis. *Physics World, 20*(1), 32.

Morton, S., Berg, A., Levit, L., & Eden, J. (2011). *Finding what works in health care: Standards for systematic reviews*. National Academies Press.

National Opinion Research Center (NORC). (2016). *Investigating how Americans navigate the modern information environment.* NORC at the University of Chicago.

Nutley, S., Jung, T., & Walter, I. (2008). The many forms of research-informed practice: A framework for mapping diversity. *Cambridge Journal of Education*, *38*(1), 53–71.

Nutley, S. M., Walter, I., & Davies, H. T. (2007). *Using evidence: How research can inform public services*. Policy Press.

O'Dell, C., Dallman, D., Vesely, M., & Vigen, J. (2004). Fifty years of experience in making grey literature available: Matching the expectations of the particle physics community. *Publishing Research Quarterly 20*(1), 84–91.

Orton, L., Lloyd-Williams, F., Taylor-Robinson, D., O'Flaherty, M., & Capewell, S. (2011). The use of research evidence in public health decision making processes: Systematic review. *PloS One*, *6*(7), e21704.

Pelzer, N. L., & Wiese, W. H. (2003). Bibliometric study of grey literature in core veterinary medical journals. *Journal of the Medical Library Association: JMLA*, *91*(4), 434–441.

Ramsey, S., & Schickedanz, A. (2010). How should we define value in cancer care? *The Oncologist, 15 Suppl* 1, 1–4.

Reitz, J. M. (2004). *Dictionary for library and information science*. Libraries Unlimited.

Revere, D., Turner, A. M., Madhavan, A., Rambo, N., Bugni, P. F., Kimball, A., et al. (2007). Understanding the information needs of public health practitioners: A literature review to inform design of an interactive digital knowledge management system. *Journal of Biomedical Informatics*, *40*(4), 410–421.

Rodrigues-Krause, J., Farinha, J. B., Krause, M., & Reischak-Oliveira, Á. (2016). Effects of dance interventions on cardiovascular risk with ageing: Systematic review and meta-analysis. *Complementary Therapies in Medicine*, *29*, 16–28.

Ross, J. S., Mocanu, M., Lampropulos, J. F., Tse, T., & Krumholz, H. M. (2013). Time to publication among completed clinical trials. *JAMA Internal Medicine*, *173*(9), 825–828.

Rothstein, H. R., & Hopewell, S. (2009). Grey literature. In H. Cooper, L. V. Hedges, & J. C. Valentine (Eds.), The handbook of research synthesis and meta-analysis (pp. 103–25). New York: Russell Sage Foundation.

Rothstein, H. R., Sutton, A. J., & Borenstein, M. (2006). *Publication bias in meta-analysis: Prevention, assessment and adjustments*. John Wiley & Sons.

Sackett, D. L. (1997). *Evidence-based medicine: How to practice and teach EBM*. W.B. Saunders Company.

Schöpfel, J. (2013). Adding value to electronic theses and dissertations in institutional repositories. *DLib Magazine*, *19*(3/4).

Schöpfel, J. & Farace D. J. (2010). Grey Literature. In M. J. Bates *&* M. N.. Maack (*eds.*), *Encyclopedia* of *Library* and *Information Sciences, Third Edition*, pp. 2029–2039. CRC Press.

Schöpfel, J., & Stock, C. (2008). Grey foundations in information landscape: A report on the 9th International Conference on Grey Literature, Antwerp, 10–11 December 2007. *Interlending & Document Supply*, *36*(2).

Seymour, D. J. (2010). *In the Trenches around the Ivory Tower: Introduction to Black-and-White Issues about the Grey Literature*,

Sibbald, S. L., MacGregor, J. C., Surmacz, M., & Wathen, C. N. (2015). Into the gray: A modified approach to citation analysis to better understand research impact. *Journal of the Medical Library Association: JMLA*, *103*(1), 49–54.

Soule, M. H., & Ryan, R. P. (1999). Gray literature, technical briefing. *Information Technology summIT.* Retrieved from http://www.Dtic.mil/summit/tb07.Html.

Straus, S. E., Tetroe, J., & Graham, I. (2009). Defining knowledge translation. *CMAJ: Canadian Medical Association Journal = Journal De l'Association Medicale Canadienne*, *181*(3–4), 165–168.

Sturges, P., & Cooke, L. (2007). Finding the grey in the blue: Transparency and disclosure in teaching. The Grey Journal: An International Journal on Grey Literature, 4(1), pp.21–28.

Sulouff, P., Bell, S., Briden, J., Frontz, S., & Marshall, A. (2005). Learning about grey literature by interviewing subject librarians: A study at the university of Rochester. *College & Research Libraries News, 66*(7), 510–515.

Tenopir, C., King, D. W., Clarke, M. T., Na, K., & Zhou, X. (2007). Journal reading patterns and preferences of pediatricians. *Journal of the Medical Library Association: JMLA, 95*(1), 56–63.

Turner, A. M., Liddy, E. D., & Bradley, J. (2002). *Breathing life into digital archives: Use of natural language processing to revitalize the grey literature of public health.* Proceedings of the 2nd ACM/IEEE-CS Joint Conference on Digital Libraries, p. 411.

UK Health Forum Research & Information Services. (2013). *Discussion paper: Grey literature in public health: Valuable evidence?*

Van Moorsel, G. (2005). Client value models provide a framework for rational library planning (or, phrasing the answer in the form of a question). *Medical Reference Services Quarterly, 24*(2), 25–40.

Wernli, K. J., Henrikson, N. B., Morrison, C. C., Nguyen, M., Pocobelli, G., & Blasi, P. R. (2016). Screening for skin cancer in adults: Updated evidence report and systematic review for the US preventive services task force. *JAMA, 316*(4), 436–447.

Wessels, R. (2003). Grey literature. *International Encyclopedia of Information and Library Science.* Routledge.

Chapter 4

Searching for Dissertations/Theses

Dissertations and theses are defined as documents "submitted in support of candidature for an academic degree or professional qualification presenting the author's research and findings" (Wikipedia, "Thesis," retrieved March 27, 2017, from https://en.wikipedia.org/wiki/Thesis). The terms "dissertation" and "thesis" are often used interchangeably (Germano, 2014); additionally, a dissertation or thesis may be written to fulfill the degree requirements for either an undergraduate degree, graduate degree, or Ph.D. (Academia Stack Exchange, "What Makes a Bachelor's Thesis Different from Master's and PhD Theses?," retrieved March 27, 2017, http://academia.stackexchange. com/questions/18665/what-makes-a-bachelors-thesis-different-from-masters-and-phd-theses), and the educational purpose of a thesis or dissertation has remained unchanged over time (Južnič, 2010).

LEARNING OUTCOMES

This chapter will focus on Ph.D. dissertations as a grey literature document type. The goals of this chapter are to provide librarians and information professionals with:

- dissertations' strengths as a document type to be included as part of a grey literature search
- dissertations' weaknesses as a document type to be included as part of a grey literature search
- a list of select bibliographic databases that include dissertations, including the following information:
  - producer of the database

- temporal coverage
- cost
- scope of database and dissertation content
- other sources for Ph.D. dissertations
- a proposed decision-making aid for including dissertations in a grey literature search

After reading this chapter, readers should also have a basic understanding of dissertations as one component of a grey literature search. The following introductory overview of dissertations should enable librarians and information professionals to facilitate discussions with their information users on including dissertations as part of a grey literature search.

ADVANTAGES OF INCLUDING DISSERTATIONS AS PART OF A GREY LITERATURE SEARCH

There are many reasons to include dissertations as part of a grey literature search. This time, let's use a Top Five framework to examine both the benefits and drawbacks of including dissertations as part of a grey lit search.

1. As a grey literature document type, dissertations offer quality and are salient resources.

Dissertations are often considered inferior sources of evidence, especially when compared to such published resources as journal articles and books. Publication of research is often used to determine study quality (Moyer et al., 2010; Conn et al., 2003), therefore dissertations may be dismissed as unreliable sources of evidence. Yet dissertations should not be banished so readily. Dissertations can be considered a peer-reviewed resource: although dissertations are not submitted to the same peer-review process as a manuscript submitted to a journal article, candidates are still required to submit their work for review to a dissertation committee, and generally the members of a dissertation committee are scholarly experts in the candidate's area of study (Germano, 2014). This may help ensure a dissertation's reliability as a quality resource because, "often the culmination of months or years of work, the dissertation is the concrete manifestation of a doctoral student's best thinking, guided and refined by the sage suggestions of the student's committee members" (Conn, 2008). Candidates research and write their dissertations with the help and insight of an advisor and committee, which provide them with support during the research and writing process (Davis, 2004; Conn, 2008). Additionally, research has identified dissertations as providing a valuable methodology and clinical source of information, even more so than some published studies (McLeod & Weisz, 2004). Overall, there is ample evidence that dissertations at least should be considered as an information source worthy of inclusion in a search. Although it is said that the best dissertation is a *finished* dissertation, the finished product may indeed be a quality research resource.

2. Dissertations often provide highly detailed information.

Dissertations are generally *not* short pieces of work—the average length is 100 to 200 pages ("How Long Is the Average Dissertation?," retrieved March 27, 2017, from https://beckmw.wordpress.com/2013/04/15/how-long-is-the-average-dissertation/), allowing for much background research and supporting references. Universities may have specific word count restrictions for dissertations, but the total word count is much more generous than for journal articles. Candidates writing dissertations may also demonstrate knowledge of a topic by providing hundreds of references (Germano, 2014). As a result, dissertations can be preceptive sources providing detailed background information on previously completed research. Thus, dissertations as part of a grey literature search may provide key information that would not be identified in other published sources.

3. Dissertations are often open access.

Many dissertations are available for free online. Much of this can be linked to the rise of institutional depositories. Additionally, there are web portals that have been established specifically to provide access to dissertations. So not only do dissertations provide detailed information, often that information is available for free online. An example is a search for dissertations on the topic of genomic profiling for cancer. A quick search on this topic in Library and Archives Canada's Thesis Canada Portal identifies thirty dissertations available for download.

4. Dissertations can provide information on a topic when the published literature does not.

Dissertations can be a source for research on a topic when there is only limited information available in published literature, because dissertations generally address very narrow topics that others have not researched in detail (Germano, 2014). The result of this narrow research focus is that dissertations may be excellent sources for research on specific geographical locations, emerging interventions, new initiatives, and special populations, among other areas. Dissertations may even be groundbreaking sources of information on original topics and new ideas (Germano, 2014; Foster & Jewell, 2017). For example, dissertations may be a key source of evidence for such topics as HIV gene therapy or balance training for fall prevention.

5. Dissertations may reduce potential publication bias.

Dissertations are considered unpublished sources (although select dissertations may be published later, in a revised format). As unpublished research, dissertations may not be subject to publication bias or the "file-drawer" effect (Moyer et al., 2010; Scargle, 1999; Rosenthal, 1979) because all accredited institutions in North America that award doctoral degrees submit their dissertations to ProQuest Global Dissertations and Theses for publication or listing (ProQuest, "Dissertation Abstracts International," retrieved March 27, 2017, from http://www.proquest.com/products-services/dissertations/Dissertations-Abstract-International.html). Even if the findings of a candidate's dissertation do not support the desired research hypothesis, the dissertation will still be indexed or referenced in a bibliographic source. Research has documented that dissertations provide access to results that may never be published because of the lack of a treatment effect. This makes dissertations valuable because research with negative results is less likely to be published in journals (Fanelli, 2011). Therefore, including dissertations in a search may be an ideal way to identify research studies with negative results (Moyer et al., 2010).

DISADVANTAGES OF INCLUDING DISSERTATIONS AS PART OF A GREY LITERATURE SEARCH

1. Dissertations are from emerging researchers and authors.

Dissertations are generally not written by experts; rather, candidates are emerging experts, and dissertations may be quasi sources of professional work, rather than the output of established researchers (Germano, 2014). Despite this, there is no reason to dismiss the insight that candidates may offer—it is not far-fetched to say that some of these individuals will go on to be Nobel Prize winners like economist Joseph Stiglitz. As Maya Angelou said, "All great achievements require time," and dissertations are a quality source even though candidates do not yet have years of research and experience under their belt.

2. Dissertations may be challenging to appraise.

The quality of a dissertation is judged by the candidate's advisor, and committee and university faculty that assess dissertations may not be following explicit evaluation criteria available to others for examination (Lovitts, 2007). Compare this to the commonly used critical appraisal tools that are used to assess the quality and utility of published research, such as the quality checklist Assessing the Methodological Quality of Systematic Reviews, or AMSTAR (Shea et al., 2007). Most lists of critical appraisal tools are for evaluating published research. If the intention is to include dissertations as part of the evidence base for a systematic review, quality checklists may need to be adapted for assessing dissertations.

3. Including dissertations with other evidence may be challenging.

The research content of dissertations may differ considerably from the content in published literature on the same topic. The content in a dissertation could vary for several reasons, including the research methods used in the dissertation, the study population size, or how research results were analyzed. A specific example would be a dissertation that has a small pool of participants in its research study—dissertations are not going to have the same study population size as multisite clinical trials. Including studies with a small number of research participants in a meta-analysis may lead to an overestimated intervention effect (Kraemer et al., 1998), and if too many "underpowered" studies with a small sample size are included, statistical correction may not be possible (Coyne, Hagedoorn, & Thombs, 2011). As such, incorporating research results available from dissertations may be more complicated.

4. Dissertations are often not included in data analysis.

While many systematic reviews may include dissertations in a pool of search results, dissertations are often not included in data analysis; research has demonstrated that data from dissertations may also not contribute to the overall findings of a systematic review (Vickers & Smith, 2000).

5. Searching for dissertations takes time.

Searching for grey literature sources, including identifying relevant dissertations from both national and international sources, may require a significant time investment (Vickers & Smith, 2000). While referring a user to select dissertation sources may be a good option for a quick reference request, exhaustive searching is needed to identify all relevant dissertations on a topic. If identifying all relevant dissertations is required as part of a comprehensive search for a systematic or scoping review, librarians and information professionals may first want to inquire how the dissertation search results will be used. A search for dissertations is a waste of time if there is not a plan for how to include and analyze the information obtained from dissertations in the evidence pool.

SOURCES FOR IDENTIFYING DISSERTATIONS

The following sources can be used to identify dissertations. While some of the sources for dissertations may include undergraduate and graduate dissertations, the aim is to list sources that identify Ph.D. dissertations.

Select Databases for Identifying Dissertations

- **American Doctoral Dissertations**
  Producer: EBSCO
  Access: https://www.ebscohost.com/academic/american-doctoral-dissertations
  Temporal Coverage: 1902–Present
  Cost: Free
  Database Scope: Dissertations accepted by American universities; the only source for dissertations accepted by American universities from 1933 to 1955. Includes more than 153,000 theses and dissertations in total, including 70,000 new citations for theses and dissertations from 1902 to the present.
- **DissOnline**
  Producer: German National Library
  Access: http://www.dnb.de/EN/Home/home_node.html
  Temporal Coverage: 1902–Present
  Cost: Free
  Database Scope: Source for dissertations in German. Once a separate portal, DissOnline is now integrated into the library catalog of the German National Library.
- **Open Access Theses and Dissertations**
  Producer: Project led by Thomas Dowling, Z. Smith Reynolds Library, Wake Forest University
  Access: https://oatd.org/
  Temporal Coverage: N/A

Database Scope: This database focuses exclusively on dissertations and theses that are open access. International in scope.

- **OpenDissertations.org**
  Access: https://biblioboard.com/opendissertations/
  Producer: EBSCO Information Services & Bibiolabs
  Temporal Coverage: N/A
  Cost: Free
  Database Scope: A newly launched open access resource for dissertations and expands on the scope of American Doctoral Dissertations.
- **ProQuest Dissertations and Theses Global**
  Producer: ProQuest
  Access: http://www.proquest.com/products-services/pqdtglobal.html
  Temporal Coverage: 1861–Present
  Cost: Subscription
  Database Scope: The most substantial database source for dissertations. Includes dissertations from Canada, the United States, and the United Kingdom. Overall, over 3.8 million dissertations are included, many available in full text. This resource may also be referred to as ProQuest Dissertations and Theses.
- **ProQuest Dissertations and Theses—UK & Ireland**
  Producer: ProQuest
  Access: http://www.proquest.com/products-services/pqdt_uk_ireland.html
  Temporal Coverage: 1716–Present
  Cost: Subscription
  Database Scope: Only includes doctoral theses from the United Kingdom and Ireland.

Other Sources

- **DART-Europe E-theses Portal**
  Producer: Partnership of research libraries and library consortia who are working together to improve global access to European research theses, including the European Working Group of the Networked Digital Library of Theses and Dissertations (NDLTD).
  Access: http://www.dart-europe.eu/basic-search.php
  Temporal Coverage: N/A
  Scope: A web portal for electronic theses and dissertations (ETDs) from Europe.
- **Global ETD Search**
  Producer: Networked Digital Library of Theses and Dissertations (NDLTD)
  Access: http://search.ndltd.org/
  Temporal Coverage: N/A

Scope: Provides access to electronic theses and dissertations contained in the NDLTD archive. International in scope.
- **Theses Canada Portal**
  Producer: Library and Archives Canada
  Access: http://www.bac-lac.gc.ca/eng/services/theses/Pages/theses-canada.aspx
  Temporal Coverage: 1965–Present
  Cost: Free
  Scope: Aims to acquire and make available a comprehensive collection of Canadian theses and dissertations. This resource may also be referred to as Theses Canada.

Other Databases Providing Dissertation Content

- **African Index Medicus**
  Producer: World Health Organization and the Association for Health Libraries in Africa
  Access: http://indexmedicus.afro.who.int/
  Temporal Coverage: 2000–Present
  Cost: Free
  Database Scope and Dissertation Content: Index for health literature published in Africa or about Africa. Includes select dissertations.
- **Australian Indigenous Health*InfoNet***
  Producer: Australian Indigenous Health*InfoNet*
  Access: http://www.healthinfonet.ecu.edu.au/
  Temporal Coverage: N/A
  Cost: Free
  Database Scope and Dissertation Content: Source for research on Aboriginal and Torres Strait Islander health. Includes select dissertations.
- **EconLit**
  Producer: American Economic Association
  Access: https://www.aeaweb.org/econlit/
  Temporal Coverage: 1886–Present
  Cost: Subscription
  Database Scope and Dissertation Content: Database for scholarly economic literature. Includes select dissertations.
- **eHRAF World Cultures**
  Producer: Human Relations Area Files, Inc. at Yale University
  Access: http://ehrafworldcultures.yale.edu/ehrafe/
  Temporal Coverage: N/A
  Cost: Subscription

    Database Scope and Dissertation Content: Cross-cultural and ethnographic database that contains historical and recent information on all aspects of cultural and social life. Includes select dissertations.

- **GambLIB database**
  Producer: International Gambling Research Institute
  Access: http://www.gamblib.org/
  Temporal Coverage: 1680–Present
  Cost: Free
  Database Scope and Dissertation Content: Includes dissertations on gambling research.

- **Google Scholar**
  Producer: Google
  Access: https://scholar.google.ca/
  Temporal Coverage: N/A
  Cost: Free
  Database Scope and Dissertation Content: Scope is multidisciplinary and select dissertations are included.
  Note: Please see Chapter 9 for more detailed information on Google Scholar.

- **IDP Database of Research on International Education**
  Producer: Australian Council for Educational Research (ACER)
  Access: http://opac.acer.edu.au/IDP_drie/
  Temporal Coverage: 1990–Present
  Cost: Free
  Database Scope and Dissertation Content: Database on international education; includes select dissertations.

- **Indigenous Studies Portal**
  Producer: University of Saskatchewan
  Access: iportal.usask.ca
  Temporal Coverage: 2005–Present
  Cost: Free
  Database Scope and Dissertation Content: Database focusing primarily on First Nations and Aboriginals of Canada with a secondary focus on North American materials and beyond. Select dissertations are included.

- **LILACS**
  Producer: Latin American and Caribbean Center on Health Sciences Information, or BIREME
  Access: lilacs.bvsalud.org/en
  Temporal Coverage: N/A
  Cost: Free

Database Scope and Dissertation Content: LILACS is an index of scientific and technical literature of Latin America and the Caribbean. Select dissertations are included.

- **Minority Health and Health Equity Archive**
  Producer: Center for Health Equity, University of Maryland; hosted by the University Library System, University of Pittsburgh
  Access: http://minority-health.pitt.edu/
  Temporal Coverage: 1882–Present
  Cost: Free
  Database Scope and Dissertation Content: Information on minority health and health disparities research and policy. Select dissertations are included.
- **Open Grey (formerly OpenSIGLE)**
  Producer: INIST-CNRS
  Access: www.opengrey.eu
  Temporal Coverage: 1980–Present
  Cost: Free
  Database Scope and Dissertation Content: Access to 700,000 bibliographical references of grey literature produced in Europe. Includes select dissertations.
- **PILOTS Database (Published International Literature on Traumatic Stress)**
  Producer: National Center for PTSD (U.S.)
  Access: www.ptsd.va.gov/professional/pilots-database
  Temporal Coverage: N/A
  Cost: Free
  Database Scope and Dissertation Content: Electronic index to the worldwide literature on PTSD and other mental health consequences of exposure to traumatic events. Includes select dissertations.
- **PsycInfo**
  Producer: American Psychological Association
  Access: http://www.apa.org/pubs/databases/psycinfo
  Temporal Coverage: 1860–Present
  Cost: Subscription
  Database Scope and Dissertation Content: Psychology and behavioral health–related content. Includes select dissertations in psychology from the 1950s onward.
- **SafetyLit**
  Producer: SafetyLit Foundation
  Access: www.safetylit.org
  Temporal Coverage: Mid-17th Century–Present
  Cost: Free

Database Scope and Dissertation Content: SafetyLit indexes research on preventing and researching unintentional injuries, violence, and self-harm. Includes select dissertations.

* ***SciTech Connect***
Producer: U.S. Department of Energy, Office of Science and Technical Information
Access: www.osti.gov/scitech
Temporal Coverage: N/A
Cost: Free
Database Scope and Dissertation Content: SciTech provides access to science, technology, and engineering research information from the U.S. Department of Energy. Includes select dissertations.

SOURCES FOR IDENTIFYING DISSERTATIONS RECOMMENDED BY HEALTH CARE AGENCIES AND ORGANIZATIONS THAT CREATE KNOWLEDGE SYNTHESIS

Several health care agencies and organizations that support the development of evidence-based practice publications list recommended grey literature search sources. These recommendations are generally included in their guidelines on information retrieval. The following is an overview of search sources for dissertations that are recommended by select agencies producing knowledge synthesis. As we will see, the list of recommended search sources for identifying dissertations is quite limited, but the available documentation can be used as a starting point to select appropriate search sources.

Cochrane

Cochrane (previously known as the Cochrane Collaboration) is a global independent, not-for-profit, NGO comprised of Cochrane contributors from over 130 countries. Cochrane's goals include producing up-to-date systematic reviews and other knowledge synthesis, and making that evidence available and accessible to a worldwide population (Cochrane, "About Us," 2017, retrieved from http://www.cochrane.org/about-us). Cochrane produces the *Cochrane Handbook for Systematic Reviews of Interventions* Version 5.1.0, which is a guide on the process of preparing and updating Cochrane systematic reviews. Section 6.2.3 provides guidance on locating unpublished research and stresses that identifying relevant unpublished research and including it in a review is essential for minimizing bias. The following sources are included in the recommendations:

- ProQuest Dissertations & Theses Database (note: this resource may also be referred to as ProQuest Dissertations & Theses Global)
- Index to Theses in Britain and Ireland (note: this resource may also be referred to as ProQuest Dissertations & Theses—UK & Ireland)
- DissOnline

The Campbell Collaboration

The Campbell Collaboration is an international, not-for-profit, non-governmental organization and "aims to help people make well-informed decisions about the effects of interventions in the social, behavioral, and educational arenas" (Campbell Collaboration, "Better Evidence for a Better World," retrieved from https://www.campbellcollaboration.org/). The Campbell Collaboration produces and disseminates systematic reviews on social and behavioral interventions, with the aim of helping the policy makers, practitioners, researchers, and members of the general public identify what interventions work. The Campbell Collaboration Information Retrieval Group has published a guide on information retrieval methods for systematic reviews: *Searching for Studies: A Guide to Information Retrieval for Campbell Systematic Reviews*. Section 3.3.4 and Section 3.3.5 of the guide recommends searching sources for unpublished research. The recommendations include the following sources for locating dissertations:

- DissOnline
- Index to Theses in Great Britain and Ireland (note: this resource may also be referred to as ProQuest Dissertations UK & Ireland)
- Networked Digital Library of Theses and Dissertations (note: NDLTD currently provides access via Global ETD Search)
- ProQuest Dissertations & Theses (note: this source may also be referred to as ProQuest Dissertations & Theses Global)
- Theses Canada (note: this resource is also referred to as Theses Canada Portal)

The Health and Medicine Division (HMD) of the National Academies of Sciences, Engineering, and Medicine

The HMD of the National Academies of Sciences, Engineering, and Medicine (formerly the Institute of Medicine) is a private U.S. not-for-profit institution with the aim of providing "independent, objective analysis and advice to the nation and conduct[ing] other activities to solve complex problems and inform public policy decisions related to science, technology, and medicine" (National Academies of Sciences, Engineering, and

Medicine—HMD, "About HMD," September 2016, retrieved from http://www.nationalacademies.org/hmd/About-HMD.aspx). HMD has published recommended standards for conducting systematic reviews, and its publication *Finding What Works in Health Care: Standards for Systematic Reviews* outlines twenty-one standards for developing high-quality systematic reviews on comparative effectiveness research. Standard 3.2 recommends searching sources for unpublished study information, but sources for specifically identifying dissertations are not mentioned.

The Agency for Health Care Research and Quality (AHRQ)

The AHRQ is a U.S. governmental agency that is part of the U.S. Department of Health and Human Services. AHRQ's mission is "to produce evidence to make health care safer, higher quality, more accessible, equitable, and affordable, and to work within the U.S. Department of Health and Human Services and with other partners to make sure that the evidence is understood and used." The AHRQ Effective Health Care Program published the *Methods Guide for Effectiveness and Comparative Effectiveness Reviews*. The chapter titled "Finding Grey Literature Evidence and Assessing for Outcome and Analysis Reporting Biases When Comparing Medical Interventions: AHRQ and the Effective Health Care Program" does not include specific sources for identifying relevant dissertations.

National Institute for Health and Care Excellence (NICE)

The NICE is a nondepartmental public body (NDPB) that is accountable to its sponsor department, the Department of Health, United Kingdom. NICE's mission is to improve outcomes for people using the National Health Service and other public health and social services. NICE produces evidence guidance and advice, including NICE guidelines and other evidence summaries. The publication *Developing NICE Guidelines: The Manual* mentions that searching sources for identifying grey literature publications may be principle for certain reviews. Appendix G, "Sources for Evidence Reviews," lists recommended sources for searching grey literature, but specific sources for dissertation searches are not listed.

SEARCH TIPS FOR LOCATING DISSERTATIONS

Search Databases with Both Published and Dissertation Content

Also known as the "Two Birds with One Stone" tip. Many databases, such as ERIC and PsycInfo, will index both published content and dissertations. However, a comprehensive search for all dissertations on a given topic will require searching other sources.

Adapt Your Search Strategy

Also known as the "KISS—Keep It Simple, Searcher" tip. Librarians and other information professionals are likely to be familiar with complicated Medline, PubMed, and Embase search strategies that use numerous subject headings, keywords, and search filters. However, the search interface of most sources that index dissertations does not provide the same level of detailed searching. As a result, simple search strategies in grey literature databases are more likely to retrieve better search results than overly complicated detailed search strategies.

Select Your Geographical Focus First

Otherwise known as the "Decide to Travel Abroad or Stay at Home" tip. If you are going to do a comprehensive search for all dissertations on a specific topic, it is best to decide if your search is only going to include dissertations from a specific country before you start searching. Certain sources for dissertations only include those from a specific country or region (for example, Thesis Canada or American Doctoral Dissertations), so a search for all relevant English language dissertations would need to include multiple sources.

Textbox 4.1. A Decision Aid for Including Dissertations in a Grey Literature Search

1. Is there very little information on your search topic?

Also known as the "Are You Looking for a Needle in a Haystack?" question. If a search of the published literature identifies few sources, searching for relevant dissertations may provide much-needed additional information. Dissertations are frequently the only source of information on new and emerging topics, as they contain information that may not be available in a journal article or book (Foster & Jewell, 2017).

---

2. Do you need to identify unpublished research?

As mentioned earlier, dissertations are considered a source of unpublished studies (Moyer et al., 2010). If the aim of the search is to locate both published and unpublished original research, then dissertations should be included in the search.

3. Do you need information from international sources?

Is the aim of your search to locate information from a diverse geographical range of sources? There are several sources that can be used to identify dissertations from non-U.S. sources, including both ProQuest Global Dissertations & Theses and Open Access Theses and Dissertations. Including dissertations in a search is a simple method for capturing data from other countries.

CONCLUSION

Dissertations can be a meritful grey literature document type, but dissertations do have their limitations. A searcher can include dissertations as one component of a comprehensive search to identify all relevant grey literature publications. Dissertation sources can also searched for more focused searches, especially when there is little information on a topic or for newly emerging topics. A great number of search sources for identifying relevant dissertations are available, including several free ones. Incorporating dissertations into a grey literature search may be a straightforward search method for including unpublished research, which aids with ensuring against potential publication bias and in the end, provides a more diverse pool of search results.

BIBLIOGRAPHY

Boote, D. N., & Beile, P. (2005). Scholars before researchers: On the centrality of the dissertation literature review in research preparation. *Educational Researcher*, *34*(6), 3–15.

Conn, V. S. (2008). The light under the bushel basket: Unpublished dissertations. *Western Journal of Nursing Research*, *30*(5), 537–538.

Conn, V. S., Valentine, J. C., Cooper, H. M., & Rantz, M. J. (2003). Grey literature in meta-analyses. *Nursing Research*, *52*(4), 256–261.

Coyne, J. C., Hagedoorn, M., & Thombs, B. (2011). Most published and unpublished dissertations should be excluded from meta-analyses: Comment on Moyer et al. *Psycho-Oncology*, *20*(2), 224–225.

Davis, G. B. (2004). Advising and supervising doctoral students: Lessons I have learned. University of Minnesota, Retrieved May, 13, 2016.

de-Miguel, M. (2010). The evaluation of doctoral thesis: A model proposal. RELIEVE, v. 16, n. 1, pp. 1–17. Retrieved from http://www.uv.es/RELIEVE/v16n1/RELIEVEv16n1_4.htm

Fanelli, D. (2011). Negative results are disappearing from most disciplines and countries. *Scientometrics, 90*(3), 891–904.

Fitt, M., Bentley, J., & Gardner, J. (2008). *Rays of change: Towards a better framework for doctoral dissertation literature reviews in instructional technology.* Proceedings of the Conference of the Association for Educational Communications and Technology, 1.

Fitt, M. H., Walker, A. E., & Leary, H. M. (2009). Assessing the quality of doctoral dissertation literature reviews in instructional technology. *ITLS Faculty Publications, 8.*

Foster, M. J. & Jewell, S. T. (2017). *Assembling the pieces of a systematic review: Guide for librarians.* Rowman & Littlefield.

Germano, W. (2014). *From dissertation to book.* University of Chicago Press.

Hart, C. (2014). *Doing a literature review: Releasing the social science research imagination.* Sage.

Holbrook, A., Bourke, S., Fairbairn, H., & Lovat, T. (2007). Examiner comment on the literature review in Ph.D. theses. *Studies in Higher Education, 32*(3), 337–356.

Jewell, S. T., Fowler, S., & Foster, M. J. (2017). Identifying the studies, part 2. *Assembling the Pieces of a Systematic Review: A Guide for Librarians, 85.*

Južnič, P. (2010). Grey literature produced and published by universities: A case for ETDs. *SCHÖPFEL, Joachim a FARACE, Dominic John.Grey Literature in Library and Information Studies,* 39–51.

Kraemer, H. C., Gardner, C., Brooks III, J. O., & Yesavage, J. A. (1998). Advantages of excluding underpowered studies in meta-analysis: Inclusionist versus exclusionist viewpoints. *Psychological Methods, 3*(1), 23.

Lovitts, B. E. (2007). *Making the implicit explicit: Creating performance expectations for the dissertation.* Stylus Publishing.

McLeod, B. D., & Weisz, J. R. (2004). Using dissertations to examine potential bias in child and adolescent clinical trials.*Journal of Consulting and Clinical Psychology, 72*(2), 235.

Moyer, A., Schneider, S., Knapp-Oliver, S. K., & Sohl, S. J. (2010). Published versus unpublished dissertations in psycho-oncology intervention research. *Psycho-oncology, 19*(3), 313–317.

Rosenthal, R. (1979). The file drawer problem and tolerance for null results. *Psychological Bulletin, 86*(3), 638.

Scargle, J. D. (1999). Publication bias (the "file-drawer problem") in scientific inference. *arXiv preprint physics/9909033.*

Schneider, S., Moyer, A., Knapp-Oliver, S., Sohl, S., Cannella, D., & Targhetta, V. (2010). Pre-intervention distress moderates the efficacy of psychosocial treatment for cancer patients: A meta-analysis. *Journal of Behavioral Medicine, 33*(1), 1–14.

Shea, B. J., Grimshaw, J. M., Wells, G. A., Boers, M., Andersson, N., Hamel, C., et al. (2007). Development of AMSTAR: A measurement tool to assess the methodological quality of systematic reviews. *BMC Medical Research Methodology*, *7*(1), 10.

Vickers, A. J., & Smith, C. (2000). Incorporating data from dissertations in systematic reviews. *International Journal of Technology Assessment in Health Care*, *16*(2), 711–713.

Chapter 5

Searching for Unpublished Clinical Trials

Clinical trials are research studies that explore whether a medical strategy, treatment, or device is safe and effective for humans. Clinical trials are also crucial for identifying which interventions are the most effective for certain illnesses and diseases, or what types of interventions are best for specific populations. Clinical trials have been identified as providing the best available data source for health care decision making and the best study type for determining the effectiveness of an intervention (National Heart, Lung, and Blood Institute, "What Are Clinical Trials?," retrieved from https://www.nhlbi.nih.gov/studies/clinicaltrials; Chamers, 1998). While an abundant number of clinical trials are available in published literature, unpublished clinical trials are considered a type of grey literature (Conn et al., 2003). Since unpublished clinical trials are a source of research that is unavailable in the white literature of books and journal articles, grey literature sources should be considered for inclusion when conducting a literature search.

LEARNING OUTCOMES

Although there are numerous types of clinical research, such as observational studies or case reports, this chapter will focus on unpublished clinical trials as a grey literature document type. However, the research and sources presented in this chapter may also be applicable to other types of unpublished clinical research studies. The goals of this chapter are to provide librarians and information professionals with:

- a brief history of how unpublished clinical trial data has become more readily available via clinical trial registries and other sources

- the strengths of the unpublished clinical trial as a document type to be included as part of a grey literature search
- the weaknesses of the unpublished clinical trial as a document type to be included as part of a grey literature search
- a list of select clinical trial registries and other sources for identifying relevant unpublished clinical trials, including the following information:
  - producer
  - access
  - scope and search tips
- a proposed decision-making aid for including unpublished clinical trials in a grey literature search

After reading this chapter, readers should have a basic knowledge of why and how to include unpublished clinical trials as one component of a grey literature search. The following introductory overview of unpublished clinical trials should also enable librarians and information professionals to facilitate discussions with their information users on the rationale for including or excluding unpublished clinical trials as part of a grey literature search.

WHY ARE SOME CLINICAL TRIALS NOT PUBLISHED?

Research has identified different reasons why certain clinical trials are never published: scientists may be unwilling to publish research with negative results, and journal publishers may not want to publish research studies with negative results if those results contradict earlier studies on the topic that yielded positive outcomes (Kannan & Gowri, 2014; Fanelli, 2010; DeCoursey, 2016). Pharmaceutical companies may find that publishing clinical trials with negative results conflicts with findings from past trials, which could potentially have economic repercussions. Also, industry-funded clinical trials are more unlikely to remain unpublished than trials that do not receive such funding (Jones et al., 2013; Goldacre, 2014). Even so, the results from these unpublished clinical trials are still paramount to informing medical decisions, because the unpublished data may provide the only source of information on such topics as adverse events or drug efficacy. Relying solely on the published medical literature to assess treatment efficacy often excludes critical evidence (Dickersin & Rennie, 2003).

UNPUBLISHED CLINICAL TRIAL DATA: ONCE COMPLETELY HIDDEN, NOW (A BIT) LESS SO

Via the Food and Drug Administration Modernization Act of 1997, the National Institutes of Health (NIH) in the United States was required to produce and maintain a publicly available source for information on clinical trials. The intention was to provide public access to information on publicly or federally funded clinical trial research regulated by the Food and Drug Administration (FDA). This publicly available information would be in the form of a clinical trial registry, which would include information on clinical trials for new drugs for serious diseases or life-threatening conditions (ClinicalTrials.gov, "History, Policies, and Laws," retrieved from https:// clinicaltrials.gov/ct2/about-site/history#CongressPassesLawFDAMA). The platform for making this information available, ClinicalTrials.gov, was launched at the end of February 2000 and was the first publicly available clinical trial registry—and it is still the most exhaustive clinical trial registry currently available (ClinicalTrials.gov, "History, Policies, and Laws"). In 2005, as a condition of consideration for future publication, the International Committee of Medical Journal Editors also began requiring that clinical trials be registered in a public trials registry at or before the time of first patient enrollment (ClinicalTrials.gov, "History, Policy and Laws"). A significant increase in the research community's registered clinical trials followed (Laine et al., 2007). Additionally, several federal funding agencies in the United States and other countries began requiring registration of clinical trials as a condition for receiving funding (National Institutes of Health, "Draft NIH Policy on Dissemination of NIH-Funded Clinical Trial Information," November 19, 2014, retrieved from http://grants.nih.gov/grants/guide/notice-files/NOT-OD-15-019.html). There has been much research on the history and evolution of clinical trial registration, and readers seeking more detailed background history can consult Laine et al.'s *Clinical Trial Registration—Looking Back and Moving Ahead* (2007), and Pansieri, Pandolfini, and Bonati's *The Evolution in Registration of Clinical Trials: A Chronicle of the Historical Calls and Current Initiatives Promoting Transparency* (2015).

ADVANTAGES OF UNPUBLISHED CLINICAL TRIALS AS PART OF A GREY LITERATURE SEARCH

There is a strong rationale for supporting the addition of unpublished clinical trials to a grey literature search. As Zora Neale Hurston said, "Research is formalized curiosity. It is poking and prying with a purpose." If a clinical trial has remained unpublished, it may be because the intended outcome of the studies was not achieved. Yet sometimes including unpublished clinical trials in a search may not have much added benefit. This time, let's use a Top Three framework to examine both the benefits and the drawbacks of including unpublished clinical trials as part of a grey lit search.

Benefits

1. Searching for unpublished clinical trial data provides access to a more diverse range of results.

Clinical trials provide indefensible evidence for informed health care decision making, and identifying clinical trials in published literature is almost effortless and straightforward—searchers just need to be familiar with relevant bibliographic sources, such as PubMed and Embase, and how to limit their search results to clinical trials. Searches of medical literature may often be limited to published clinical trials since clinical trials are frequently considered the gold standard for determining the efficacy of an intervention (Bothwell et al., 2016). Nevertheless, a great number of clinical trial results are *not* published—a study in PLoS Medicine found that only 40 percent of industry-sponsored clinical trials and 47 percent of trials funded by the NIH are published (Ross et al., 2009). Since such a substantial percentage of clinical trials are unpublished, searches that only retrieve clinical trials published in white literature may not capture all available information. A search that only includes results from published literature has a number of limitations: the results in the published literature may have overexaggerated rates of intervention efficacy and may have underestimated harms or adverse events (Chan, 2012). Broadening a search to include unpublished clinical trial results identifies a more diverse pool of available information and ensures that publication bias or the "file-drawer" effect will be avoided (Moyer et al., 2010; Scargle, 1999; Rosenthal, 1979).

2. Unpublished clinical trial data may provide information that is not available in the published version.

The available data from an unpublished clinical trial may be dissimilar to the documentation of the clinical trial's results in published literature. A 2016 study in PLoS Medicine found that the data on the number and range of adverse events available in unpublished clinical trials was not always included in the published version of the study (Golder et al., 2016). The information available from unpublished clinical trials can also be used to identify discrepancies between unpublished and published methods (Chan, 2012). Searching sources that contain unpublished clinical trial data can be used to supplement other sources of published information (Scherer et al., 2015). Thus, including unpublished data available from clinical trials may mean the search results will help inform a more precise analysis of the available evidence.

3. Unpublished clinical trials are a source for emerging and new interventions.

Studies available in published literature may not provide much data on topics such as drugs or medical devices, which are still in the investigational stage (Cottingham, Kalbaugh, & Fisher, 2014; Chang et al., 2015). Additionally, once a clinical trial has been completed, time until publication (if it is published at all) can vary—studies have found that the average time until publication can be two or more years (Ross et al., 2013; Ross et al., 2012). If searchers want to provide a set of results that includes the most up-to-date data, searching for unpublished clinical trial data is imperative.

Drawbacks

1. Searching for unpublished clinical trial data may not identify all relevant information.

Clinical trial registries, such as ClinicalTrials.gov, are the main source for identifying unpublished clinical trial results. However, the information available from clinical trial registries may not truly represent all the available information. Studies have documented that it is not uncommon for clinical trials to be registered *after* the trial has been completed but before publication (Harriman & Patel, 2016). A substantial number of clinical researchers are not complying with the requirement to register their clinical trial results in a clinical trial registry—one study found that only 22 percent of publicly funded trials were registered in ClinicalTrials.gov, even though those trials were subject to mandatory reporting in a clinical trial registry. Research has also identified a lack of methods to guarantee adherence to standards for clinical trial registration or clinical trial results disclosure (Viergever et al., 2014). Other sources for identifying unpublished clinical trial data may also provide incomplete information. For example, unpublished clinical trial data from regulatory agencies' reports, such as the FDA's drug approval packages, may often contain redacted information because the data is considered intellectual property (Kesselheim & Mello, 2007). As a result, a search for unpublished clinical trial data may not truly accomplish the goal of identifying all relevant unpublished clinical trial data.

2. Other information sources may be superior to clinical trials.

The type of grey literature search that is required depends on the type of unpublished clinical trial data that is needed. As Chapter 10 will explain, not all types of grey literature publication need to be included in a search: it simply is not practical, and searching for unpublished clinical trial data may not add any value to search results if the intention of the grey literature search is to locate relevant government publications, NGO publications, pilot projects, epidemiological studies, or guidelines. While clinical trials have been highlighted as a source for providing the highest level of evidence, other sources of medical knowledge, such as case reports, are also a crucial source of information (Bothwell et al., 2016). Searchers who want to include unpublished clinical trials in a grey literature search need to first assess what type of results, what types of studies, or what kinds of information they want their grey literature search to retrieve.

3. Unpublished clinical trials may provide very limited data.

A search for clinical trial data in sources such as ClinicalTrials.gov may retrieve several results for completed clinical trials and their results. Yet unlike a journal article documenting the findings of a clinical trial, the data in clinical trial registries is exceedingly limited. Information will be available on such topics as the study design, baseline characteristics, outcome measures, and adverse events, but the information is not analyzed in great detail, nor does it provide much context. Compare this to the information available in a journal article—the average word count of an academic paper is 3,000 to 10,000 words (Bjork, Roos, & Lauri, 2009), which is much more than what is available in the unpublished version in a clinical trial registry. Additionally, the available data may need to be analyzed by a subject specialist or statistician since the outcome results are not discussed or explained.

SOURCES FOR IDENTIFYING UNPUBLISHED CLINICAL TRIAL DATA

Clinical Trial Registries and Clinical Trial Results Databases

Clinical trial registries are one source of unpublished clinical trials. A clinical trial registry is an internationally agreed-upon record containing minimal information about a clinical trial, and a clinical trial registry is the data source for individual clinical trial registers (International Clinical Trials Registry Platform, "Frequently Asked Questions," retrieved from http://www.who.int/ictrp/faq/en/). The purpose of clinical trial registries is multifold: while a clinical trial registry can be searched like a database to identify relevant studies, registries are also responsible for ensuring the accuracy of information about clinical trials, as the registered information is expected to be used to inform health care decisions (International Clinical Trials Registry Platform, "Frequently Asked Questions"). Information obtained from unpublished clinical trials may vary depending on which clinical trial registry is searched. Clinical trial result databases are sometimes a separate source from clinical trial registries, or the clinical trial results database may be part of a larger clinical trial registry. The function of the clinical trial results database is specifically to provide access to research results from completed clinical trials.

Regulatory Agencies

Industry submissions to regulatory agencies, such as the British Medicines and Healthcare products Regulatory Agency (MHRA), the FDA, and the European Medicines Agencies can also be used to identify data from unpublished clinical trials. Regulatory agencies only provide access to their reports for drugs or devices that have received regulatory approval, not for ones in which approval is still pending or has been rejected (Chan, 2012). Regulatory agencies have expanded public access to their information (Chan, 2012; Asamoah & Sharfstein, 2010), and regulatory agencies may have publicly available online searchable databases for their approval reports. These agency reports can be used to identify unpublished clinical trial results that are included as part of a pharmaceutical company's application for drug approval. Although research has documented the value of drug or device approval reports as key sources for identifying unpublished clinical trial data (Chan, 2012; Schroll, Abdel-Sattar, & Bero, 2015), these sources also have limitations such as poor searchability, redacted data, missing methodology data, and lack of standardized fields or information on older drugs (Chan, 2012). But information from regulatory agencies should not be overlooked, as "regulatory agencies have access to substantially more clinical trial information than the health care providers, patients, and researchers who use and evaluate the interventions" (Chan, 2012).

Conference Abstracts

Conference abstracts from papers presented at conferences can be a source for identifying unpublished clinical trial results (Citrome, 2014). Research has identified that only 63 percent of clinical trial results presented at conferences are published as peer-reviewed articles in medical literature; additionally, positive results reported in conference abstracts are more likely to be published (Scherer, Langenberg, & von Elm, 2005). The inclusion of conference abstracts that contain unpublished clinical trial data can be used to broaden the pool of relevant research, but the data available from conference abstracts does have limitations, such as lack of available details about the study or reported outcomes (Sandelowski, Docherty, & Emden, 1997; University of York Centre for Reviews and Dissemination, 2009). Sources for identifying relevant unpublished clinical trial results include both bibliographic databases that index conference abstracts and individual websites of relevant conferences (Higgins & Green, 2011; Citrome, 2014).

SEARCH SOURCES

The following includes sources for clinical trial registries, clinical trial results databases, and regulatory agencies, along with other sources. Sources for identifying conference papers will be discussed in Chapter 7. Please note that subject-specific clinical trial registries for specific health conditions, such as cancer or HIV/AIDS, are not included.

- **AmgenTrials**
  Producer: Amgen
  Access: http://www.amgentrials.com/amgen/study.aspx
  Scope and Search Tips: Use to search clinical trials sponsored by Amgen. Search by condition, drug name, or protocol number. Unpublished clinical trial results can be accessed by checking for results in the status section.
- **AstraZeneca Clinical Trial Website**
  Producer: AstraZeneca
  Access: https://astrazenecagrouptrials.pharmacm.com/ST/Submission/ Search
  Scope and Search Tips: Use to search for clinical trials sponsored by AstraZeneca. Advanced Search interface is best, and limiting to completed studies will retrieve some clinical trials with posted results.
- **Australian and New Zealand Clinical Trial Registry (ANZCTR)**
  Producer: NHMRC Clinical Trials Centre
  Access: http://www.anzctr.org.au/
  Scope and Search Tips: Includes clinical trials being undertaken in Australia and New Zealand, along with clinical trials in other countries. Use Advanced Search to locate completed clinical trials with results. Search results can also be limited to clinical trials that focus on such topics as diagnosis/prognosis, early detection/screening, drugs, surgery,

devices, rehabilitation, and lifestyle. ANZCTR and Clinicaltrials.gov can also be searched concurrently.

- **Bayer HealthCare Clinical Trials Registry and Results**

  Producer: Bayer AG

  Access: http://pharma.bayer.com/en/innovation-partnering/clinical-trials/trial-finder/

  Scope and Search Tips: Use to search for clinical trials sponsored by Bayer. The clinical study synopsis provides results information from individual trials.

- **Bristol-Myers Squibb Clinical Study Reports**

  Producer: Bristol-Myers Squibb

  Access: https://www.bms.com/researchers-and-partners/clinical-trials-and-research.html

  Scope and Search Tips: Information on clinical trial outcomes sponsored by Bristol-Myers Squibb. Clinical trial outcomes can only be browsed by the following topics: cardiovascular, immunoscience, oncology, and virology.

- **British Medicines and Healthcare Products Regulatory Agency (MHRA)**

  Producer: UK government

  Access: https://www.gov.uk/government/organisations/medicines-and-healthcare-products-regulatory-agency

  Scope and Search Tips: MHRA is responsible for regulating all medicines and medical devices in the UK. Public Assessment Reports for approved drugs can be searched. Locating individual unpublished clinical trial data can be tricky, but it may be listed in the clinical efficacy and safety section of the Public Assessment Reports.

- **CenterWatch**

  Producer: CenterWatch

  Access: https://www.centerwatch.com/clinical-trials/

  Scope and Search Tips: Includes clinical trials in the United States and other countries. Focus is primarily on industry-sponsored trials actively seeking research participants, and limited information is available on completed clinical trials with results.

- **ClinicalStudyDataRequest**

  Producer: IdeaPoint

  Access: https://www.clinicalstudydatarequest.com/Default.aspx

  Scope and Search Tips: Not a clinical trial registry, but the largest clinical trial data–sharing repository. Users must first register before searching. Data from clinical studies can be requested once the search has been completed, but a single research proposal must be submitted first. May include mostly clinical trials with industry support.

- **ClinicalTrials.gov**

Producer: National Library of Medicine

Access: https://clinicaltrials.gov/

Scope and Search Tips: Includes clinical research studies in all 50 states and in 200 countries. ClinicalTrials.gov is both a clinical trial registry and a clinical trial results database. It includes clinical trials sponsored by the U.S. federal government and industry, as well as non-profit organizations from around the world. Use Advanced Search to locate completed clinical trials with results.

- **clinicaltrials.ie**

  Producer: Irish Platform for Patient Organisations, Science (IPPOSI)

  Access: http://www.clinicaltrials.ie/

  Scope and Search Tips: Focus is mostly on providing residents of Ireland with information about clinical trials. It does not include information on completed clinical trials with available results.

- **Devices@FDA**

  Producer: Food and Drug Administration (U.S.)

  Access: https://www.accessdata.fda.gov/scripts/cdrh/devicesatfda/

  Scope and Search Tips: Use to search for information on FDA-approved medical devices. Devices@FDA includes agency reports for approved medical devices from 1994 onward. Information on the device's approval, safety and effectiveness summaries, and relevant clinical trials is included.

- **Drugs@FDA**

  Producer: Food and Drug Administration (U.S.)

  Access: https://www.accessdata.fda.gov/scripts/cder/daf/

  Scope and Search Tips: Use to access drug products approved by the FDA. Only drugs approved after 1997 are included. Searching both the specific drug's generic name and trade name is advised rather than searching by drug class or active ingredient. Drug approval letters, labels, and review package are available, all of which may contain unpublished clinical trial data.

- **European Medicines Agency**

  Producer: European Union

  Access: http://www.ema.europa.eu/ema/

  Scope and Search Tips: Use to search for information on drugs approved in the European Union. European Public Assessment Reports for human medicines may contain information from unpublished clinical trials in the Scientific Discussion section. Clinical data submitted to the European Medicines Agency may also be searched at https://clinicaldata.ema.europa.eu/web/cdp/home, but users must create an account before searching.

- **European Union Clinical Trials Database (EudraCT)**

Producer: European Medicines Agency

Access: https://eudract.ema.europa.eu/

Scope and Search Tips: The European Clinical Trials Database contains information about interventional clinical trials on medicines that were conducted in European Union member countries or the European Economic Area (EEA). Coverage starts after May 1, 2004. Use Advanced Search to locate completed clinical trials with results.

- **European Union Clinical Trials Register**

Producer: European Medicines Agency

Access: https://www.clinicaltrialsregister.eu/

Scope and Search Tips: The EU Clinical Trials Register contains information about interventional clinical trials on medicines that were conducted in European Union member countries or the European Economic Area. Use Advanced Search to locate completed clinical trials with results.

- **Federal RePORTER**

Producer: An initiative of STAR METRICS®, under the auspices Office of Science and Technology Policy (OSTP)

Access: https://federalreporter.nih.gov/

Scope and Search Tips: A source for locating information on federally funded research, including publications listed in PubMed, PubMed Central, and Google Scholar. Unpublished clinical trial data is not included, but Federal RePORTER can be used to identify publication status of a trial.

- **GlaxoSmithKline (GSK) Clinical Study Register**

Producer: GlaxoSmithKline

Access: https://www.gsk-clinicalstudyregister.com/

Scope and Search Tips: The GlaxoSmithKline (GSK) Clinical Study Register is a repository of data from GSK-sponsored clinical studies. Protocol summaries, scientific results summaries, protocols, and clinical study reports are included.

- **Health Canada Drug Product Database (DPD)**

Producer: Health Canada

Access: https://www.canada.ca/en/health-canada/services/drugs-health-products/drug-products/drug-product-database.html

Scope and Search Tips: Lists basic information about all prescription, nonprescription, and veterinary drugs approved by Health Canada. Very limited clinical trial data is available.

- **HSRProj (Health Services Research Projects in Progress)**

Producer: National Library of Medicine

Access: https://wwwcf.nlm.nih.gov/hsr_project/home_proj.cfm

Scope and Search Tips: Information on in-progress research projects receiving governmental and foundation funding. International in scope and can be searched for the names of performing and sponsoring agencies, names and addresses of principal investigators, and beginning and ending years of a project. Also includes information about study design and methodology, including demographic characteristics of a study group, number of subjects in a study population, population base of a study sample, and the source of project data. This source focuses more on unpublished health services research than on unpublished clinical trial data.

- **International Federation of Pharmaceutical Manufactures & Associations Clinical Trial Portal**
  Producer: International Federation of Pharmaceutical Manufactures & Associations
  Access: https://www.ifpma.org/
  Scope and Search Tips: All in one portal, search for ongoing clinical trials or results of completed trials conducted by the international pharmaceutical industry. Can be searched by medical condition or drug name.
- **ISRCTN registry**
  Producer: ISRCTN, registry hosted and published by BioMed Central
  Access: https://www.isrctn.com/
  Scope and Search Tips: Clinical trial registry that is international in scope. Use the Advanced Search option to locate completed clinical trial results with basic reporting.
- **NIHR Central Portfolio Management System (CPMS)**
  Producer: National Institute for Health Research
  Access: https://www.nihr.ac.uk/research-and-impact/nihr-clinical-research-network-portfolio/
  Scope and Search Tips: Replaces the UK CRN Portfolio Database, which was previously used for accessing clinical trial information from the UK Clinical Research Network. Users must register prior to searching, and access to data may be limited to specific users in the CRN network. Public access to clinical research studies is available from the UK Clinical Trial Gateway.
- **NIH RePORTER**
  Producer: National Institutes of Health
  Access: https://projectreporter.nih.gov/reporter.cfm
  Scope and Search Tips: A source for locating information on NIH research activities, reports, data, and analyses. Unpublished clinical trial data is not included, but NIH RePORTER can be used to identify publication status of a trial.
- **Novartis**
  Producer: Novartis
  Access: https://www.novctrd.com/CtrdWeb/terms.nov

Scope and Search Tips: Novartis provides the results from their interventional trials for innovative products within one year after the trial
has completed. Search options include study identification number,
browsing by sponsor, or searching by product. Most information is
included in the technical results summary.

- **OpenTrials (Beta)**
Producer: Open Knowledge
Access: https://explorer.opentrials.net
Scope and Search Tips: Online database of information about clinical
research trials worldwide. This source will host and match such information as registry entries, links, abstracts or texts of academic journal
papers, regulatory documents describing individual data for each trial,
clinical study reports, and research protocols. Advanced Search can be
used to search for studies with results.

- **OpenTrialsFDA (Beta)**
Producer: Open Knowledge
Access: https://fda.opentrials.net/search
Scope and Search Tips: OpenTrialsFDA works on making clinical trial data
from the U.S. Food and Drug Administration (FDA) more easily accessible and searchable. OpenTrialsFDA extracts the relevant data from FDA
documents and links it to other clinical trial data. The goal is to increase
access to the information in the FDA's Drug Approval Packages.

- **Pfizer Clinical Study Report Synopses**
Producer: Pfizer
Access: http://www.pfizer.com/science/research_clinical_trials/trial
_results
Scope and Search Tips: Includes Clinical Study Reports (CSRs) submitted
by Pfizer to regulatory agencies. Search options are limited to selecting
the generic or brand name of a drug from the drop-down menu or
searching by the ClinicalTrials.gov unique identifier.

- **UK Clinical Trials Gateway**
Producer: National Institute of Health Research, on behalf of NHS England,
NHS Wales, NHS Scotland, and Health Social Care in Northern Ireland
Access: https://www.ukctg.nihr.ac.uk/
Scope and Search Tips: The focus is on clinical trials located in the United
Kingdom that are actively recruiting participants. An Advanced Search
option is not available.

- **WHO International Clinical Trials Registry Platform (ICTRP)**
Producer: World Health Organization (WHO)
Access: http://apps.who.int/trialsearch/
Scope and Search Tips: International in scope. Search results cannot be
limited to completed clinical trials with available results. Also may be

referred to as the WHO International Clinical Trial Registry Platform Search Portal or the Clinical Trials Registry Platform.

- **YODA Project (Yale University Open Data Access)**
  Producer: Yale University
  Access: http://yoda.yale.edu/
  Scope and Search Tips: An open science sharing project. Information on unpublished clinical trials is included, along with other types of data. Trials can be browsed by generic drug name, and requests can be submitted for specific information.

SEARCH TIPS FOR LOCATING UNPUBLISHED CLINICAL TRIALS

Adapt Your Search Strategy

Also known as the "KISS—Keep It Simple, Searcher" tip. Librarians and other information professionals are likely to be familiar with complicated Medline, PubMed, and Embase search strategies that use numerous subject headings, keywords, and search filters. Nevertheless, the search sources for locating unpublished clinical trial data do not provide the same level of detailed searching. An example of this would be the limited number of fields available in the clinical trial registry ICTRP, which only allows a search for intervention or disease and does not include a "search all fields" option. As a result, simple search strategies are more likely to retrieve higher-quality search results than overly complicated detailed search strategies. Additionally, the search interface of many clinical trial registries may require specific terms—such as names of conditions, interventions, or population age—to be entered in predetermined fields. Less is always more when searching clinical trial registries—sometimes it may be preferable to execute a broad search on a specific drug or condition, providing the searcher with the most extensive pool of available results. Also, if a free text field is available, you may want to execute a specific search that has been modified appropriately. When searching regulatory agency reports for unpublished clinical trials, it is best to just search the specific drug or device rather than searching by disease or drug class. Searchers should attempt variations of a search so they can determine which search string identifies the best set of results or if using multiple search strategies is required.

Don't Assume All Sources for Identifying Unpublished Clinical Trials Are Created Equal

Otherwise known as the "Don't Make an Ass Out of You and Me" rule. Some clinical trial registries support such search functions as phrase searching and truncation (or the ability to limit search results by recruitment status or to completed clinical trials that are reporting available study results). Searchers should be prudent and check for search tips listed on individual clinical trial registries web pages. Additionally, when searching other sources, such as regulatory agencies, see if there are any search tips available that outline specific strategies.

Try to Search More Than One Source

As the Renaissance Italian poet Petrarch said, "Sameness is the mother of disgust, variety is the cure." A search for unpublished clinical trials will benefit from the inclusion of more than one source or search method to ensure the most optimal retrieval of results. For example, you may want to search for information from both clinical trial registries and regulatory agencies.

Researchers or Study Sponsors May Need to Be Contacted Directly

Although Woody Allen said "80 percent of success is showing up," identifying unpublished data may require exhaustive effort. For example, the Cochrane review on Neuraminidase inhibitors for preventing and treating influenza in healthy adults and children (Jefferson et al., 2014) included unpublished clinical studies on Tamiflu (Oseltamivir), but the data was obtained not by simply searching clinical trial registries. Freedom of Information Requests were also filed with the FDA and the European Medicines Agency in order to obtain more than 70 Tamiflu reports consisting of over 100,000 pages (Wolford, 2014).

SOURCES FOR IDENTIFYING UNPUBLISHED CLINICAL TRIALS OR OTHER SIMILAR RESEARCH RECOMMENDED BY HEALTH CARE AGENCIES AND ORGANIZATIONS THAT CREATE KNOWLEDGE SYNTHESIS

Several health care agencies and organizations that support the development of evidence-based practice publications will list recommended sources for unpublished research. These recommendations are generally included in their guidelines on information retrieval. The following is an overview of search sources that are recommended by select agencies producing knowledge synthesis. As we will see, the list of recommended search sources for identifying unpublished clinical trials and other unpublished research studies is quite limited, but the available documentation can be used as a starting point to select which databases should be used for a grey literature search.

Cochrane

Cochrane (previously known as the Cochrane Collaboration) is an independent, global, not-for-profit, NGO comprised of Cochrane contributors from over 130 countries. Cochrane's goals include producing up-to-date systematic reviews and other knowledge synthesis, and making that evidence available and accessible to a worldwide population (Cochrane, "About Us," 2017, retrieved from http://www.cochrane.org/about-us). Cochrane produces the *Cochrane Handbook for Systematic Reviews of Interventions* Version 5.1.0, which is a guide on the process of preparing and updating Cochrane systematic reviews. Section 6.2.3 provides guidance on locating unpublished and ongoing studies and stresses that identifying relevant unpublished studies and including them in a review is essential for minimizing bias. The following sources are included in the recommendations:

- National and international trial registers, such as Clinicial.Trials.gov and the CenterWatch
- Subject-specific trial registers, such as Cancer Research UK
- Pharmaceutical industry trial registers, such as Roche Clinical Trials Results Database
- Trial results registers, such as the International Federation of Pharmaceutical Manufacturers and Associations (IFPMA) Clinical Trials Portal
- Current controlled trials, such as *meta*Register of Controlled Trials (*m*RCT) (note: this source is currently under review and unavailable)

Cochrane also outlines additional detailed search methods for tracking unpublished studies, such as contacting researchers, subject specialists, or pharmaceutical companies directly for information on completed but never published studies.

The Campbell Collaboration

The Campbell Collaboration is an international, not-for-profit, NGO that "aims to help people make well-informed decisions about the effects of interventions in the social, behavioral, and educational arenas" (Campbell Collaboration, "Better Evidence for a Better World," retrieved from https://www.campbellcollaboration.org/). The Campbell Collaboration produces and disseminates systematic reviews on social and behavioral interventions, with the aim of helping policy makers, practitioners, researchers, and members of the general public identify what interventions work. The Campbell Collaboration Information Retrieval Group has published a guide on information retrieval methods for systematic reviews: *Searching for Studies: A Guide to Information Retrieval for Campbell Systematic Reviews*. Section 3.3.4 and Section 3.3.5 of the guide recommend searching sources for both unpublished and ongoing studies. The recommendations include the following sources:

- ClinicalTrials.gov
- EU Clinical Trials Register
- Social Care Online (note: this resource is listed in Chapter 3)
- World Health Organization (WHO) International Clinical Trials Registry Platform Search Portal (note: Social Care Online and World Health Organization [WHO] International Clinical Trials Registry Platform Search Portal are specifically recommended as sources for reviewers to identify ongoing studies)

Other recommended search methods include contacting researchers and subject specialists directly.

The Health and Medicine Division (HMD) of the National Academies of Sciences, Engineering, and Medicine

The HMD of the National Academies of Sciences, Engineering, and Medicine (formerly the Institute of Medicine) is a private U.S. not-for-profit institution with the aim of providing "independent, objective analysis and advice to the nation and conduct[ing] other activities to solve complex problems and inform public policy decisions related to science, technology, and medicine" (National Academies of Sciences, Engineering, and Medicine—HMD, "About HMD," September 2016, retrieved from http://www.nationalacademies.org/hmd/About-HMD.aspx). HMD has published recommended standards for conducting systematic reviews, and its publication *Finding What Works in Health Care: Standards for Systematic Reviews* outlines twenty-one standards for developing high-quality systematic reviews on comparative effectiveness research. Searching sources for unpublished and ongoing studies is recommended in Standard 3.2.1. The following sources are included in the recommendations:

- ClinicalTrials.gov
- WHO International Clinical Trials Registry Platform
- Information available from regulatory agencies, such as the FDA

Contacting researchers and study sponsors for information on published or ongoing studies is also included in the recommendations.

The Agency for Health Care Research and Quality (AHRQ)

The AHRQ is a U.S. governmental agency that is part of the U.S. Department of Health and Human Services. AHRQ's mission is "to produce evidence to make health care safer, higher quality, more accessible, equitable, and affordable, and to work within the U.S. Department of Health and Human Services and with other partners to make sure that the evidence is understood and used." The AHRQ Effective Health Care Program has published the *Methods Guide for Effectiveness and Comparative Effectiveness Reviews*, and the chapter "Finding Grey Literature Evidence and Assessing for Outcome and Analysis Reporting Biases When Comparing Medical Interventions: AHRQ and the Effective Health Care Program" recommends searching trial registries for information on unpublished studies. The following sources are included in the recommendations:

- ClinicalTrials.gov
- World Health Organization (WHO) International Clinical Trials Registry Platform (ICTRP)
- Information available from regulatory agencies, such as the FDA

National Institute for Health and Care Excellence (NICE)

The NICE is a nondepartmental public body (NDPB) that is accountable to its sponsor department, the Department of Health, United Kingdom. NICE's mission is to improve outcomes for people using the National Health Service and other public health and social services. NICE produces evidence guidance and advice, including NICE guidelines and other evidence summaries. The publication *Developing NICE Guidelines: The Manual* mentions that searching sources for identifying grey literature publications may be principle for certain reviews. Appendix G, "Sources for Evidence Reviews," includes lists of unpublished and ongoing studies as recommended sources for the grey literature. The following sources are included:

- ClinicalTrials.gov

- Current Controlled Trials (note: also referred to as International Clinical Trials Registry Platform [ICTRP])
- United Kingdom Clinical Research Network's (UKCRN) Portfolio Database (note: this resource has been replaced by the NIHR Central Portfolio Management System [CPMS] and the UK Clinical Trial Gateway)
- Campbell Collaboration Social, Psychological, Educational & Criminological Trials Register (C2-SPECTR) (note: this resource is no longer available from the Campbell Collaboration)

Textbox 5.1. A Decision Aid for Including Unpublished Clinical Trials in a Grey Literature Search

Is Your Grey Literature Search for a Systematic Review?

Systematic reviews are considered the best source for evidence-based clinical decisions (Cook, Mulrow, & Haynes, 1997), but if relevant clinical trials are not included in a systematic review, the results will be biased (Scherer, Langenberg, & von Elm, 2005). Clinical trial registries are considered a critical search source for systematic reviews (Higgins & Green, 2011; Moher et al., 2009), and including unpublished clinical trials strengthens the validity of a systematic review's assessment of an intervention (Jones et al., 2014). Reports from both the FDA and the European Medicines Agency have unpublished clinical trial data that can be used for meta-analysis (Schroll, Abdel-Sattar, & Bero, 2015). Research has also demonstrated the value of searching regulatory agencies' reports. A study found that the inclusion of unpublished data located by searching available data from regulatory agencies changed the conclusion of the systematic review's meta-analysis, when compared to just including published clinical trials (Hart, Lundh, & Bero, 2012).

Additionally, quality checklists for appraising systematic reviews, such as AMSTAR—Assessing the Methodological Quality of Systematic Reviews (Shea et al., 2007)—may list the inclusion of unpublished sources as one measure of quality. A systematic review search that does not include unpublished studies, such as unpublished clinical trials, will receive a lower AMSTAR score than one that does. If you are involved with a search for a systematic review and do not include unpublished clinical trials or other sources for unpublished research, peer reviewers may question the validity of your search methods. In short, including unpublished clinical trial data from the onset of a search avoids a potential snafu later, because it prevents the entire data extraction process from having to be restarted in order to incorporate results from unpublished research.

Unfortunately, past research has documented that unpublished clinical trial results are often not included in systematic reviews, and sources for identifying unpublished clinical trials, such as clinical trial registries, are commonly not included as part of the search process (Jones et al., 2014). But overall, a systematic review search that includes unpublished clinical trial results will draw upon a wider-reaching research base than one that does not.

WHAT IS THE TOPIC OF YOUR SEARCH?

If the intention of your search is to identify negative research results or adverse treatment effects, to find research on emerging drugs or medical devices, or to inform decision making, unpublished clinical trial data may provide perspicacious information. Unpublished clinical trials have been identified as a key source for locating information on such topics as negative research results or adverse events (Schroll, Abdel-Sattar, & Bero, 2015), so unpublished clinical trials should be added to a grey literature search. But if the intention is to identify detailed, synthesized sources of information, such as evidence briefs or treatment guidelines, then searching for unpublished clinical trials may not be a worthwhile time investment.

DO YOU NEED TO FOLLOW RECOMMENDED SEARCH GUIDELINES?

A librarian or information professional may often follow specific published search guidelines to select search sources. If your overall search plan requires following published search guidelines, check to see if including unpublished clinical trials is listed as a recommendation. For example, the *Cochrane Handbook for Systematic Reviews of Interventions* does recommend including unpublished studies in a systematic review search as fundamental to minimizing the potential risk of bias.

CONCLUSION

The addition of relevant unpublished clinical trials and other related unpublished research may provide a vital contribution to the research landscape on a topic and can be essential for avoiding publication bias or identifying negative or null results. The research cited in this chapter also should help librarians and information professionals have detailed conversations with their users on the elemental value of including search sources for unpublished clinical trials and other related unpublished research. Yet identifying relevant unpublished clinical trials and other related unpublished research may be a tedious and complex endeavor. While there are numerous online sources that may be used to search for unpublished clinical trials, contacting study authors or filling Freedom of Information Requests may also be necessary in order truly obtain complete information (Greenhalgh & Peacock, 2005; Royle & Milne, 2003).

BIBLIOGRAPHY

Asamoah, A. K., & Sharfstein, J. M. (2010). Transparency at the Food and Drug Administration. *New England Journal of Medicine, 362*(25), 2341–2343.

Baudard, M., Yavchitz, A., Ravaud, P., Perrodeau, E., & Boutron, I. (2017). Impact of searching clinical trial registries in systematic reviews of pharmaceutical treatments: Methodological systematic review and reanalysis of meta-analyses. *BMJ (Clinical Research Ed.), 356,* j448.

Bjork, B., Roos, A., & Lauri, M. (2009). Scientific journal publishing: Yearly volume and open access availability. *Information Research: An International Electronic Journal, 14*(1).

Bothwell, L. E., Greene, J. A., Podolsky, S. H., & Jones, D. S. (2016). *Assessing the Gold standard—lessons from the History of RCTs.* New England Journal of Medicine, 374(22), 2175–81.

Chan, A. W. (2012). Out of sight but not out of mind: How to search for unpublished clinical trial evidence. *BMJ (Clinical Research Ed.), 344,* d8013.

Chang, L., Dhruva, S. S., Chu, J., Bero, L. A., & Redberg, R. F. (2015). Selective reporting in trials of high risk cardiovascular devices: Cross sectional comparison between premarket approval summaries and published reports. *BMJ (Clinical Research Ed.), 350,* h2613.

Citrome, L. (2014). Beyond PubMed: Searching the "grey literature" for clinical trial results. *Innovations in Clinical Neuroscience, 11*(7–8), 42–46.

Conn, V. S., Valentine, J. C., Cooper, H. M., & Rantz, M. J. (2003). Grey literature in meta-analyses. *Nursing Research, 52*(4), 256–261.

Cook, D. J., Mulrow, C. D., & Haynes, R. B. (1997). Systematic reviews: Synthesis of best evidence for clinical decisions. *Annals of Internal Medicine, 126*(5), 376–380.

Cottingham, M. D., Kalbaugh, C. A., & Fisher, J. A. (2014). Tracking the pharmaceutical pipeline: Clinical trials and global disease burden. *Clinical and Translational Science, 7*(4), 297–299.

DeCoursey, T. E. (2006). It's difficult to publish contradictory findings. *Nature, 439*(7078), 784.

Dickersin, K., & Rennie, D. (2003). Registering clinical trials. *JAMA, 290*(4), 516–523.

Fanelli, D. (2010). "Positive" results increase down the hierarchy of the sciences. *PloS one, 5*(4), e10068.

Goldacre, B. (2014). *Bad pharma: How drug companies mislead doctors and harm patients.* Macmillan.

Golder, S., Loke, Y., Wright, K., Norman, G., & Bland, M. (2016). *P18 the Extent of Hidden or Unpublished Adverse Events Data: A Methodological Review*. PLoS Med 13(9): e1002127.

Golder, S., Loke, Y. K., Wright, K., & Norman, G. (2016). Reporting of adverse events in published and unpublished studies of health care interventions: A systematic review. *PLoS Medicine, 13*(9), e1002127.

Goodman, M. (2015). Most of the web is invisible to Google. Kere's what it contains. *Popular Science.*

Greenhalgh, T., & Peacock, R. (2005). Effectiveness and efficiency of search methods in systematic reviews of complex evidence: audit of primary sources. *Bmj, 331*(7524), 1064–1065.

Harriman, S. L., & Patel, J. (2016). When are clinical trials registered? An analysis of prospective versus retrospective registration. *Trials, 17*(1), 187.

Hart, B., Lundh, A., & Bero, L. (2012). Effect of reporting bias on meta-analyses of drug trials: Reanalysis of meta-analyses.*BMJ (Clinical Research Ed.), 344*, d7202.

Higgins, J. P., & Green, S. (2011). *Cochrane handbook for systematic reviews of interventions.* John Wiley & Sons.

Jefferson, T., Jones, M. A., Doshi, P., Del Mar, C. B., Hama, R., Thompson, M., ... & Howick, J. (2014). Neuraminidase inhibitors for preventing and treating influenza in healthy adults and children. *Sao Paulo Medical Journal, 132*(4), 256–257.

Jones, C. W., Handler, L., Crowell, K. E., Keil, L. G., Weaver, M. A., & Platts-Mills, T. F. (2013). Non-publication of large randomized clinical trials: Cross sectional analysis. *BMJ (Clinical Research Ed.), 347*, f6104.

Jones, C. W., Keil, L. G., Weaver, M. A., & Platts-Mills, T. F. (2014). Clinical trials registries are under-utilized in the conduct of systematic reviews: A cross-sectional analysis. *Systematic Reviews, 3*(1), 126.

Kannan, S., & Gowri, S. (2014). Contradicting/negative results in clinical research: Why (do we get these)? Why not (get these published)? Where (to publish)?. *Perspectives in clinical research, 5*(4), 151.

Kesselheim, A. S., & Mello, M. M. (2007). Confidentiality laws and secrecy in medical research: Improving public access to data on drug safety. *Health Affairs (Project Hope), 26*(2), 483–491.

Laine, C., Horton, R., DeAngelis, C., & Godlee, F. (2007). Update on trials registration: Clinical trial registration: Looking back and moving ahead. N Engl J Med. 2007;356:2734–2736.

Light, R. J., & Pillemer, D. B. (2004). *Summing Up: The Science of Reviewing Research*. S.L: Harvard University Press.

Mathieu, S., Chan, A. W., & Ravaud, P. (2013). Use of trial register information during the peer review process. *PloS One, 8*(4), e59910.

McCord, A. (2003). Institutional repositories: Enhancing teaching, learning, and research. *EDUCAUSE Evolving Technologies Committee white paper.* URL: http:// sitemaker. umich. edu/dams/files/etcom-2003-repositories. pdf [December 4, 2003].

Moher, D., Liberati, A., Tetzlaff, J., Altman, D. G., & PRISMA Group. (2009). Preferred reporting items for systematic reviews and meta-analyses: The PRISMA statement. *Journal of Clinical Epidemiology, 62*(10), 1006–1012.

Moyer, A., Schneider, S., Knapp-Oliver, S. K., & Sohl, S. J. (2010). Published versus unpublished dissertations in psycho-oncology intervention research. *Psycho-oncology, 19*(3), 313–317.

Pansieri, C., Pandolfini, C., & Bonati, M. (2015). The evolution in registration of clinical trials: A chronicle of the historical calls and current initiatives promoting transparency. *European Journal of Clinical Pharmacology, 71*(10), 1159–1164.

Rosenthal, R. (1979). The file drawer problem and tolerance for null results. *Psychological Bulletin, 86*(3), 638.

Ross, J. S., Mocanu, M., Lampropulos, J. F., Tse, T., & Krumholz, H. M. (2013). Time to publication among completed clinical trials. *JAMA Internal Medicine, 173*(9), 825–828.

Ross, J. S., Mulvey, G. K., Hines, E. M., Nissen, S. E., & Krumholz, H. M. (2009). Trial publication after registration in ClinicalTrials.gov: A cross-sectional analysis. *PLoS Medicine, 6*(9), e1000144.

Ross, J. S., Tse, T., Zarin, D. A., Xu, H., Zhou, L., & Krumholz, H. M. (2012). Publication of NIH funded trials registered in ClinicalTrials.gov: Cross sectional analysis. *BMJ (Clinical Research Ed.), 344*, d7292.

Royle, P., & Milne, R. (2003). Literature searching for randomized controlled trials used in Cochrane reviews: Rapid versus exhaustive searches. *International journal of technology assessment in health care, 19*(4), 591–603.

Sandelowski, M., Docherty, S., & Emden, C. (1997). Focus on qualitative methods qualitative metasynthesis: Issues and techniques. *Research in Nursing and Health, 20*, 365–372.

Scargle, J. D. (1999). Publication bias (the "file-drawer problem") in scientific inference. *ArXiv Preprint physics/9909033,*

Scherer, R. W., Huynh, L., Ervin, A., & Dickersin, K. (2015). Using ClinicalTrials.gov to supplement information in ophthalmology conference abstracts about trial outcomes: A comparison study. *PloS One, 10*(6), e0130619.

Scherer, R., Langenberg, P., & von Elm, E. (2005). Full publication of results initially presented in abstracts: The Cochrane database of reviews, issue 2. *Art. no.: MR000005.Doi, 10,* 14651858.

Schneider, S., Moyer, A., Knapp-Oliver, S., Sohl, S., Cannella, D., & Targhetta, V. (2010). Pre-intervention distress moderates the efficacy of psychosocial treatment for cancer patients: A meta-analysis. *Journal of Behavioral Medicine, 33*(1), 1–14.

Schroll, J. B., Abdel-Sattar, M., & Bero, L. (2015). The food and drug administration reports provided more data but were more difficult to use than the European medicines agency reports. *Journal of Clinical Epidemiology, 68*(1), 102–107.

Shamir, L. (2010). The effect of conference proceedings on the scholarly communication in Computer Science and Engineering. *Scholarly and Research Communication, 1*(2).

Shea, B. J., Grimshaw, J. M., Wells, G. A., Boers, M., Andersson, N., Hamel, C., et al. (2007). Development of AMSTAR: A measurement tool to assess the methodological quality of systematic reviews. *BMC Medical Research Methodology, 7*, 10–2288–7–10.

Siegel, G. E. (2010). Institutional Grey Literature in the University Environment. *Grey Literature in Library and Information Studies*, 69.

Stone & Poladia (2014) . Meet the Deep Web: Inside the Hidden Internet. That Lies beyond Google. International Business Times.

Viergever, R. F., Karam, G., Reis, A., & Ghersi, D. (2014). The quality of registration of clinical trials: still a problem. *PLoS One, 9*(1), e84727.

Zarin, D. A., Tse, T., Williams, R. J., Califf, R. M., & Ide, N. C. (2011). The ClinicalTrials.gov results database: Update and key issues. *New England Journal of Medicine, 364*(9), 852–860.

Chapter 6

Repositories for Grey Literature

Repositories play a key role in scholarly communication, by both disseminating knowledge output and ensuring the preservation of that knowledge. This knowledge includes research from grey literature publications. The volume of content and the diversity of the content available from repositories is vast, and the number of repositories is increasing. Repositories can be useful, if imperfect, sources for identifying relevant grey literature publications.

LEARNING OUTCOMES

The goals of this chapter are to provide librarians and information professionals with:

- information on institutional and open access repositories as a grey literature search source
- the strengths of repositories as search sources locating grey literature publications
- the weaknesses of repositories as grey literature search sources
- a list of select sources for identifying repositories with grey lit content
- tips for searching repositories
- a proposed decision-making aid for selecting and including repositories as a grey literature search source

After reading this chapter, readers should also have a basic knowledge of the search functionality of repositories in regard to grey literature, including benefits and drawbacks. This chapter should also help librarians and information professionals facilitate discussions with their information users on selecting and evaluating repositories as a grey literature search source.

INSTITUTIONAL REPOSITORIES AND OPEN ACCESS REPOSITORIES

Institutional Repositories

An institutional repository is an archive for collecting, preserving, and disseminating digital copies of the intellectual output of an institution, in particular a research or academic institution (Crow, 2002). Institutional repositories are, essentially, online archives, and the mandate of institutional repositories is to collect, preserve, and disseminate the research output of an institution (Oladiran, Bentley, & Jain, 2013). Most institutional repositories are created and hosted by a research or academic institution, such as a university or college. The content of an institutional repository "consists of formally organized and managed collections of digital content generated by faculty, staff, and students at an institution" and can include such items as journal manuscripts and research data and reports (McCord, 2003). Examples of institutional repositories include Deep Blue at the University of Michigan, TSpace at the University of Toronto, and the Digital Repository of the Pan American Health Organization.

Open Access Repositories

An open access repository may also be an institutional repository, or it may be a repository that focuses on a specific discipline or government publications (Oasis, "Open Access Repositories," retrieved from http://www.openoasis. org/index.php%3Foption%3Dcom_content%26view%3Darticle%26id%3D1 37%26Itemid%3D333). Examples of open access repositories include RePEc (Research Papers in Economics), which focuses on business and economics, and the NRC Publications Archive, an institutional repository for articles, technical reports, and conference publications authored by the National Research Council of Canada.

Advantages for Using Repositories for Grey Literature

While storing grey literature is not the primary reason for the existence of repositories—as stated earlier, they are largely to archive various digital materials—there are still compelling reasons to locate grey literature publications within institutional or open access repositories. Again, let us use a Top Three framework to examine both the benefits and drawbacks of using institutional or open access repositories as a grey literature research resource.

1. They are a documented source for grey literature.

Institutional and open access repositories have been identified as a source for grey literature (Schöpfel & Farace, 2010). Although repositories do not just include grey literature, a survey of content type available in OpenDOAR repositories identified the following types of grey literature publications: theses, conference papers, working papers, unpublished reports, data sets, and patents. Grey literature publications may comprise a sizeable percentage of repository content since institutional repository project managers quickly identified grey literature as an ideal document type to boost the number of items in repositories (Siegal, 2010).

2. Institutional and open access repositories identify as keeper of the grey literature.

Institutional and open access repositories also play an imperative role in enabling access to grey literature publications, as well as preserving them (LaFleur & Rupp, 2005). Institutional repositories also have been noted as a key source for sharing an institution's grey literature publications (Bell, Fried, Foster, & Gibbons, 2005). Additionally, repositories have been identified as having a mission to preserve access to grey literature (Shreeves & Cragin, 2008). There is even a "Conference on Grey Literature and Repositories," with the goal of the conference to provide communication research and news on grey literature. Since repositories have identified themselves as a prime source for grey literature, searchers should consider repositories when selecting a grey literature search source.

3. They are a search tool for Deep Web searching.

The Deep Web has been defined as a "class of content on the Internet that, for various technical reasons, is not indexed by search engines" (Chertoff & Simon, 2015). The Deep Web has been estimated as being 4,000 to 5,000 times greater than the everyday and easily searched surface web, and it has been "growing at a rate that defies quantification" (Bright Planet, "Deep Web: A Primer," June 4, 2012, retrieved from https://brightplanet. com/2012/06/deep-web-a-primer/). When relying solely on search engines—such as the perennial favorite, Google—to identify relevant results, you are only searching the visible web: in other words, you are only searching 4 percent of what is available (Stone & Poladian, 2014; Goodman, 2015; Bergman,

2001). Searching individual institutional repositories may identify grey literature content that otherwise would not be retrieved in a general Internet
search such as a Google search. Google, including Google Scholar, may not
crawl the complete contents of an institutional repository—in other words,
the metadata used by institutional repositories cannot always be identified
by Googlebot to connect the results to Google. Adding institutional or open
access repositories to a grey literature search provides a documented example
of Deep Web search techniques.

Drawbacks to Institutional Depositories

While institutional repositories are a source for identifying grey literature
publications, they do have noted limitations.

1. An embarrassment of riches: Over 3,000 repositories and still counting.

There are numerous institutional and open access repositories—the directory for open access repositories, OpenDOAR, lists over 3,000 repositories
worldwide—and while the diversity of sources for repositories is a bonus, it
is unfeasible to search all of the available institutional or open access repositories in a grey literature search. Even searching the repositories from a specific country or region may be problematic. OpenDOAR lists over 400 open
access repositories in the United States, 81 in Canada, and 255 in the United
Kingdom. While there are select sources for searching across the content of
numerous repositories, such as SHERPA Search for searching across all UK
repositories, such search tools may not identify all relevant content.

2. They have limited grey literature content.

The grey literature content of institutional depositories may be quite limited.
Peer-reviewed journal articles are the largest content type in both institutional
and open access repositories (Oasis, "Open Access Repositories," retrieved
from http://www.openoasis.org/index.php%3Foption%3Dcom_content%26v
iew%3Darticle%26id%3D137%26Itemid%3D333). Journal articles constitute 71 percent, and books or book chapters constitute 38 percent of repository content. While grey literature content such as dissertations, unpublished
reports, and working papers may indeed be included in an institutional repository, these are not the primary document content types. As a result, the
number of grey literature publications retrieved in an institutional repository
search may be dwarfed by hits from published literature. Although grey

literature has been identified as a content type in repositories, the percentage of grey literature content in individual repositories may be ambiguous.

3. They have no-frills search functionality.

Many institutional repositories may not have the search functionality of other sources such as databases. For example, there may not be an Advanced Search option or the ability to limit by document types such as dissertations. Such search functions as Boolean operators or truncation may also not be supported. And the inability to *exclude* documents from white literature is even more of a hassle. Thus, locating grey literature hits in a repository may be like trying to find a four-leaf clover in a sea of grass. As J. R. R. Tolkien said, "Not all those who wander are lost," and searching for grey literature in repositories may require quite a bit of "search pottering." Institutional repositories may indeed be a source for grey literature publications, but searching specifically for grey literature publications might be easier said than done.

SOURCES FOR IDENTIFYING INSTITUTIONAL REPOSITORIES AND OPEN ACCESS REPOSITORIES

The following sources can be used to identify institutional and open access repositories. Individual institutional and open access repositories are not listed. Note also that there is no individual source listing all repositories.

- **Canadian Association of Research Libraries**
  Producer: Canadian Association of Research Libraries
  Access: http://www.carl-abrc.ca/advancing-research/institutional
     -repositories/repos-in-canada/
  Scope: Provides a list of repositories in Canada, including federal, provincial, and regional repositories.
- **Digital Commons Network**
  Producer: bepress
  Access: https://network.bepress.com/
  Scope: Allows users to search across over 500 repositories using the Digital Commons institutional repository platform. Grey literature publications such as working papers and conference proceedings are included. Alas, search functionality is limited, so locating grey literature content may be a herculean task.
- **DSpace User Registry**
  Producer: DURASPACE
  Access: http://registry.duraspace.org/registry/dspace

Scope: A who's who listing of institutions using the DSpace open access software for their institutional repository. Results can be filtered by country, type of content, and type of institution, along with other search filters.

- **OpenDOAR: Directory of Open Access Repositories**
  Producer: University of Nottingham
  Access: http://www.opendoar.org/
  Scope: A directory of academic open access repositories, OpenDOAR is a project that lists and categorizes academic open access research repositories. The directory of repositories can be searched by repository type, location, subject content, and language, along with other search fields. The embedded Google Custom Search can be used to search full text material held in open access repositories listed in OpenDOAR.

- **Ranking Web of Repositories**
  Producer: Cybermetrics Lab
  Access: http://repositories.webometrics.info/en
  Scope: Good for identifying repositories worldwide. Ranking reflects a repository's global visibility and impact.

- **ROAR: Registry of Open Access Repositories**
  Producer: Hosted by the University of Southampton
  Access: http://roar.eprints.org/
  Scope: This directory of repositories can be searched by repository type, location, subject content, and language, along with other search fields. Full text material held in open access repositories listed in OpenDOAR can be searched using the embedded Google Custom Search.

- **SHERPA Search**
  Producer: Centre for Research Communications, University of Nottingham
  Access: http://www.sherpa.ac.uk/
  Scope: Use the trial SHERPA Search for a simple search for full text materials held by UK open access repositories. SHERPA Search is powered by a Google Custom Search.

SEARCH TIPS FOR REPOSITORIES

Do a General Search First

Also known as the Yogi Berra "If You Don't Know Where You Are Going, You'll End Up Someplace Else" search tip. Before you start searching a repository, see if you can easily locate grey literature content. If you cannot, then proceeding with a more extensive search may not be a worthy investment of time.

Decide to Be Perspective, Not Subscripted

Otherwise known as Benjamin Franklin's "Lost Time Is Never Found Again" tip. Directories that list repositories, such as OpenDOAR or ROAR, list a great many sources; thus, it is not practical or fruitful to search all of the possible sources. Before starting a search, see if there is a rationale for narrowing the list of search sources—for example, by focusing only on discipline-specific repositories, such as Cogprints, a subject-based repository for cognitive science.

Check for Recent Content

Otherwise known as the "Keeping Up with the Joneses" tip. Librarians and information professionals are often trusted to direct users to the most recent information on a topic. Many repositories containing grey literature content may not be frequently updated, and search results may be outdated. Search results should provide current grey literature publications rather than a retro snapshot of grey literature publications from ten years ago. Confirming the currency of the content in a repository is a key step, otherwise much relevant content may be missed.

Beware of Cross-Searching across Multiple Sources

Or maybe just be aware. A number of directories for repositories use Google Custom Search to power a search across repository contents. Not all of the relevant content may be retrieved, and search functionality may be limited. In order for repository content to be retrieved, Googlebot (Google's web spider) must be able to crawl repository content. Even if the cross-searching option is not powered by a Google Custom Search, the search results still may be lacking. Therefore, it is best to do a general search first—search a broad term, like "economics" or "cats," to see if any content is retrieved—to tentatively check the content of the results. (For more information on Google Custom Search limitations, see Chapter 9.)

SEARCHING REPOSITORIES FOR GREY LITERATURE: RECOMMENDATIONS BY HEALTH CARE AGENCIES AND ORGANIZATIONS THAT CREATE KNOWLEDGE SYNTHESIS

Several health care agencies and organizations that support the development of evidence-based practice publications will list recommended grey literature search sources. These recommendations are generally included in their guidelines on information retrieval. The following is an overview of available guidance, including institutional repositories in a grey literature search. The list of recommended search sources is quite limited, but the available documentation can be used as a starting point to select appropriate search sources.

Cochrane

Cochrane (previously known as the Cochrane Collaboration) is an independent, global, not-for-profit, NGO comprised of Cochrane contributors from over 130 countries. Cochrane's goals include producing up-to-date systematic reviews and other knowledge synthesis, and making that evidence available and accessible to a worldwide population (Cochrane, "About Us," 2017, retrieved from http://www.cochrane.org/about-us). Cochrane produces the *Cochrane Handbook for Systematic Reviews of Interventions*, which is a guide on the process of preparing and updating Cochrane systematic reviews. Section 6.2 provides guidance on sources to search, and searching institutional repositories is not listed.

The Campbell Collaboration

The Campbell Collaboration is an international, not-for-profit, NGO that "aims to help people make well-informed decisions about the effects of interventions in the social, behavioral, and educational arenas" (Campbell Collaboration, "Better Evidence for a Better World," retrieved from https://www.campbellcollaboration.org/). The Campbell Collaboration produces and disseminates systematic reviews on social and behavioral interventions, with the aim of helping policy makers, practitioners, researchers, and members of the general public identify what interventions work. The Campbell Collaboration Information Retrieval Group has published a guide on information retrieval methods for systematic reviews: *Searching for Studies: A Guide to Information Retrieval for Campbell Systematic Reviews*. Section 3.3.6 notes that repositories may be a mixture of both published and grey literature. Specific institutional repositories are not listed, but the following sources are recommended for searching listings of repositories or searching the content of repositories:

* Directory of Open Access Repositories (OpenDOAR)
* Register of Open Access Repositories (ROAR)
* Canada

THE HEALTH AND MEDICINE DIVISION
(HMD) OF THE NATIONAL ACADEMIES OF
SCIENCES, ENGINEERING, AND MEDICINE

The HMD of the National Academies of Sciences, Engineering, and Medicine (formerly the Institute of Medicine) is a private U.S. not-for-profit institution with the aim of providing "independent, objective analysis and advice to the nation and conduct[ing] other activities to solve complex problems and inform public policy decisions related to science, technology, and medicine" (National Academies of Sciences, Engineering, and Medicine—HMD, "About HMD," September 2016, retrieved from http://www.nationalacademies.org/hmd/About-HMD.aspx). HMD has published recommended standards for conducting systematic reviews, and its publication *Finding What Works in Health Care: Standards for Systematic Reviews* outlines twenty-one standards for developing high-quality systematic reviews on comparative effectiveness research. Searching sources for unpublished information about studies is recommended in standard 3.2, but searching institutional repositories is not included in the recommendations.

The Agency for Health Care Research and Quality (AHRQ)

The AHRQ is a U.S. governmental agency that is part of the U.S. Department of Health and Human Services. AHRQ's mission is "to produce evidence to make health care safer, higher quality, more accessible, equitable, and affordable, and to work within the U.S. Department of Health and Human Services and with other partners to make sure that the evidence is understood and used." The AHRQ Effective Health Care Program has published the *Methods Guide for Effectiveness and Comparative Effectiveness Reviews*, and the chapter titled "Finding Grey Literature Evidence and Assessing for Outcome and Analysis Reporting Biases When Comparing Medical Interventions: AHRQ and the Effective Health Care Program" does not include searching institutional repositories for grey literature.

National Institute for Health and Care Excellence (NICE)

The NICE is a nondepartmental public body (NDPB) that is accountable to its sponsor department, the Department of Health, United Kingdom. NICE's mission is to improve outcomes for people using the National Health Service and other public health and social services. NICE produces evidence guidance and advice, including NICE guidelines and other evidence summaries. The publication *Developing NICE Guidelines: The Manual Manual* mentions that searching sources for identifying grey literature publications may be principle for certain reviews. Appendix G, "Sources for Evidence Reviews," lists recommended sources for the searching grey literature, but searching institutional repositories is not included.

Textbox 6.1. A Decision Aid for Searching Repositories: Grey Literature Checklists for a Grey Literature Search

As discussed earlier in this chapter, there are over 3,000 institutional and open access repositories listed in OpenDOAR. But it is neither feasible nor fruitful to search all the available institutional repositories for grey literature publications. The following is a proposed decision aid for selecting who, when, where, what, and why not to search repositories.

Are you Looking for Grey Literature Content from Specific Institutions?

If so, check to see if they have an institutional repository. It may be a trouble-free way to search across content from multiple departments and authors.

Is There a Subject-Specific Repository Available That Matches Your Search Topic?

As mentioned, there are several discipline-specific repositories, and these sources can be searched to identify topic-specific publications. OpenDOAR or ROAR can be easily searched to identify subject-specific repositories worldwide. For example, Policy Online is a discipline-specific repository for unpublished public policy documents, with a focus on Australia and New Zealand. If the aim of a search is to identify international policy documents on a topic such as migration, Policy Online could be a key source to search.

Do You Need to Identify a Specific Grey Literature Publication Type?

Just as database searches in Medline or PsycInfo can be limited to review articles, a repository search can be used to locate specific types of grey literature publications, such as data sets, theses, and papers presented at conferences. For example, if the aim of a grey literature search is to locate relevant conference presentations on a topic related to sustainably built environments (SBEs), a search in OpenDOAR can identify relevant repositories with specific grey literature publication types.

Are You Looking for Grey Literature Content from a Specific Region?

The available directories of institutional and open access repositories can be used to identify institutions by location. If you are looking for country- or location-specific grey literature, you may be able to search repositories from specific countries or regions, such as the United Kingdom or Scandinavia. But this is *not* a feasible option for locating grey literature content using an expansive geographical scope, such as all of North America, the European Union, or Canada. In short, stay focused and do not stray too far.

CONCLUSION

A growing number of research institutions are implementing institutional repositories, providing a key online source for research dissemination and long-term preservation of digital materials. Since repositories collect, preserve and provide free, unrestricted online access to all types of institutional research outputs, they may be used to identify grey literature documents, albeit imperfectly. A grey literature search may benefit from adding institutional repositories as a search source, but other grey literature search sources or methods should be included in order to obtain all of the relevant information.

BIBLIOGRAPHY

Bell, S., Fried Foster, N., & Gibbons, S. (2005). Reference librarians and the success of institutional repositories. *Reference Services Review, 33*(3), 283–290.

Bergman, M. K. (2001). White paper: The Deep Web: Surfacing hidden value. *Journal of Electronic Publishing, 7*(1).

Chertoff, M., & Simon, T. (2015). The Impact of the Dark Web on Internet Governance and Cyber Security. *The Centre for International Governance; Global Commission on Internet* Governance: Paper Series no. 6 Retrieved from https://www.cigionline.org/sites/default/files/gcig_paper_no6.pdf.

Crow, R. (2002). The case for institutional repositories: A SPARC position paper.

Jain, P., Bentley, G., & Oladiran, M. (2009). The role of institutional repository in digital scholarly communications. *African Digital Scholarship and Curation Conference*, pp. 12–14.

LaFleur, L., & Rupp, N. (2005). Making grey literature available through institutional repositories. *Grey Journal (TGJ), 1*(2).

McCord, A. (2003). Institutional repositories: Enhancing teaching, learning, and research. *EDUCAUSE Evolving Technologies Committee white paper.* URL: http://sitemaker. umich. edu/dams/files/etcom-2003-repositories. pdf [December 4, 2003].

Oladiran, M., Bentley, G., & Jain, P. (2013). The role of institutional repository in digital scholarly.

Poladian, C., & Stone, J. (2015). Tour the Deep Web: Illegal marketplaces, book clubs and Everything in between. *International Business Times.*

Rudesill, D. S., Caverlee, J., & Sui, D. (2015). *The Deep Web and the darknet: A look inside the internet's massive black box.* Ohio State Public Law Working Paper No. 314. Woodrow Wilson International Center for Scholars.

Schöpfel, J., & Farace, D. (2010). *Grey Literature in Library and Information Studies.* De Gruyter Saur.

Shreeves, S. L., & Cragin, M. H. (2008). Introduction: Institutional repositories: Current state and future. *Library Trends, 57*(2), 89–97.

Chapter 7

Conference Proceedings, Papers, and Posters for Grey Literature

Conference proceedings, papers, and posters are worthwhile grey literature publication types. Information from conferences plays a key role in disseminating new research and ideas. Additionally, research findings presented at conferences are often imparted years or months before the results are available in published literature; moreover, the results are sometimes never published (Scherer, Langenberg, & von Elm, 2007). This chapter will address how conference proceedings, papers, and posters may fill a crucial role in a grey literature search.

WHAT ARE CONFERENCE PROCEEDINGS, PAPERS, AND POSTERS?

Conference proceedings are a collection of papers presented at an individual conference. They may also be referred to as a congress, symposium, colloquium, meeting abstract, caucus, exhibition, or convention, along with other terms. Conference proceedings are the documented record of the research communications shared at a specific conference. Depending on the specific conference, the conference proceedings may provide very detailed information on papers and posters presented at the conference, or they may provide only abstracts or titles. Conference proceedings may be published as a special issue of a journal; for example, the *Proceedings of the 2009 Dallas Symposium: State of the Art of Atrial Fibrillation Ablation* was published as a supplement in the journal *HeartRhythm*. They may also be published separately, as a single volume online or in print, like the *Collected Annual Conference Proceedings 1868–2012: Complete Dental Proceedings and AAZV History* from the American Association of Zoo Veterinarians.

Sometimes conference proceedings may simply not be published at all. Conference papers are individual research papers presented at a conference. Research posters provide a visual outline of research findings, followed by an interactive one-on-one dialogue with the researcher after the poster is hung and viewed by conference attendees. All of the layers of the various types of conference publications can be muddling. In short, identifying conference proceedings, papers, and posters can be notoriously grueling, but in the end finding notable research from them can be a rewarding task.

For the sake of clarity, this chapter will use the term "conference publications" to refer collectively to conference proceedings, papers, and posters. This chapter will also address the noteworthiness of conference publications as a grey literature type.

LEARNING OUTCOMES

The goal of this chapter is to provide librarians and information professionals with the following:

- information on conference publications as a grey literature document type
- the benefits of conference publications
- the weaknesses of conference publications
- a list of select sources for identifying conference publications, including the following information:
  - producer
  - access
  - cost
  - temporal coverage
  - scope
- search tips for identifying conference publications
- a proposed decision-making aid for selecting and including conference publications

After reading this chapter, readers should have a basic knowledge of how conference publications can provide added value to a larger search, such as a systematic review or a scoping review. This chapter should also enable librarians and information professionals to facilitate discussions with their information users on why including conference publications in their search may be warranted and which sources to search.

ADVANTAGES OF INCLUDING
CONFERENCE PUBLICATIONS AS PART
OF A GREY LITERATURE SEARCH

As mentioned in previous chapters, there should be a pragmatic reason for including a grey literature document type in a search. An information source is only an advantageous addition if it truly offers a unique contribution to the overall knowledge landscape. Likewise, excluding a document type from a grey literature search is perfectly acceptable, so long as there is a defensible justification for doing so. So why should conference publications be included as part of a grey literature search? Again, let us use a Top Three framework to examine both the advantages and drawbacks of including conference publications as part of a grey lit search.

Benefits of Conference Publications

1. Conference publications provide information on emerging research.

As mentioned earlier, information presented and shared at conferences focuses on communicating new ideas, initiatives, and emerging research. It can take years to complete a research study and have its results analyzed, written up, and submitted to a journal. In fact, research has documented that it can take on average 2.5 years for the results of a clinical trial to be published (Ioannidis, 1998). Findings from conference publications may be shared with fewer time constraints as the write-up and submission process is not as lengthy. Conference publications may also be a source for research in progress (University of York, Centre for Reviews and Dissemination, 2009). All of these factors may result in information from conference papers being more up-to-date than published research, and conference papers may provide more pertinent background information on the current state of research activity than what is accessible in published literature.

Conference publications may also contain hidden research treasures that are not currently well recognized but will eventually receive worldwide acclaim (Wong, 2008). Wong provided two examples in "What Other Treasures Could Be Hidden in Conference Papers?": the work of the 2002 Nobel Prize winner in Chemistry, Koichi Tanaka, and the 1979 Nobel Prize winner in Physics, Abdus Salam. Their work was originally presented at conferences, without much fanfare, but they were later recognized as making vital contributions to their disciplines. Also, in certain disciplines, such as computer science and engineering, conference publications are the primary means of disseminating new research (Shamir, 2010).

2. *Even if the conference paper is published later as a journal article, the content may be dissimilar.*

It is a misconception that there is no need to search for a conference publication if the results were published later in a journal article. Even though both of these publication types draw on the results from the same research study, the communication of results or the type of information that is included or highlighted can differ. In addition, studies reported in conference publications may have data discrepancies when compared to the published version of a research study (Dundar et al., 2006). Including conference publications in a search may provide surprising, if not illuminating, information.

3. *They can help avoid the file drawer effect.*

The file drawer effect (Light & Pillemer, 1984; Rosenthal, 1979) pitfall provides a strong motivation for searching for relevant conference publications. As mentioned in previous chapters, one of the aims of a grey literature search is to identify and provide access to a diverse pool of results, specifically unpublished research; more than half of the research studies that report results in conference publications are not published, and the studies that are eventually published in full are systematically different from the research that remains unpublished (Scherer, Langenberg, & von Elm, 2007). Thus, incorporating unpublished research along with published research literature is a critical step for minimizing publication bias. Publication bias occurs when research from published literature is systematically unrepresentative of the population of completed studies (Borenstein, Rothstein, & Sutton, 2005). A search for conference publications has been identified as a means to minimize publication bias, especially if the aim of a search is to identify studies for a meta-analysis (Haidich, 2010).

Conference publications have also been identified as a key source for locating relevant intervention studies that report null or nonsignificant results (McAuley, Tugwell, & Moher, 2000; Hopewell, 2005; Hopewell et al., 2007), so the inclusion of conference publications may be especially crucial if the aim of the search is to locate research on the efficacy of an intervention. Also, the results of clinical trials are often presented at a conference before the results are published in full in journal literature. And since approximately 25 to 50 percent of clinical trials are not published (Dwan et al., 2008; Ross et al., 2012), conference publications may be a fitting resource for locating up-to-date information on completed but unpublished clinical trials.

Weaknesses of Conference Publications

1. Conference publications communicate research findings in a nutshell.

Conference publications—specifically research papers and posters—are a means to briefly disseminate research findings. In comparison, journal articles take much longer to produce and publish, and the end benefit is that more detailed information is provided. For example, journal articles contain statistical tables, several pages of background information, a lengthy literature review, and details on study design (Miller, 2007). Conference publications will provide *some* of the same elements as a journal article—such as information on statistical data or data sources—but the information will be much more abbreviated. So, while a search for conference publications may locate additional sources that were not included in the searches of published literature, the information is not going to be as comprehensive. For the complete research details, the primary author may need to be contacted. In the end, journal articles may provide more usable and exhaustive information.

2. The peer review process may not be extensive.

Conference publications may not be subjected to a vigorous peer-review process, especially when compared to the peer-review process for journal articles. Conference publications sometimes may not be peer-reviewed at all, or there may be a lack of transparency on the methodology for determining their academic attributes (Bossio, 2015). Peer review is an intrinsic component of the research process (Gannon, 2001) because it validates research findings. And since peer reviewers are fellow experts, their input can improve the quality of published papers (Kelly, Sadeghieh, & Adeli, 2014). Without extensive peer review, conference publications may be lacking quality control when compared to published journal articles. While this does not preclude conference publications from providing worthy information, it can be a limitation.

3. In the end, a search for information from conference publications may not add any value.

It is one thing to have the good intention of locating seemingly relevant conference publications, but a search is only truly worthwhile if the research results are useable. What is the purpose of including a search for conference publications if there is not a blueprint for utilizing the search results? It's the "If a tree falls in the forest and nobody's around to hear it" quandary. Conference publications could have missing data that may be problematic, or they may mention research that is in progress but not completed, so the results cannot be analyzed. Before including a search for conference publications, it may be prudent to address the limitations of the results. If conference publications are going to be included, there should be a strategy for analyzing the research results from them. Otherwise conference publications remain an unheard voice among the louder published research literature.

SOURCES FOR IDENTIFYING CONFERENCE PUBLICATIONS

This section will provide information on select sources for identifying conference publications, including such information as producer, access, temporal coverage, cost, and scope.

The following is a selection of multidisciplinary sources for identifying conference papers. Please note that sources focusing exclusively on a specific discipline (i.e., chemistry, international studies) may not be included.

Select Sources Identifying Conference Publications

- **BIOSIS Previews**
  Producer: Thomson Reuters
  Access: http://wokinfo.com/products_tools/specialized/bp/
  Temporal Coverage: 1926–Present
  Cost: Subscription
  Scope: Interdisciplinary database for disciplines such as medicine, biochemistry, biophysics, bioengineering, biotechnology, and other life science research. Limited inclusion of conference papers and meeting abstracts.
- **British Library Inside Conferences**
  Producer: The British Library
  Access: http://media2.proquest.com/documents/british_lib_inside_conference.pdf
  Temporal Coverage: 1993–Present
  Cost: Subscription
  Scope: Database for searching for papers from congresses, symposia, conferences, expositions, workshops, and meetings in the collection of the British Library Document Supply Centre. Interdisciplinary and international coverage.
- **The British Library: The Conference Collections**
  Producer: The British Library
  Access: http://www.bl.uk/services/bsds/dsc/conference.html
  Temporal Coverage: N/A

Cost: Free

Scope: Source for identifying a variety of conference proceedings and papers, including special supplements, on-off monographs, or regularly published proceedings. Aims to collect "worthwhile" conference publications on all subjects and/or languages.

- **CAB Abstracts**

  Producer: CABI Publishing

  Access: http://www.cabi.org/publishing-products/online-information-resources/cab-abstracts/

  Temporal Coverage: 1973–Present

  Cost: Subscription

  Scope: Database indexing publications on life sciences, including agriculture, environment, veterinary sciences, applied economics, food science and nutrition; includes conference proceedings.

- **Conference Proceedings—Web of Science Index**

  Producer: Clarivate Analytics

  Access: http://wokinfo.com/products_tools/multidisciplinary/webofscience/cpci/

  Temporal Coverage: 1990–Present

  Cost: Subscription

  Scope: Database for accessing conferences, symposia, seminars, colloquia, workshops, and conventions in a wide range of disciplines. Covers more than 148,000 journal- and book-based proceedings in science, social sciences, and humanities across 256 disciplines.

- **Conference Proceedings Citation Index**

  Access: http://wokinfo.com/products_tools/multidisciplinary/webofscience/cpci/

  Producer: ClarivateAnalytics

  Temporal Coverage: 1990–Present

  Cost: Subscription

  Scope: interdisciplinary source for conference proceedings and included in the Web of Science Core Collection database. Focus is primarily on conference proceedings that are published by an academic publisher. This source supersedes ISI Index to Social Sciences & Humanities Proceedings & ISI Index to Scientific & Technical Proceedings.

- **F1000Research**

  Producer: F1000 Research Ltd.

  Access: https://f1000research.com/

  Temporal Coverage: N/A

  Scope: Open access web repositories for articles, slides, and research posters in the life sciences, public health, education, and communication.

- **Google Books**
  Producer: Google
  Access: https://books.google.com
  Temporal Coverage: N/A
  Cost: Free
  Scope: Google search engine for searching the full text of scanned books. Google Books is especially good for locating and accessing the content of past conference publications, such as conference proceedings.
- **Google Scholar**
  Producer: Google
  Access: https://scholar.google.ca/
  Temporal Coverage: N/A
  Cost: Free
  Scope: Google search engine containing academic journals and books, conference papers, theses and dissertations, preprints, abstracts, technical reports, court opinions, and patents; scope is multidisciplinary. Locating conference publications may be challenging, as Google Scholar does not offer a publication type limit. (Note: See Chapter 9 for more detailed information on Google Scholar.)
- **Northern Lights**
  Producer: Northern Lights Group LLC
  Access: http://www.ovid.com/site/catalog/databases/13207.jsp
  Temporal Coverage: 2010–Present
  Cost: Subscription
  Scope: Database of conference abstracts and posters in the life sciences. One of the most up-to-date sources for identifying recent research presented at conferences, including conference posters.
- **OAIster**
  Producer: OCLC/University of Michigan
  Access: http://www.oclc.org/en/oaister.html
  Cost: Free
  Scope: Online catalog, specifically focused on open access materials available from open archive collections. Note that while OAIster may contain conference publications, there is not a specific command for limiting to publication type.
- **PapersFirst**
  Producer: OCLC
  Access: https://www.oclc.org/support/services/firstsearch/documentation/dbdetails/details/PapersFirst.en.html
  Temporal Coverage: 1993–Present
  Cost: Subscription

Scope: Database of papers presented at conferences worldwide. Includes every published congress, symposium, conference, exposition, workshop, and meeting received by the British Library Document Supply Centre.

- **ProceedingsFirst**
  Producer: OCLC
  Access: https://www.oclc.org/support/services/firstsearch/documentation/dbdetails/details/Proceeding.en.html
  Temporal Coverage: 1993–Present
  Cost: Subscription
  Scope: Database for conference proceedings. Includes every published congress, symposium, conference, exposition, workshop, and meeting received by the British Library Document Supply Centre.

- **Scopus**
  Producer: Elsevier
  Access: https://www.elsevier.com/solutions/scopus
  Temporal Coverage: 2005–Present
  Cost: Subscription
  Scope: Interdisciplinary database, including information on life sciences, social sciences, and the humanities. Scopus does index conference publications but is limited to subject areas where conference papers represent a substantial portion of research, such as engineering or computer science.

- **USA.gov**
  Producer: U.S. federal government
  Access: https://www.usa.gov/
  Cost: Free
  Scope: Web portal for searching federal, state, and municipal government websites. Great for locating information on federally sponsored conferences, such as those sponsored by the National Institutes of Health. Since this is a web portal for a wide range of government information, limiting search results to conference publications can be challenging.

- **Web of Conferences**
  Producer: EDP Sciences
  Access: https://www.webofconferences.org/
  Temporal Coverage: N/A
  Cost: Free
  Scope: Open access platform devoted to the publication of scientific conference proceedings. Searches must be for specific proceedings, not individual papers presented at conferences.

- **Zetoc**
  Producer: Jisc, on behalf of the British Library
  Access: http://zetoc.jisc.ac.uk/
  Temporal Coverage: 1993–Present
  Cost: Subscription
  Scope: Includes both journal articles and conference proceedings, but searches can be limited to conference proceedings. Also can be utilized as a current awareness service.

SEARCH TIPS FOR LOCATING CONFERENCE PAPERS

Short, Basic Searches

Otherwise known as the "It's a Gift to Be Simple" tip. Many of the databases that index conference papers are best searched using an abbreviated version of a search. For example, a search for the drug alogliptin for treating type 2 diabetes may best be executed using both the generic and trade names, as conference papers are not going to have the highly detailed level of indexing that journal articles have.

Scan the Past Programs of Conferences of Interest

Otherwise known as the "Don't Follow Trends, Set Them" tip, this is a shrewd search step you would use to identify conference meetings that are likely to include presenters delivering papers on your search topic. For example, if you are searching for conference papers or posters on the relatively new intervention of early palliative care integrated with cancer treatment, then scanning the conference proceedings of the International Congress of Palliative Care may be a worthy investment of your time. Also, this search method will capture conference papers or posters that may not be indexed by a database. This may be the best methodology for accessing the most recent conference papers, as there is always a delay between when a paper is presented and when it is included in a source that indexes conference publications.

Do a Preliminary Search First

While a substantial number of databases, such as Scopus and Google Scholar, may state that they include conference publications, they may not actually include much information from conferences. This is otherwise known as the "Less Than Meets the Eye" tip. It is not uncommon for the conference publications content of a database search to be limited or practically non-existent—materials such as conference proceedings simply are not frequently indexed. When selecting a database to search, a good search tip is to do a preliminary search for conference papers when you know there should be hits on your topic. One example of this would be doing a search using commonly used keywords such as "treatment" or "cancer." If there are a limited number of hits or only older hits for a search on such a broad topic, move on. The source *claiming* to index conference papers most likely includes little of the needed content.

RECOMMENDATIONS BY HEALTH CARE AGENCIES AND ORGANIZATIONS THAT CREATE KNOWLEDGE SYNTHESIS

Several health care agencies and organizations that support the development of evidence-based practice publications recommend that searches for evidence should include search methods for identifying conference publications. These recommendations are generally included in their publications on information retrieval guidelines. The following is an overview of those that are recommended by select agencies producing knowledge synthesis. The available search methodologies are not very detailed, but the available documentation can be used as a starting point.

The Campbell Collaboration

The Campbell Collaboration is an international, not-for-profit, NGO that "aims to help people make well-informed decisions about the effects of interventions in the social, behavioral, and educational arenas" (Campbell Collaboration, "Better Evidence for a Better World," retrieved from https://www.campbellcollaboration.org/). The Campbell Collaboration produces and disseminates systematic reviews on social and behavioral interventions, with the aim of helping policy makers, practitioners, researchers, and members of the general public identify what interventions work. The Campbell Collaboration Information Retrieval Group has published a guide on information retrieval methods for systematic reviews: *Searching for Studies: A Guide to Information Retrieval for Campbell Systematic Reviews*. Section 3.3.1.1 of the guide lists searching for conference proceedings and meeting abstracts as a key method for locating unpublished studies.

Cochrane

Cochrane (previously known as the Cochrane Collaboration) is an independent, global, not-for-profit, NGO comprised of Cochrane contributors from over 130 countries. Cochrane's goals include producing up-to-date systematic reviews and other knowledge synthesis, and making that evidence available and accessible to a worldwide population (Cochrane, "About Us," 2017, retrieved from http://www.cochrane.org/about-us). Cochrane produces the *Cochrane Handbook for Systematic Reviews of Interventions*, which is a guide on the process of preparing and updating Cochrane systematic reviews. Section 7.2.2.6 of the handbook advises searching for relevant studies reported in conference abstracts using databases and/or manually searching or electronically searching specific conference proceedings.

The Health and Medicine Division (HMD) of the National Academies of Sciences, Engineering, and Medicine

The HMD of the National Academies of Sciences, Engineering, and Medicine (formerly the Institute of Medicine) is a private U.S. not-for-profit institution with the aim of providing "independent, objective analysis and advice to the nation and conduct[ing] other activities to solve complex problems and inform public policy decisions related to science, technology, and medicine" (National Academies of Sciences, Engineering, and Medicine—HMD, "About HMD," September 2016, retrieved from http://www.nationalacademies.org/hmd/About-HMD.aspx). HMD has published recommended standards for conducting systematic reviews, and its publication *Finding What Works in Health Care: Standards for Systematic Reviews* outlines twenty-one standards for developing high-quality systematic reviews on comparative effectiveness research. Conference publications are a recommended grey literature document type that may contain much needed information on relevant unpublished studies.

The Agency for Health Care Research and Quality (AHRQ)

The AHRQ is a U.S. governmental agency that is part of the United States Department of Health and Human Services. AHRQ's mission is "to produce evidence to make health care safer, higher quality, more accessible, equitable, and affordable, and to work within the U.S. Department of Health and Human Services and with other partners to make sure that the evidence is understood and used." The AHRQ Effective Health Care Program has published the *Methods Guide for Effectiveness and Comparative Effectiveness Reviews*, and the chapter "Finding Grey Literature Evidence and Assessing for Outcome and Analysis Reporting Biases When Comparing Medical Interventions: AHRQ and the Effective Health Care Program" recommends searching for relevant conference publications. The specific

---

Textbox 7.1. A Decision Aid

• *Are you looking for original research or synthesized sources of information?*

Conference papers are not exhaustive sources of information, especially in comparison to other grey literature sources such as guidelines or white papers. If the aim of your search is to identify communication of original research results, such as the Precision Medicine Initiative (also referred to as the All of Us Research Program from the NIH), then conference papers may be a worthwhile grey lit document type to include. But if you are looking for grey literature sources that will summarize the results of past research on a topic such as ethical guidelines for involving aboriginal/First Nations communities in research, conference publications may provide limited information. Conference publications generally do not provide explicit background information, exhaustive discussion on the various aspects of an issue, or detailed recommendations for future research, policy, and practice. An example of a grey literature source that would provide synthesized research versus original research results would be the *CIHR Guidelines for Health Research Involving Aboriginal Peoples.*

• *Are you following prescribed search guidelines?*

Institutions such as the Campbell Collaboration recommend that searches include conference papers. If the aim of your search methodology is to follow specific search guidelines, check to see if searching for conference publications is noted in the search guidelines.

• *Will your search methodology be evaluated using established measurement tools?*

The publication rate of systematic reviews—including deficient, poorly executed systematic reviews (Ioannidis, 2016)—is increasing, and there is debate on how to evaluate the reporting or the methodological quality of systematic reviews (Faggion, 2015). Sources for appraising systematic reviews, such as AMSTAR (Shea et al., 2007), indicate that searching for conference papers provides evidence of the inclusion of unpublished literature. Systematic reviews that include a search for relevant conference papers may positively affect the overall quality of the review, as the systematic review may receive a higher score on an appraisal tool. The inclusion of a source indexing conference papers in a search also helps guard against source selection bias (Schlosser, 2007) because a source containing unpublished literature is included.

sources for identifying conference publications are listed: Conference Papers Index, Scopus, PapersFirst, ProceedingsFirst, and BIOSIS Previews.

National Institute for Health and Care Excellence (NICE)

The NICE is a nondepartmental public body (NDPB) that is accountable to its sponsor department, the Department of Health, United Kingdom. NICE's mission is to improve outcomes for people using the National Health

Service and other public health and social services. NICE produces evidence guidance and advice, including NICE guidelines and other evidence summaries. The publication *Developing NICE Guidelines: The Manual* mentions that identifying relevant conference publications may be fundamental for certain review questions. Appendix G, "Sources for Evidence Reviews," recommends searching individual conference websites as well as the following databases: Embase, British Library Inside Conferences (BLIC), and Google Scholar.

CONCLUSION

Conference publications can be a central part of research knowledge creation and communication—often, conference publications may be the only record of completed research or the dissemination of emerging ideas. Incorporating conference publications into a grey literature search may be a straightforward search method for including unpublished research, which helps ensure against potential publication bias and in the long run, may provide a more diverse pool of search results.

BIBLIOGRAPHY

Borenstein, M., Rothstein, H., & Sutton, A. (2005). *Publication bias in meta-analysis: Prevention, assessment and adjustments.* Wiley.

Bossio, D. (2015). The value of conference publications: old challenges and new opportunities. *Communication Research and Practice, 1*(3), 236–241.

Dundar, Y., Dodd, S., Dickson, R., Walley, T., Haycox, A., & Williamson, P. R. (2006). Comparison of conference abstracts and presentations with full-text articles in the health technology assessments of rapidly evolving technologies. *Health Technology Assessment (Winchester, England), 10*(5), iii–iv, ix–145.

Dwan, K., Altman, D. G., Arnaiz, J. A., Bloom, J., Chan, A., Cronin, E., et al. (2008). Systematic review of the empirical evidence of study publication bias and outcome reporting bias. *PloS One, 3*(8), e3081.

Faggion, C. M. (2015). Critical appraisal of AMSTAR: Challenges, limitations, and potential solutions from the perspective of an assessor. *BMC Medical Research Methodology, 15*(1), 63.

Gannon, F. (2001). The essential role of peer review. *EMBO reports, 2*(9), 743–743.

Haidich, A. B. (2010). Meta-analysis in medical research. *Hippokratia, 14*(Suppl 1), 29–37.

Hopewell, S., & Clarke, M. (2005). Abstracts presented at the American Society of Clinical Oncology Conference: How completely are trials reported? *Clinical Trials, 2*(3), 265–268.

Hopewell, S., Clarke, M., & Mallett, S. (2005). Grey literature and systematic reviews. *Publication Bias in Meta-Analysis: Prevention, Assessment and Adjustments*, 48–72.

Hopewell, S., Clarke, M. J., Stewart, L., & Tierney, J. (2007). Time to publication for results of clinical trials. *The Cochrane Library*,

Ioannidis, J. P. (1998). Effect of the statistical significance of results on the time to completion and publication of randomized efficacy trials. *JAMA*, *279*(4), 281–286.

Ioannidis, J. (2016). The mass production of redundant, misleading, and conflicted systematic reviews and meta-analyses. *The Milbank Quarterly*, *94*(3), 485–514.

Kelly, J., Sadeghieh, T., & Adeli, K. (2014). Peer review in scientific publications: benefits, critiques, & a survival guide. *EJIFCC*, *25*(3), 227.

McAuley, L., Tugwell, P., & Moher, D. (2000). Does the inclusion of grey literature influence estimates of intervention effectiveness reported in meta-analyses? *Lancet*, *356*(9237), 1228–1231.

Miller, J. E. (2007). Preparing and presenting effective research posters. *Health services research*, *42*(1p1), 311–328.

Richard, J., & Pillemer, D. B. (1984). *Summing up*. Harvard University Press.

Rosenthal, R. (1979). The file drawer problem and tolerance for null results. *Psychological Bulletin*, *86*(3), 638.

Ross, J. S., Tse, T., Zarin, D. A., Xu, H., Zhou, L., & Krumholz, H. M. (2012). Publication of NIH funded trials registered in ClinicalTrials.gov: Cross-sectional analysis. *BMJ (Clinical Research Ed.)*, *344*, d7292.

Scherer, R. W., Langenberg, P., & Von Elm, E. (2007). Full publication of results initially presented in abstracts. *Cochrane Database Syst. Rev.*, *2*(2), MR000005.

Schlosser, R. W., Wendt, O., & Sigafoos, J. (2007). Not all systematic reviews are created equal: Considerations for appraisal. *Evidence-Based Communication Assessment and Intervention*, *1*(3), 138–150.

Shea, B. J., Grimshaw, J. M., Wells, G. A., Boers, M., Andersson, N., Hamel, C., et al. (2007). Development of AMSTAR: A measurement tool to assess the methodological quality of systematic reviews. *BMC Medical Research Methodology*, *7*(1), 10.

University of York Centre for Reviews and Dissemination. (2009). *Systematic reviews: CRD's guidance for undertaking reviews in health care*. University of York, Centre for Reviews & Dissemination.

Wong, M. (2008). What other treasures could be hidden in conference papers? *Nature*, *456*(7221), 443.

Chapter 8

Grey Literature Search Checklists and Other Similar Sources

Grey literature search checklists can be a fruitful research tool for identifying relevant grey literature publications, and they may be especially instructive guides for identifying relevant grey literature publications. This chapter will discuss specific grey literature search checklists and other similar sources.

LEARNING OUTCOMES

The goal of this chapter is to provide librarians, information professionals, and library students with the following:

- information on grey literature search checklists created specifically to identify sources for locating grey literature publications
- the strengths and weaknesses of grey literature search checklists as search sources for locating grey literature publications
- tips for using grey literature checklists
- a list of select grey literature checklists
- other search sources that, though not identical to grey literature search checklists, are sources that can be used similarly
- a proposed decision-making aid for using grey literature search checklists and similar sources

After reading this chapter, readers should also have a basic knowledge of grey literature search checklists. This chapter should help librarians and information professionals facilitate discussions with their information users for selecting specific search tools as part of a grey literature search.

GREY LITERATURE SEARCH CHECKLISTS

A grey literature search checklist can be defined as a clearly outlined list that contains a selection of sources to be searched for grey literature publications. Grey literature search checklists are static resources that have been published by institutions that reference grey literature sources, most likely focusing on a specific subject area. Grey literature search checklists may also provide search tips for specific sources listed in the checklist.

Why Use Grey Literature Search Checklists? Why Not?

A grey literature search checklist can be a serviceable resource for identifying relevant grey literature publications. There are many advantages to using checklists for locating grey literature publications. Again, let's use a Top Three framework to examine both the benefits and drawbacks of using checklists as a grey literature research resource.

Benefits

1. They provide prêt-à-porter, ready sources to search.

If you use a grey literature checklist, all of your search sources are pre-selected—thus, you only need to search the sources outlined on the list. As all of the search sources to consult are listed, the grey literature search does not need to be made from scratch. As a result, there is no need to research and select which grey literature sources you should incorporate into your search because the legwork has already been completed for you.

2. They are frequently used and easily referenced.

Otherwise known as the "Listen to Advice and Accept Instruction, That You May Gain Wisdom in the Future" tip. If you need to outline the methodology for your grey literature search, a grey literature search checklist is a source that can be easily referenced. Using a grey literature source that can be referenced may be hugely convenient if you need to outline and provide supporting documentation for your grey literature search methodology for a grant proposal, systematic review, or scoping review protocol. For example, grey literature checklists, such as *Grey Matters: A Practical Search Tool for Evidence-Based Medicine*, published by the Canadian Institute for Drugs and Technologies in Health (CADTH), have commonly been listed as grey lit search sources in systematic reviews and published protocols (Sullivan, Coyle, & Wells, 2014; Tricco et al., 2012; Young et al., 2012).

3. They are user-friendly.

Searching can be decidedly simple, so why make it complicated? A grey literature search checklist may be a handy source to give to students or others who may be unfamiliar with grey literature searches or are in need of specific guidance on how to complete a grey literature search. A checklist can provide a considerably more straightforward path for completing a grey literature search because you only need to search a predetermined list of sources, and it can be the perfect antidote for the confusing guesswork that is often involved with a grey literature search. Grey literature checklists may also be indispensable teaching tools to explain the search process involved with a comprehensive grey literature source.

Drawbacks

1. Checklists may have a decidedly specific focus.

Grey literature search checklists are generally subject specific—it would be a Sisyphean task to create a grey literature search checklist suitable for all types of grey literature searches. Yet, while one of the strengths of a checklist is to identify sources on a specific topic, such as public health, this could also be considered a potential handicap. If your grey literature search topic is slightly outside the subject scope of the checklist, then some sources that may be relevant to your topic may be missed. For example, if your search topic is on rehabilitation services for seniors, using a grey literature search checklist that focuses only on public health sources or clinical trials may not include all of the grey literature sources that should be searched.

Grey literature search checklists also may emphasize sources that have a national presence or mandate. When deciding on whether to use a grey literature checklist, users may want to determine if the search sources listed on a checklist concentrate on a specific geographical region—this way, users can determine if using a grey literature checklist will exclude a great number of other pertinent sources. Most grey literature search checklists also primarily list search sources from larger institutions, and smaller organizations that produce grey literature may not be included. If a search needs to locate grey literature publications from organizations with a specific state/provincial or county focus, relying on a grey literature search checklist may miss other pertinent sources.

2. A checklist can be a moment frozen in time.

While one of the benefits of a grey literature search checklist is that it is a static resource containing a predetermined list of sources, its fixed state may also be considered a hindrance. For example, an unchanging checklist will not include newly emerging sources for grey literature or take into account sources that are no longer available. For example, the *Grey Literature Report*, from the New York Academy of Medicine, ceased adding new publications at the end of 2016, but it is cited as a source for grey literature on some checklists.

3. A checklist can be time-consuming.

Like Dr. Seuss said, "How did it get so late so soon?" While a grey literature search checklist may provide a detailed roadmap for completing a grey literature search, using a search checklist can be time-consuming. Although one of the benefits of a grey literature checklist is that it may provide an exhaustive list of subject-specific sources that can be searched, this might translate into an extraordinarily lengthy time commitment to search all of the sources. Before using a grey literature search checklist, users should ensure that the time investment will be worthwhile. The use of a grey literature search checklist may not need to be prescriptive; instead, searchers may need to select which sources on the checklist should be searched.

GREY LITERATURE CHECKLISTS

Sources

- **Grey Matters: A Practical Tool for Searching Health-Related Grey Literature**
  Producer: CADTH—Canadian Agency for Drugs and Technologies in Health
  Access: https://www.cadth.ca/resources/finding-evidence/grey-matters
  Checklist Scope: Currently the most comprehensive search checklist for executing a grey literature search. The focus of the checklist is on Canadian and international health technology assessment sources, but the checklist also lists sources relevant to health economics, clinical practice guidelines, clinical trials, and health statistics. The checklist is available as a downloaded MS Word file, so users can easily document a search strategy and identify which sources were searched.
- **Grey Matters Light**
  Producer: CADTH—Canadian Agency for Drugs and Technologies in Health
  Access: https://www.cadth.ca/sites/default/files/is/cadth_Handout_ greymatters_light_e.pdf

Checklist Scope: Lists the top 14 sources from "Grey Matters: A Practical Tool for Searching Health-Related Grey Literature." The focus is on health technology assessment organizations, safety/advisory resources, and clinical practice guidelines.

- **Physical Rehabilitation: Grey Literature Search Checklist**
  Producer: Katie McLean (Nova Scotia Health Authority) and Sarah Visintini (Maritime SPOR SUPPORT Unit)
  Access: http://library.nshealth.ca/ld.php?content_id=11110859
  Checklist Scope: Lists sources for identifying grey literature publications on physical rehabilitation; also includes a link to a Google Custom Search engine for searching select organizational sources. Includes Canadian, U.S., and other international sources.

- **Public Health Grey Literature Sources**
  Producer: Ontario Public Health Libraries Association
  Access: http://www.ophla.ca/pdf/Public%20Health%20Grey%20 Literature%20Sources.pdf
  Checklist Scope: Lists sources for identifying grey literature publications on public health–related topics. Checklist includes repositories, health services research and policy organizations, and public health organizations, along with other sources. The main focus is on Canadian sources but also includes U.S. and international sources.

- **SRC Grey Literature: Tips and Checklist**
  Producer: Robin Paynter (Scientific Research Center [SRC], Oregon Health & Science University)
  Access: https://mclibrary.duke.edu/sites/mclibrary.duke.edu/files/public/ guides/SRC%20Grey%20Literature%20Checklist.pdf
  Checklist Scope: lists grey literature sources searched by the SRC, and focuses on U.S., Canadian, and other international sources. Checklist includes sources for regulatory information, clinical trials, and conference publications. Includes quite constructive (and entertaining) search tips for each source listed.

Other Similar Sources

Some select organizations provide lists of recommended websites that can be searched for grey literature publications. The lists of recommended sources may not be available in a PDF or Word file that can be downloaded as a search guide, and they also may not provide detailed search tips. Even so, these sources can still provide invaluable guidance.

Subject-specific online directories can also be searched to identify organizations that produce grey literature. Since the listings of online directories may also be organized thematically or geographically, or searched by using specific keywords, they can also be worthwhile research tools for muddling through the key organizations in a specific subject area. And just browsing the listing in a directory can aid with deciding on the scope of a grey literature search.

The following is a list of select sources:

- **A–Z Index of U.S. Government Departments and Agencies**
  Producer: U.S. federal government
  Access: https://www.usa.gov/federal-agencies/a
  Cost: Free
  Scope: Alphabetical listing of all federal governmental departments and agencies.
- **Associations Canada**
  Producer: Grey House Publishing Canada
  Access: http://www.greyhouse.ca/assoc.htm
  Cost: Subscription
  Scope: Listing of associations in Canada, including organizational activities.
- **CharityVillage Directories**
  Producer: Charity Village
  Access: https://charityvillage.com/directories.aspx
  Cost: Free
  Scope: Topical listing of registered charities in Canada.
- **Developing NICE Guidelines: Appendix G, Sources for Evidence Reviews**
  Producer: National Institute for Health and Care Excellence (NICE)
  Access: https://www.nice.org.uk/process/pmg20/resources/developing-nice-guidelines-the-manual-appendices-ag-i-2549710189/chapter/appendix-g-sources-for-evidence-reviews
  Cost: Free
  Scope: From the publication *Developing NICE Guidelines: The Manual.* Outlines general search guidelines for those involved with NICE Evidence Reviews. Includes a brief list of specific websites that can be used as a general starting point for a search.
- **Directory of Australian Organizations**
  Producer: ConnectWeb
  Access: http://connectweb.com.au/pages/directory-of-australian-associations.aspx
  Cost: Subscription
  Scope: Online directory of organizations in Australia, including organization purpose.
- **Directory of Charities and Nonprofit Organizations**
  Producer: GuideStar

Access: https://www.guidestar.org/NonprofitDirectory.aspx

Cost: Free

Scope: Source for identifying charities and other non-profit organizations in the United States.

- **Directory of Development Organizations**

    Producer: The Organization for Economic Co-operation and Development (OECD)

    Access: http://www.oecd.org/dev/pgd/directoryofdevelopmentorganizations.htm

    Cost: Free

    Scope: Lists developmental governmental organizations. Search limits include organization type, location, and activities.

- **Directory of Health Technology Assessment Organizations Worldwide**

    Producer: International Society for Pharmacoeconomics and Outcomes Research

    Access: https://www.ispor.org/HTADirectory/Index.aspx

    Cost: Free

    Scope: An international directory of HTA organizations. Can be searched by region, country, or organization name.

- **Directory of Organizations in Prevention**

    Producer: International Centre for the Prevention of Crime

    Access: http://www.crime-prevention-intl.org/nc/en/directory-organizations-prevention.html

    Cost: Free

    Scope: International directory; includes both governmental and non-governmental organizations.

- **Encyclopedia of Associations**

    Producer: Gale Research

    Access: http://www.gale.com/ebooks

    Cost: Subscription

    Scope: Detailed information on associations, including research activity. There are separate volumes for multinational, international, national, regional, state, and local organizations.

- **Encyclopedia of Governmental Advisory Originations**

    Producer: Gale Research

    Access: http://www.gale.com/ebooks

    Cost: Subscription

    Scope: Directory for identifying the organizations and committees that function to advise the U.S. federal government.

- **Grey Literature Report: Publishers List**

    Producer: The New York Academy of Medicine

    Access: http://www.greylit.org/publishers/list

Cost: Free

Scope: Provides an alphabetical list of organizations producing grey literature. Topic focus is on health services research and urban health; includes U.S., Canadian, and other international sources. (Note: Since the Grey Literature Report ceased updating in 2016, newer organizations may not be included.)

- **Grey Source Index**
  Producer: GreyNet
  Access: http://www.greynet.org/greysourceindex.html
  Cost: Free
  Scope: Topical list of organizations that produce grey literature. Includes organizations from Canada, the United States, Europe, and other international sources. The listing of organizations is not intended to be comprehensive, but rather is meant to provide examples of producers of grey literature in specific subject areas.

- **GuideStar UK**
  Producer: GuideStar
  Access: http://www.guidestar.org.uk/default.aspx
  Cost: Free
  Scope: Online directory listing registered charities in England and Wales.

- **healthfinder.gov: Find a Health Organization**
  Producer: Office of Disease Prevention and Promotion, Department of Health and Human Services
  Access: https://healthfinder.gov/FindServices/Organizations/default.aspx
  Cost: Free
  Scope: List of health-related organizations in the United States. It is especially good for identifying relevant federal and state organizations.

- **International Directory of Organizations in Grey Literature**
  Producer: GreyNet
  Access: http://www.greynet.org/images/GreyNet_International_Directory.pdf
  Cost: Free
  Scope: Directory listing over 200 organizations in 40 countries worldwide associated with GreyNet. Organizations are listed alphabetically.

- **MedlinePlus: A Collection of Organizations Providing Health Information**
  Producer: National Library of Medline
  Access: https://medlineplus.gov/organizations/all_organizations.html
  Cost: Free
  Scope: List of organizations that supply health information, including ones that produce grey literature. Focus is primarily on U.S. organizations,

but international sources are also included. List can be sorted either alphabetically or by topic.

- **Methods Guide for Effectiveness and Comparative Effectiveness Reviews: Finding Evidence for Comparing Medical Interventions**
  Producer: Agency for Health Care Research and Quality
  Access: https://effectivehealthcare.ahrq.gov/topics/cer-methods-guide/overview/
  Cost: Free
  Scope: A publication outlining methods for conducting reviews. The chapter titled "Finding Grey Literature Evidence and Assessing for Outcome and Analysis Reporting Biases When Comparing Medical Interventions" briefly outlines specific websites that should be searched.
- **National Directory of Nonprofit Organizations**
  Producer: Gale Research
  Access: http://www.gale.com/ebooks
  Cost: Subscription
  Scope: Detailed information on nonprofit organizations in the United States, including organization type and affiliation.
- **Pro Bono Australia Guide to Giving**
  Producer: Pro Bono Australia
  Access: https://probonoaustralia.com.au/guide-to-giving/
  Cost: Free
  Scope: Online listing of charities in Australia. Can be searched by organization name, or listings can be browsed by topic.
- **Searching for Studies: A Guide to Information Retrieval for Campbell Systematic Reviews—Appendix II: Grey Literature**
  Producer: Campbell Collaboration
  Access: https://www.campbellcollaboration.org/images/Campbell_Methods_Guides_Information_Retrieval.pdf
  Cost: Free
  Scope: Appendix II outlines organizations primarily from Great Britain, Canada, Europe, and the United States that can be searched. Focus is on organizations relevant to the social, behavioral, and educational sciences.
- **United States Government Internet Directory 2017**
  Producer: Rowman & Littlefield
  Access: https://rowman.com/ISBN/9781598889048/The-United-States-Government-Internet-Directory-2017#
  Cost: Purchase
  Scope: Lists U.S. federal government websites by subject; also includes information on websites from congressional committees.
- **World Directory of Think Tanks**

Producer: National Institute for Research Advancement (NIRA)

Access: http://www.nira.or.jp/past/ice/nwdtt/2005/index.html

Cost: Free

Scope: An international directory of think tanks. Can be searched by organization title or browsed by country.

- **Worldwide NGO Directory**

  Producer: World Association of Non-Governmental Organizations (WANGO)

  Access: http://www.wango.org/resources.aspx?section=ngodir

  Cost: Free

  Scope: An international listing of NGOs. Can either be browsed by region or searched by keywords.

SEARCH TIPS FOR GREY LITERATURE CHECKLISTS AND OTHER SIMILAR SOURCES

"Nearly" Is *Not* There

As Coco Chanel said, "Don't spend time beating on a wall, hoping to transform it into a door." Do you think the search sources listed on a checklist will have information on your topic? Before you start searching the sources outlined on a checklist, see if you can easily locate grey literature content on your search topic using just a sample of the sources listed on the checklist. If you can't, then proceeding with a more extensive search may not be a worthy investment of time. If a checklist does not list sources that will be beneficial for your grey literature search, it will be of no use to you, and other methods of grey literature searching—such as databases or structured Google searching—may be more advantageous.

Decide to Be Prescriptive, Not Subscripted

Otherwise known as the "A Back Does Not Break from Bending" search tip. Grey literature search checklists may list an almost countless number of sources, and it is not practical or fruitful to search all of the possible sources. There is room for flexibility when using grey literature search checklists, as long as you are transparent and forthright about your search methods. Before starting a search, see if there is a rationale for whittling down the list of search sources. For example, are you specifically interested in guidelines, or more so in emerging research or drug information?

Check for Recent Content

Otherwise known as the "Unlike a Fine Wine, Some Sources Do Not Get Better with Age" tip. Librarians and information professionals are often trusted to direct users to the most current information on a topic. Web checklists or online directories may not be frequently updated, which results in the sources being potentially outdated. Confirming the latest update of the web checklist or online directory is a key step, because the content may not be relevant due to age.

Avoid the Squirrel Syndrome and Don't Be Tempted by Distraction

Web checklists may list numerous potential sources to search for grey literature, and there are numerous online organizational directories with a multitude of entries. But these sources should only be an *aid* for crafting a grey literature search, especially since it is unfeasible or unreasonable to search every listing. For example, if utilizing a directory to select sources, try to determine a specific scope for your search—focus, for example, on organizations that only have a national or international mandate rather than including all local affiliates.

RECOMMENDATIONS BY HEALTH CARE AGENCIES AND ORGANIZATIONS THAT CREATE KNOWLEDGE SYNTHESIS

Most health care agencies and organizations that support the development of evidence-based practice publications do not list web checklists or online directories as search sources in their information retrieval guidelines. Their recommendations are quite brief, and most do not provide detailed guidance.

Cochrane

Cochrane (previously known as the Cochrane Collaboration) is an independent, global, not-for-profit, NGO comprised of Cochrane contributors from over 130 countries. Cochrane's goals include producing up-to-date systematic reviews and other knowledge synthesis, and making that evidence available and accessible to a worldwide population (Cochrane, "About Us," 2017, retrieved from http://www.cochrane.org/about-us). Cochrane produces *Cochrane Handbook for Systematic Reviews of Interventions* Version 5.1.0, which is a guide on the process of preparing and updating Cochrane systematic reviews. Section 6.2.1.8 of the handbook provides a brief overview of identifying grey literature publications. Specific web checklists for use in a search are not listed, but the search guidelines suggest searching professional associations' or governmental websites as a method for identifying research in progress.

The Campbell Collaboration

The Campbell Collaboration is an international, not-for-profit, non-governmental organization that "aims to help people make well-informed decisions about the effects of interventions in the social, behavioral, and educational arenas" (Campbell Collaboration, "Better Evidence for a Better World," retrieved from https://www.campbellcollaboration.org/). The Campbell Collaboration produces and disseminates systematic reviews on social and behavioral interventions, with the aim of helping the policy makers, practitioners, researchers, and members of the general public identify what interventions work. The Campbell Collaboration Information Retrieval Group has published a guide on information retrieval methods for systematic reviews: *Searching for Studies: A Guide to Information Retrieval for Campbell Systematic Reviews—Appendix II: Grey Literature*. The guide recommends that specific websites should be searched to ensure retrieval of grey literature publications, but the use of specific web checklists is not mentioned in the search guidelines. *Appendix II: Grey Literature* provides an extensive list of websites that should be included in a search; the list is cited as a source earlier in this chapter.

The Health and Medicine Division (HMD) of the National Academies of Sciences, Engineering, and Medicine

The HMD of the National Academies of Sciences, Engineering, and Medicine (formerly the Institute of Medicine) is a private U.S. not-for-profit institution with the aim of providing "independent, objective analysis and advice to the nation and conduct[ing] other activities to solve complex problems and inform public policy decisions related to science, technology, and medicine" (National Academies of Sciences, Engineering, and Medicine—HMD, "About HMD," September 2016, retrieved from http://www.nationalacademies.org/hmd/About-HMD.aspx). HMD has published recommended standards for conducting systematic reviews, and its publication *Finding What Works in Health Care: Standards for Systematic Reviews* outlines twenty-one standards for developing high-quality systematic reviews on comparative effectiveness research. Standard 3.2.5 lists scanning relevant websites rather than using an

Internet search engine for identifying relevant studies, but web checklists and searching of specific websites are not mentioned.

The Agency for Health Care Research and Quality (AHRQ)

The AHRQ is a U.S. governmental agency that is part of the U.S. Department of Health and Human Services. AHRQ's mission is "to produce evidence to make health care safer, higher quality, more accessible, equitable, and afford-able, and to work within the U.S. Department of Health and Human Services and with other partners to make sure that the evidence is understood and used." The AHRQ Effective Health Care Program has published the *Methods Guide for Effectiveness and Comparative Effectiveness Reviews*, and the chapter "Finding Grey Literature Evidence and Assessing for Outcome and Analysis Reporting Biases When Comparing Medical Interventions: AHRQ and the Effective Health Care Program" recommends sources for identifying the grey literature on conventional drugs and devices. Specific web checklists for use in a search are not listed in the recommendations. The chapter *Finding Grey Literature Evidence and Assessing for Outcome and Analysis Reporting Biases When Comparing Medical Intervention* has a short list of recommended websites for locating clinical trials or regulatory information, including Drugs@FDA, Devices@FDA, European Medicine Agency, and ClinicalTrials.gov.

National Institute for Health and Care Excellence (NICE)

The NICE is a nondepartmental public body (NDPB) that is accountable to its sponsor department, the Department of Health, United Kingdom. NICE's mission is to improve outcomes for people using the National Health Service and other public health and social services. NICE produces evidence guidance and advice, including NICE guidelines and other evidence sum-maries. The publication *Developing NICE Guidelines: The Manual* mentions that searching sources for identifying grey literature publications may be in-dispensable for certain reviews. *Appendix G: Sources for Evidence Reviews*, recommends that individual websites should be searched for relevant infor-mation, including the websites of UK national organizations, websites of pro-fessional bodies, and websites of organizations for service users, caregivers, and family members. Using specific web checklists for locating grey litera-ture is not mentioned in the search guidelines.

Textbox 8.1. A Decision Aid for Using Grey Literature Checklists or Other Similar Sources

---

The following is a proposed decision aid for adding a grey literature search checklist or similar sources to your grey literature search.

1. Do you need to outline the methods for the grey lit search?

If your overall search plan requires publishing and documenting your grey search techniques, a grey literature search checklist is a suitable source to reference in a search methodology write-up. Some grey literature checklists, such as CADTH's Grey Matters, also supply a ready-made worksheet to outline the search terms used and space to document results, which may especially be appreciated later if detailed information on the search methods is required.

2. Do you need to provide guidance to someone else doing a grey literature search?

This is also known as outsourcing, unloading, or *avoiding* doing a grey literature search. All kidding aside, sometimes librarians and information professionals may be more involved with teaching search methods than with being responsible for completing a search. A grey literature checklist is a fine search source to suggest to others, as long as the benefits and limitations of the checklist are explained. Sources similar to grey literature search checklists can also be employed to help explain to users how an abundant number of organizations produce grey literature and grey literature's international presence, and they can also aid with devising the scope of a grey literature search.

CONCLUSION

Grey literature search checklists and other similar sources may provide much needed specific guidance on how to determine a clearly defined scope for grey literature search. When searchers use grey literature search checklists, they have a clear idea of the limitations and exclusions of the search scope. They also may not need to draft a grey literature search strategy from scratch. Having a predetermined scope for a grey literature search may be a much needed tool for successful search completion, especially for novice searchers or when detailed documentation of the search methods are required. Other similar sources, such as directories, may also be helpful for identifying potential producers of grey literature to include the sources in a search.

BIBLIOGRAPHY

Sullivan, S. M., Coyle, D., & Wells, G. (2014). What guidance are researchers given on how to present network meta-analyses to end-users such as policymakers and clinicians? A systematic review. *PloS one*, *9*(12), e113277.

Tricco, A. C., Ivers, N. M., Grimshaw, J. M., Moher, D., Turner, L., Galipeau, J., et al. (2012). Effectiveness of quality improvement strategies on the management of diabetes: A systematic review and meta-analysis. *Lancet*, *379*(9833), 2252–2261.

Young, M. M., Stevens, A., Porath-Waller, A., Pirie, T., Garritty, C., Skidmore, B., . . . & Reardon, R. (2012). Effectiveness of brief interventions as part of the screening, brief intervention and referral to treatment (SBIRT) model for reducing the non-medical use of psychoactive substances: a systematic review protocol. *Systematic reviews*, *1*(1), 22.

Chapter 9

Google for Grey Literature

"I'll Google that" has become part of our conversational lexicon, and Googling is now synonymous with searching the Internet. The Internet search engines prior to Google's debut are but a faint memory to most (rest in peace, Alta Vista; Infoseek, we hardly knew ya), and Google is more likely than not our first point of contact to locate recipes, news, instructions on how to fix things, reviews, and, of course, research. Google can also be an especially potent research tool for grey literature. Google searching can find a great number of pertinent and nonpareil grey literature hits, and it can be a superior grey literature search source, especially when compared to other more traditionally used grey literature search sources. This chapter will address how using Google can play a crucial role in a grey literature search.

LEARNING OUTCOMES

The goal of this chapter is to provide librarians and information professionals with:

- the benefits of Google in locating grey lit
- the limitations of Google in locating grey lit
- structured Google searching for grey lit
- Google Scholar for grey lit searching
- topic-specific Google Custom Search (GCS) engines for grey lit searching
- alternatives (gasp!) to Google
- a proposed decision-making aid for using Google, Google Scholar, or a GCS as a grey literature search source

After reading this chapter, readers should have a basic knowledge of how Google can be a key research tool for quick grey literature searches, or how Google can be an advantageous additional source for a comprehensive grey literature search—such as a systematic review or a scoping review—that includes a multitude of grey literature search sources. This chapter should also enable information professionals to facilitate discussions with their information users on methods for employing Google for grey literature searches.

ADVANTAGES OF USING GOOGLE FOR GREY LITERATURE SEARCHES

As discussed in previous chapters, a grey literature search source should only be used when there is a clear gain for doing so. So why Google for a grey literature search? This time, let's use a Top Ten framework to examine both the advantages and drawbacks of using Google to identify grey literature.

Benefits of Google

1. *A Google search can be helpful for locating grey lit publications that are not indexed by databases.*

Although databases can be a meritorious source for identifying grey literature publications, they are not always ideal sources for locating recent grey lit publications, or grey lit publications from smaller or very location-specific producers such as local affiliates of national or international organizations. This is where a Google search for grey literature can shine—the sheer size and strength of Google clearly indicates it has a heavyweight, Joe Louis–like champion advantage. An example of such a search would be, say, grey literature publications on best practices for creating community partnerships for public health issues. This type of search is quite challenging to do in one database as the topic is broad and could potentially include publications from a wide range of institutions and disciplines in such areas as health, criminal justice, and education. There is also not one specific database that would capture all the possible grey literature hits as the range of potential sources is quite vast. For example, some grey literature documents on creating community partnerships may be government publications from the Centers for Disease Control and Prevention (CDC); others could be published by charities such as the March of Dimes. Yet a Google search on such a topic retrieves over 4,620,000 potential search hits—and the search can be refined to retrieve grey literature hits by specific formats, regions, or year range. It's speedy and simple, too.

2. Google is ideal for quick searches.

Grey literature searches can be tremendously time-consuming—there simply is not one all-inclusive source that can be searched. But if you are familiar with Advanced Google Search commands—which we will examine later in this chapter—it is fairly uncomplicated to do a quick grey literature search and locate grey lit publications relevant to your topic. Grey literature searches are often only included as part of an exhaustive and more detailed search for such projects as systematic reviews or scoping reviews. Google searches can quickly be utilized to add grey literature search results to less complicated search requests. Again, it just requires a smidgen of supplementary search steps to retrieve truly distinctive hits. A quick grey literature search in Google can also be beneficial for providing structure to a more comprehensive literature review. For example, particular search request topics, such as a search request for information on evaluating patient education strategies, are extraordinarily broad. A quick Google grey literature search can be used to ferret out key grey literature publications that then can be used to help draft database searches.

3. Its search results are relevant.

Google's super-secret search algorithm often allows it to deliver remarkably relevant results, and the algorithm is continually being improved (Levy, 2010). While other grey lit sources, such as databases or institutional repositories, will provide hits based on the occurrence of search terms, neither will typically sort hits by relevancy as accurately as Google will. A listing of search terms by relevancy helps identify key grey literature publications quickly.

4. It is a well-recognized source to suggest to users.

As Kennedy and Price insightfully wrote: "College students AND professors might not know that library databases exist, but they sure know Google." Google is a household name and the de facto generic searching standard: there are over 3.5 billion searches per day and 1.2 trillion searches per year worldwide ("Google Search Statistics," retrieved from http://www.internetlivestats.com/google-search-statistics/). Since the majority of users are already accustomed to Google, it can easily be proposed as a search source. Although adapting Google searching to retrieve grey literature hits may require specific training, the majority of users are going to be familiar with the fundamentals of the search process. Countless users may already have been using Google to locate grey literature publications but may have been unaware of or unfamiliar with the publication type.

5. It is good for locating regional information.

The grey literature publications of region-specific grey literature–producing organizations, such as local affiliates of charities, food banks, counties, municipalities, or public health units, can be laborious to locate. These publications are not often included in available grey literature databases or institutional repositories, even though there are immeasurable numbers of these publications. Google searches can easily be structured to locate information by location, so Google is an ideal source for identifying geographically relevant information. Often, a Google search may be one of the few hassle-free methods for identifying relevant region-specific organizations and their grey literature publications.

6. You can find publications from smaller organizations.

Many smaller NGOs or other organizations produce grey literature, but these publications can often be hard to identify using other grey literature search methods. The organizations simply may not have a sizeable grey literature publication output or an international focus. One example would be the research from iDAPT at the Toronto Rehabilitation Institute. This research rates winter boots for slip resistance in various winter conditions—it is research that is only available in grey literature ("Rate My Treads," retrieved from http://www.ratemytreads.com/). Google searches are preeminent search sources for identifying these publications that may otherwise not be accessible from databases or institutional repositories.

7. It is the ultimate discovery tool.

We as users Google topics daily that we want to be more knowledgeable about. Or we use Google to learn something new, from how to fix a broken window, to how to boil an egg, to how to use chopsticks ("How to Fix a Toilet and Other Things We Could Not Do Without Search," retrieved from http://how-to-fix-a-toilet.com/). Google can also be an ideal source to discover organizations producing grey literature that we are not familiar with. A search on improving patient safety, for example, can help identify key national and international grey literature producers in the area. This "A-ha!" moment of discovery can also help add structure to more targeted and precise grey literature searches in the future. Google searches for grey literature publications are also superb for identifying new initiatives, interventions, or approaches.

8. It provides up-to-date search results.

Google search results are in a constant state of change. Google's indexing system allows it to quickly crawl and index the web for new content (Amit Singhal, "Giving You Fresher, More Recent Search Results," November 3, 2011, retrieved from https://googleblog.blogspot.ca/2011/11/giving-you-fresher-more-recent-search.html), and Google's ranking algorithm provides more recent relevant results, especially for up-to-the-minute events or trending topics. Recently updated results are key for grey literature searches, and not just for finding out the latest match updates to the Liverpool F.C. versus Manchester United tilt. A grey literature search for publications on the opiate addiction crisis is one example of a search that would benefit from including the most current search results.

9. It is a global search tool.

Google searches can be easily structured to identify grey literature searches from far abroad. A Google search can be easily adapted to identify grey literature publications from Australia, Ireland, and the United Kingdom, along with other countries. Google has invested heavily in being recognized as an international source of information. Developing an international search presence has been a key focus of Google, enabling Google searches for all spoken languages (Udi Manber, May 20, 2008, "Introduction to Google Search Quality," retrieved from https://googleblog.blogspot.ca/2008/05/introduction-to-google-search-quality.html). As a result, Google is a stellar source for locating grey literature hits worldwide, not just from North America. Google's wide scope of indexing enables it to be a forceful search tool for locating grey literature publications that provide international insights on a wide range of issues, including HIV/AIDS, health systems research, and treatment guidelines.

10. Its sheer size.

Google currently indexes over 130 trillion web pages (Barry Schwartz, November 14, 2016, "Google's Search Knows About Over 130 Trillion Pages," http://searchengineland.com/googles-search-indexes-hits-130-trillion-pages-documents-263378). Obviously, this number potentially includes countless web pages that contain grey literature sources, from varied sources in an assortment of countries. In comparison, other grey literature sources, such as databases or repositories, contain a smaller and usually more tightly focused pool of information. Having the vastness of Google's indexing breadth is an added bonus when searching for grey literature, simply because of the immense scope of available sources.

Drawbacks to Google

1. It is challenging to document the search process.

Unlike a search in a database, repository, or on specific websites such as best practice portals, it is a challenge to outline the Google search terms you used and have someone else reproduce your strategy based on your documentation. Google search results can change quickly, especially the ranking of results. Fluctuating search results are a major challenge to Google searching for grey literature publications—it can be difficult to retrace search steps and retrieve the same results from past searches.

2. The number of results can be overwhelming.

The number of search results retrieved in a Google search can appear endless. The sheer size of Google means that there is a likelihood of a Google Search identifying an abundance of grey literature content on such topics as fall prevention or surgical safety checklists. But it is another can of worms to actually review *all* of that content, which is why 91 percent of Google searchers do not go past the first page of their search results, and 50 percent of Google searchers do not go past the first three search results listed on page one (Van Deursen & Van Dijk, 2009). The magnitude of Google is an asset because of the available content, but an immeasurable number of search results requires foresight on how to prioritize results that will be examined in greater detail.

3. There is too much of everything and anything.

Google can deliver the ultimate junk drawer of search results—everything and anything is there. There are search methods and limits available to whittle down search results to a more manageable number, but excluding irrelevant hits can be a complicated and troublesome process.

4. Google personalized searching.

Google customizes everyone's search results, even when a user is not signed in to a Google account (Danny Sullivan, "Google Now Personalizes Everyone's Search Results," December 4, 2009, retrieved from, http://searchengineland. com/google-now-personalizes-everyones-search-results-31195).   Among other factors, search results are personalized by location, previous search queries, and 180 days of search activity linked to an anonymous cookie in an individual browser (Bryan Horling & Matthew Kulick, "Personalized Searching for Everyone," December 4, 2009, retrieved from https:// googleblog.blogspot.ca/2009/12/personalized-search-for-everyone.html). Personalized searching was launched in 2009 and has become ubiquitous in Google searching today. The aim of Google personalized search results is to get to "the heart of who you are, the kinds of sources you gravitate to, and the content that will most satisfy you as a searcher" (Heather Physioc, "The Complex Web of Personalized Search," retrieved from http://tentacleinbound.com/articles/personalized-search). Before the launch of Google's personalized search results, every user would receive identical search results for a topic, from the 1973 coup d'états in Chile, to genetically modified organisms, to gun safety, to bullfighting, to diabetes, to Sumo wrestling, to the first election of President Barack Obama. Now, Google search results for the above-mentioned topics are personalized, and one person may retrieve vastly contrasting search results when compared to someone else's search. Personalized search results are a barrier to locating diverse sources of information because particular results are selectively displayed over others based on what is seen to be the most central to a user's specific search. This results in a "filter bubble" source where an algorithm determines what results are displayed, and searchers are not exposed to search results from diverse perspectives (Pariser, 2011).

5. The "echo chamber of results."

There has been much debate on how Google's personalized search results create an "echo chamber" where results are displayed depending on previous searches, and search results are primarily from information sources that simply reinforce currently held beliefs instead of introducing new or divergent viewpoints (Mostafa M. El-Bermawy, "Your Filter Bubble Is Destroying Democracy," November 18, 2016, retrieved from https://www.wired.com/2016/11/filter-bubble-destroying-democracy/). New and heterogeneous sources of information are not favored; instead, sources of information that have been visited before are ranked more prominently. Personalized Google search results can also be an unneeded hassle in a grey literature search. Google personalized searching means that search hits from unknown sources are less likely to be displayed than search results from pages you have visited in the past. For a quick example, just Google "NICE." If you are a health science librarian who has visited the web page for the National Institute for Health and Care Excellence, that hit will most likely receive top ranking. If you have not visited that site, chances are that information on weather and travel to "Nice, France" will be ranked first. Google's personalized results can be counterproductive because the whole aim of a search is to unearth grey literature publications and sources that you were previously unfamiliar with, rather than to retrieve a result list cluttered up by hits from the usual suspects. To effectively use Google for locating grey literature, steps must be taken to bypass the impact of personalized search results and to purposefully seek out information that will be from undiscovered sources.

6. *Google searching is not Deep Web searching.*

Internet search engines, including Google, only index 4 percent of available information (Poladian & Stone, 2015; Goodman, 2015; Bergman, 2001). Google is an impressive resource for searching the surface web, but if Deep Web searching is required, a search should incorporate other sources besides Google. While a Google search for grey literature may be apropos for a quick search or as one component of a more in-depth grey literature search, Google is not a one-stop source for identifying all grey literature. For example, a Google search for adverse drug effects is not likely to identify relevant regulatory documents from the Food and Drug Administration or the European Medicines Agency.

7. *Expert searching is necessary.*

While Google is familiar to many, most people do not use the Advanced Search option. The crowd of those using Advanced Search commands is most likely remarkably small: fanatical users, professional librarians, spooks, and private investigators (Tim Bray, "On Search: The Users," June 17, 2003, retrieved from https://www.tbray.org/ongoing/When/200x/2003/06/17/ SearchUsers). Unless a searcher utilizes the Google Advanced Search interface or is cognizant of Google search commands, only a minuscule number of grey literature publications may be retrieved. Advanced Google Search techniques are vital because, unlike a PubMed search where the hits can be limited to clinical trials or review articles, a search in Google cannot be limited to grey literature hits. The grey literature hits can indeed be teased out from the broader pool of results, but extra legwork is required.

8. *Managing Google Search results is a challenge.*

Unlike a database search, it is not easy to send someone else the results of a Google search. This can be a major barrier to sharing results, especially if more than one person is responsible for scanning a list of results to determine relevancy for inclusion. For more comprehensive grey literature searches for systematic reviews, this may mean it could be burdensome to include Google as a search source. Additionally, it is onerous to update a Google search because of the vast amount of information that is available. The content of web pages can change quickly and often—the information on a page, such as link to a report, may easily disappear tomorrow. While this is no fault of

Google, the lack of static results is a challenge for capturing search results to view later.

9. Bias.

Google search results are often dominated by the usual suspects—for example, searches for health-related topics will mostly likely retrieve hits from large organizations (hello, Mayo Clinic and WebMD). If you are searching a topic within the United States or Canada, your search results will be dominated by such sources. The "usual suspects" pitfall can only be avoided by adapting your search methods—for example, by using search commands to retrieve country-specific information and publications from specific locations or domains.

10. Its search quality might be slipping.

For years, Google has dominated the Internet search engine marketplace (Danny Sullivan, "Google versus Everyone," July 6, 2007, retrieved from http://searchengineland.com/nielsen-netratings-august-2007-search-share-puts-google-on-top-microsoft-holding-gains-12243), commanding over 80 percent of the market (Sourthern, 2016). But Google's spot as the optimum search engine is becoming more frequently debated (Danny Sullivan, "A Deep Look at Google's Biggest-Ever Search Quality Crisis," April 3, 2017, retrieved from http://searchengineland.com/google-search-quality-crisis-272174). At the heart of the debate is the validity of the information displayed in the prominently featured "snippets in search"—these are search results that are displayed in a block at the top of the search page in response to a user typing a search question. Past examples of Google leading users to spurious sources of information include a search snippet indicating that dinosaurs are being used to indoctrinate children and adults into the idea of millions of years of earth history ("Go Ahead, Ask Google 'What Happened to the Dinosaurs,'" June 10, 2015, retrieved from https://motherboard.vice.com/en_us/article/pga4wg/go-ahead-ask-google-what-happened-to-the-dinosaurs), as well as assigning high ranking to Holocaust-denial websites (Adrianne Jeffries, "Why Does Google Think Obama Is Planning a Coup D'etat?," March 5, 2017, retrieved from https://theoutline.com/post/1192/google-s-featured-snippets-are-worse-than-fake-news). Part of the predicament is that Google has transformed from a research tool supplying web pages of potentially relevant sources to providing the one true answer to a question (Eva Flores, "Google's 'One True Answer' Problem—When Featured Snippets Go Bad," March 5, 2017, retrieved from http://latessearchengineupdatestoday.blogspot.ca/2017/03/googles-one-true-answer-problem-when.html). All of the previously supplied arguments for Google's robustness as a tool for grey lit are based on its capacity to highlight a diverse array of valid information rather than a limited list of dubious or sketchy sources.

ADAPTING A GOOGLE SEARCH FOR GREY LITERATURE

Grey literature searches in Google cannot be executed utilizing the identical methods as more common Google searches. Searches must be adapted, and specific search commands need to be employed in order to tease out the concealed grey literature content; otherwise, the grey lit hits are adrift in the sea of results from all of the other sources. Structured Google searching is distinct from commonplace, everyday Google searches—instead of simply entering search terms to capture any or every type of search hit, specific search criteria are determined before searching. The specific criteria could include results limited by region, search terms in the title page domain, file types, phrase search, or exclusion of search hits from specific websites. A structured Google search is also helpful if search-specific steps need to be executed or outlined in a search methodology.

Steps for Structured Grey Literature Google Searching

Look for Information from International Sources

Going to Google Advanced Search and limiting search results from a specific region is one of the easiest ways to access a varying range of grey literature hits. It is also an almost effortless method for ensuring that your search hits are not dominated by your specific location. Australia, Canada, and the United Kingdom all produce vast numbers of grey literature publications that may be relevant to a search topic, but unless specific search steps are used to pinpoint these results, the search hits will remain buried.

Limit to File Type

Limiting the file type to Adobe Acrobat PDF or MS Word may be especially good for structuring a search to only retrieve hits with more detailed content, such as evidence briefs or white papers. While limiting to file types will possibly miss some grey literature hits, it will exclude a vast number of irrelevant hits. Limiting to file type is also ideal for more comprehensive grey literature publications, since these items generally are not available in HTML format. Additionally, limiting the file type to MS PowerPoint presentations is often a savvy search strategy for locating information on topics such as newly launched programs, initiatives, or conference publications.

Text Box 9.1. Best Bets Domain Limits

Educational institutions (U.S.-focused): edu
International treaty-based organizations: int
Non-commercial organizations: org
Non-governmental organizations: ngo/ong
U.S. federal, state, county, and municipal government agencies: gov
U.S. military: mil

Textbox 9.2. Select Country-Specific Domains

Australia: au
Canada: ca
European Union: eu
Ireland: ie
New Zealand: nz
United Kingdom: uk
United States: us

Limit by Domain

Limiting by search domain is another means to exclude search hits from irrelevant sources, such as commercial sources. The best step is to use top-level domain extensions, such as country-specific domains. Top-level domains are controlled and assigned by the Internet Assigned Numbers Authority, and domain limits can be used to limit to sources such as educational institutions or the U.S. military

Google Alerts

Google search alerts can also be used to keep current with new and emerging sources of grey literature. Google search alerts can be limited to web alerts, news alerts, or alerts that contain information from multiple sources. Google Alerts are convenient for keeping up with recently released grey literature publications on specific topics or organizations. Advanced Search commands can also be used when setting up a Google Alert.

When to Stop Searching?

As previously mentioned, it is tricky to surmise when to stop sifting through the results of a Google search. Even an extremely structured Google search

---

Textbox 9.3. Quick Search Terms for Googling Grey Literature

Care Pathway
Evaluation
Evidence
Framework
Guideline
Policy
Rapid Review
Steering Group
Strategic Plan
Strategy
Task Force
Toolkit
White Paper

Textbox 9.4. Select Google Search Commands

---

allintext: to search for documents with specific words in the text
allinurl: to find search terms in url
cache: to find Google's backup version of a page
inauthor: to find books written by specific author
intitle: to find your term in the title and document
link: to find sites that link to a desired URL
location: to find results from a location (Google News only)
related: to find web pages that are similar to a URL (a great way to find organizations you are not familiar with)
site:country code: to search for results from a specific country
source: to find results from a specific source
*: to execute a search when you want to substitute any search term in a phrase; for using a wildcard
-: to exclude a search term from your results
" ": to search by phrase

---

could potentially retrieve numerous results. There has been a limited amount of research of only viewing the first fifty search results, because the most relevant search results will most likely be identified (Hepworth et al., 2013; Bielska, 2009; Hamilton Lopez, Singer Cohen, & Holve, 2012; Kelly et al., 2008).

GOOGLE SCHOLAR FOR GREY LITERATURE

What Is Google Scholar?

Google Scholar was launched in 2004 and is a free search engine that can be used to search across a wide range of academic sources. Recent estimates of Google Scholar's content have found that it indexes more than 160 million items (Orduña-Malea et al., 2014). As a search source, Google Scholar can be an alternative to costly subscription databases, and its free and easy-to-use search interface is a benefit (Neuhaus et al., 2006). Uptake of Google Scholar has been increasing at an exponential rate since its launch (Herrera, 2011; Quint, 2008).

Google Scholar has many of its own merits to offer for searching grey literature, separate from Google searches for grey literature. This time, let's use a quick Top Three list to evaluate Google Scholar for locating grey literature.

1. There's been a considerable amount of research on Google Scholar.

When Google Scholar was first released in 2004, significant research activity on the validity of Google Scholar as an academic search source soon followed. Google Scholar has received its fair share of scrutiny. Research studies have investigated the appropriateness of Google Scholar as a worthy source to include in systematic reviews, how it compares to PubMed as a search source, and the reproducibility of Google Scholar searches (Gehanno, Rollin, & Darmoni, 2013; Giustini & Boulos, 2013; Falagas et al., 2008). Research has also documented Google Scholar's strength for locating grey literature (Haddaway et al., 2015). The wide range of available research is highly constructive for learning more about the appropriateness and limitations of Google Scholar searching and when its use is warranted.

2. It is frequently cited as a source for grey literature in systematic reviews.

It is not uncommon to see Google Scholar cited as a source for grey literature in the search methodologies of systematic reviews. A quick search in PubMed will retrieve several recent systematic reviews that list Google Scholar as the source searched for grey literature (Haas Junior et al.; Capriglione et al.; Meireles et al.; Van der Roest et al.; Eliyahu et al.). As a result, Google Scholar is becoming a routinely used and trusted source for grey literature.

3. *Unlike most academic databases, Google Scholar includes diverse types of grey literature, from a wide range of disciplines.*

Most academic databases focus on peer-reviewed published literature, and academic databases are generally quite topic-specific. Some databases may selectively index specific publication types of grey literature—an example of this is PsycInfo, which includes select dissertations. Not long after Google Scholar's debut, it was identified as a source containing numerous types of grey literature (Kesselman & Watstein, 2005), and Google Scholar continues to include diverse sources of grey literature today. The scope of grey literature documents included in Google Scholar is quite broadly defined, and a Google Scholar search on a given topic may retrieve the following types of grey literature publications: conference proceedings, conference papers, dissertations, and reports (Google Scholar, "About," retrieved from https://scholar.google.ca/intl/en/scholar/about.html).

Google Scholar also represents itself as a multidisciplinary source for research rather than as a source that simply focuses on one topic area. Google Scholar does not just focus on publications in the humanities or science; therefore, it can be used to identify grey literature publications for a wide range of searches on various topics. As result, a Google Scholar search can be used to identify a broad spectrum of grey literature publications from various subject areas, such as education or medicine.

Weaknesses of Google Scholar

1. *Grey literature is in Google Scholar, but where?*

While Google Scholar may indeed be a source to locate grey literature, search results cannot be limited to grey literature content. Unlike academic databases, there is not an option to limit search results by specific publication types or sources. So, while grey literature publications of presented conference papers may indeed be retrieved by a Google Scholar search, results cannot be limited only to that type of publication. A search could include such keywords as "conference paper" or "report," since these are terms frequently used in grey literature, but these are not validated filters for grey literature. Rather, search terms for retrieving grey literature hits in Google Scholar are clunky and primitive at best. There are no tried-and-true search filters for locating grey literature in Google Scholar, and using keywords to identify grey literature relies on pure guesswork.

Even if Google Scholar searches include keywords to potentially identify grey literature publications, grey literature hits may still be buried among all the results from the published literature. Google Scholar does indeed contain grey literature content, but the grey literature content may be arduous to identify. So while research has evaluated Google Scholar as a source for grey literature, the majority of grey literature results are located at page 80 (Haddaway et al., 2015). Thus, Google Scholar's focus is still on published academic literature.

2. The unreliability of Google Scholar.

The information provided by Google Scholar is vast and valuable. It is also tricky to put your finger on. Depending on the search method used, the number of search results may change, and past research has noted this as a problem when Google Scholar is used for complex searches. Another challenge is Google Scholar's limited search function and search options—it has no controlled vocabulary, no authority files, no quality control, and no way to limit results by publication or study type (Schroeder, 2007). Google Scholar's hits are ranked by relevancy, which is another obstacle; its ranking of a search hit depends on how often a source has been cited by other research, which favors older research over newly emerging ideas. As put by librarian Keven O'Kelly, "As a thought experiment, imagine an alternate universe in which Google Scholar existed in the late seventeenth century. A student searching for basic information on physics, such as the laws of motion, would retrieve works by and about Aristotle. . . . Meanwhile, the work of a Cambridge scholar named Isaac Newton probably wouldn't even appear on the first page of results." The relevancy algorithm focuses on a search hit's "citedness" rather than simply sorting results by descending publication date (Hartman & Mullen, 2008). Since Google Scholar's ranking of results favors older research that has been frequently cited, it can be a faulty and clumsy search source for locating recent grey literature publications. While Google Scholar may indeed be a source for grey literature, it is wanting as a source for new grey literature publications such as updated treatment guidelines or recently presented conference publications. Research has documented that Google Scholar is likely to miss many grey literature sources, and a comprehensive grey literature search must also employ a search of individual websites in addition to Google Scholar (Haddaway et al., 2015). Ruefully, Google Scholar is *not* the much-needed one-stop source for grey literature publications.

3. The black box of databases.

Google Scholar has been criticized for its lack of transparency—little is known about Google Scholar's content updating and subject coverage (Jacsó, 2005). Unlike traditional databases such as Web of Science, Embase, or ERIC, Google Scholar has no clearly defined list of indexed document types or journals. We simply do not know what, specifically, is included in Google Scholar, or the criteria for inclusion or exclusion (Antell et al., 2013). So much in Google Scholar is uncertain, and it is unclear what types of grey literature Google Scholar includes, on which topics, and which organizations produce it. Determining if Google Scholar is a suitable source for identifying conference presentations on cancer-related research—or if it is better for locating reports by U.S. think tanks on health care disparities—is mere guesswork. The murkiness of Google Scholar's grey literature content means that assessing its topical coverage is challenging.

The percentage of grey literature content in Google Scholar is also unclear. For example, unlike PsycInfo, which unequivocally states that dissertations comprise 10 percent of its database content, Google Scholar does not indicate how much dissertation content it includes (American Psychological Association, "PsycInfo: A World-Class Resource for Behavioral and Social Science Research," retrieved from http://www.apa.org/pubs/databases/psycinfo/psycinfo-printable-fact-sheet.pdf). It is also unclear whose grey literature content is included. For example, does Google primarily include grey literature publications from U.S. sources, or can it also be searched reliably to identify grey literature publications from international sources, such as the World Health Organization or the World Bank? Since Google Scholar is vague at best about what is and is not included, gauging the content of Google Scholar can be puzzling. Additionally, it is unknown if all of an organization's grey literature output will be identified by a Google Scholar search or just select ones. As a result, a high proportion of grey literature can potentially be missed by Google Scholar.

GOOGLE CUSTOM SEARCH

GCS allows individuals to create a Google-powered search engine for a specific website or blog, or a topic search engine for websites ("What Is Google Custom Search?," retrieved from https://developers.google.com/custom-search/). GCS was launched in 2006, and many libraries created topic-specific GCSs on a wide range of topics. In short, a topic-specific GCS is the equivalent of limiting search results to preselected websites. The sources listed in GCSs are frequently producers of grey literature publications.

While available GCSs can be a hassle-free way to search for grey literature publications, they have their own strengths and weaknesses, like the other Google-powered grey lit search sources. Again, let's use a Top Three framework to examine both the benefits and drawbacks of using GCSs as a grey literature research resource.

Strengths

1. GCS takes the guesswork out of searching.

GCS provides a curated list of sources: you simply enter the search terms in a GCS, and a list of results limited to specific sites is delivered. No need for the hassle of wading through endless pages of results. The creators of a GCS select specific sources to highlight the most relevant content. There are also additional bonuses to searching a curated list of sites—sites that otherwise would be buried in a standard Google search may be prominently featured in a GCS.

2. GCS supports use of Advanced Search commands.

GCS functionality is the same as Google or Google Scholar searches, and expert searching is an option. All of the Advanced Search commands, such as domain limits or file type limits, can be used, along with phrase searching or excluding search terms. As a result, searching a well-designed GCS can be an alternative to searching all of Google, and can help to avoid deciding how to wrestle through numerous results.

3. No personalized searching.

Everyone and anyone searching a GCS will retrieve the same number of search results. Search results are not personalized according to location, past search history, or use of social networks. This means there are no worries that search results on the topic of measles will display results from anti-vaccination sources, or that a search on minority health will link to dubious sources. GCSs from well-respected sources can be an unbiased search source to suggest. Of course, the catch is to only use GCSs that include search results from a diverse array of sources or GCSs created and curated by reputable organizations.

Weaknesses

1. GCS only lists ten pages of results.

Whether a search topic entered in a GCS is a narrowly defined topic such as the Mediterranean Diet for prehypertension, or a broadly defined topic such as cancer, only ten pages of results will be retrieved. This handicap means that GCS cannot be relied on to identify all relevant grey literature publications, even if a GCS includes all of the websites that could be potential sources of information.

> **Textbox 9.5. It's relatively simple to identify GCS on a given topic:**
>
> - Use the search term "Google Custom Search" and enter the desired search topic.
> - Search for Google Custom Search embedded on LibGuides.
> - Search the topic of interest and use the Google search command site https://cse. google.com to limit your search results to GCS.

2. *Google's relevancy ranking pushes popular sites to the top.*

A GCS is still a Google Search—the most popular sites will still be favored and will receive a higher ranking. For example, if the creators of a GCS include tremendously popular websites such as Medline Plus or the Mayo Clinic in their GCS, it is likely that the results from such large and popular sources will dominate the search results. While the high ranking is warranted because of the organization's immense information output and influence, it is a shortcoming because less-known sources will not be prominently displayed.

3. *The black box strikes again.*

While excellent GCSs, such as the NGOs GCS from Yale University Library, will search several worthy sources, a detailed listing of websites that have been searched is generally not available. This is through no fault of the creators of the GCS—it is simply a drawback of the GCS design: searchers cannot scrutinize all of the websites behind the curtain of a GCS interface. GCS can potentially include up to 5,000 sites, but there is no option to view the sites that are being searched or to de-select sites from the GCS search list. Also, unlike a database, there generally is no information on the currency of a GCS. For example, is the GCS regularly updated to test for dead links, or was the GCS created years ago as part of a well-intentioned library student practicum project that was neglected? These drawbacks are similar to those associated with Google Scholar: there is limited information about the sources being searched or whether this resource can be relied upon to identify the most paramount and up-to-date information.

ALTERNATIVES TO GOOGLE

In 2006, "Google" officially became a verb in the *Oxford English Dictionary* (Barry Schwartz, "Google Now a Verb in the Oxford English Dictionary," June 29, 2006, retrieved from https://searchenginewatch.com/sew/news/2058373/ google-now-a-verb-in-the-oxford-english-dictionary), and "Googling" is often used to describe the activity of looking something up on the

---

Textbox 9.6. Select Google Custom Search Engines

- **Carleton University**
  Canadian Government Documents
  https://cse.google.com/cse/home?cx=007843865286850066037:3ajwn2jlweq

- **Harvard Kennedy School Library and Knowledge Services**
  Think Tanks and Research Centers
  http://guides.library.harvard.edu/hks/think_tank_search/

- **Nova Scotia Health Authority Hospital Library Services**
  Physical Rehabilitation Literature

- **Ontario Public Health Libraries Association**
  Canadian Public Health Information
  http://www.ophla.ca/customsearchcanada.htm
  U.S. State Public Health Information
  http://www.ophla.ca/customsearchusstates.htm
  Ontario Public Health Unit Websites
  http://www.ophla.ca/customsearchoph.htm
  Canadian Public Health Associations
  http://www.ophla.ca/customsearchcpha.htm

- **ScHARR Library—University of Sheffield**
  Netting the Evidence
  https://cse.google.com/cse/home?cx=004326897958477606950:djcbsrxkatm

- **University of Saskatchewan Library**
  Canadian Public Policy
  http://libguides.usask.ca/c.php?g=16374&p=90287

- **Virginia Commonwealth University**
  Drug Courts & Drug Policy Resources
  https://cse.google.com/cse/home?cx=004668642609100521661:i1udxn_28pc
  Drug and Alcohol Resources
  https://cse.google.com/cse/home?cx=004668642609100521661:baynin0u0bo&h
  l=en

- **Yale University Library**
  Non-Governmental Organizations
  https://cse.google.com/cse/home?cx=012681683249965267634%3Aq4g16p05-ao

---

Internet—more often than not using Google. While Google-powered search tools can be formidable resources for locating grey literature publications, there are—gasp—Google alternatives that offer their own noteworthy value.

Dogpile Web Search

http://www.dogpile.com/

Dogpile is a metasearch engine that returns search results from all of the best search engines, including Bing, Google, and Yahoo (Dogpile, "About Dogpile," retrieved on September 13, 2017, from http://www.dogpile.com/support/aboutus). The objective is to deliver a set of search results that is more comprehensive than the user would get using individual Internet search engines. An Advanced Search interface is not available, so targeted searching options are limited. A search in Dogpile can be used to compare search results from a Google search.

DuckDuckGo

https://duckduckgo.com/

Launched in 2008 ("About DuckDuckGo," retrieved on September 13, 2017, from https://duckduckgo.com/about), DuckDuckGo is an alternative search engine to Google. Privacy of searches is a priority for DuckDuckGo—personal information on searches is not collected or shared. There is no personalized searching either—the search results for a topic in DuckDuckGo will be the same, no matter if the search location is Bumpass, Pennsylvania; Moose Factory, Ontario; or Melbourne, Australia. If you are using structured Google searches to locate grey literature, also try entering your search terms in DuckDuckGo to see how your results vary.

MedNar

http://mednar.com/mednar

MedNar is a free federated search engine for Deep Web searching. Search results are ranked by relevancy and can be sorted by publication, author, topic, and source. An Advanced Search option is available, which is useful for focusing search results on grey literature.

Million Short

https://millionshort.com

Million Short's motto is "What Haven't You Found?," and this specialized search engine allows users to filter off the top web sites from search results ("About Million Short," retrieved on September 13, 2017, from https://millionshort.com/about).

A Million Short search provides the option to remove the top hundred, thousand, ten thousand, hundred thousand, or one million of the otherwise buried results. The aim of Million Short is to allow users to discover sites that are not highly ranked and to take the road less traveled. Results can be limited to location or language, along with other available settings. For grey literature searches, Million Short can be put to use to locate elusive hits from smaller organizations or as a supplement to a Google search to obtain more unbiased search hits.

Tor

https://www.torproject.org/

Tor is a free and open network that guards against Internet surveillance, for example, while communicating over a public network (Tor, "Tor: Overview," from https://www.torproject.org/about/overview.html.en). Tor works by masking your IP address and using Tor guards to prevent others from knowing the source and destination of your Internet searches. It keeps your searching behavior and interests anonymous. The Tor Bundle is an open access software and can be downloaded on a computer or mobile device. For grey literature searches, Tor offers an option to see what types of search results you can obtain when your search habits are not being tracked at all—Tor is the ultimate in depersonalized searching. Of course, there may be limited opportunities to install Tor on a workplace computer.

TURN OFF PERSONALIZED SEARCH RESULTS

Want to keep using Google, but not so up close and personal? If you are signed in to your Google account, your settings can be changed to turn off personalized search results. SEO Global for Google search is another option—it's an available Firefox extension that allows you to see search results from other geographical locations aside from your own (Redfly SEO Global for Google Search, retrieved on September 13, 2017, from https://addons.mozilla.org/en-US/firefox/addon/google-global/). The plug-in allows viewers to see both organic and paid Google search results as they appear in different countries, cities, regions, zip codes, and IP addresses.

SEARCH TIPS FOR GOOGLE-POWERED
SOURCES FOR GREY LITERATURE

Search Tips for Google

*Have a Clearly Defined Scope Before You Start a Google Grey
Literature Search*

Otherwise known as the "You Can't Have Your Cake and Eat It Too" search
tip. While it may be tempting to decide that a Google search should include
all sources from everywhere and produced by everybody—and Google cer-
tainly includes a lot of everything—it's not an attainable goal. A Google
search for grey literature is more likely to be fruitful if the search results are
limited to information from specific locations, countries, domains, or file
types. Also, deciding on the scope of your search from the beginning helps to
target sources that you know will be relevant.

*Remember the Difference between American and British
Vocabulary and Spelling*

Otherwise known as E. B. White's "Be Obscure Clearly" search tip. When
searching for grey literature publications from other countries, be mindful
that terminology can differ. And it's not as simple as changing the spelling of
"center" to "centre." For example, the term "college students" is commonly
used in the United States, while Australia, Canada, and the United Kingdom
use "university students." Another example would be search terms to capture
grey literature on Indigenous populations—in Canada, frequently used terms
would be "First Nations" or "First Peoples," but in the United States, the
terms "Native Americans" or "American Indians" are used. If the aim of your
grey literature search is to capture search results from international sources,
ensure that you are familiar with the nuances of vocabulary.

Have Advanced Search Commands at the Ready

Also known as the "Avoid the Maslow's Hammer" search tip: if all you have
is a hammer, then everything looks like a nail. A standard Google search is
simply ineffective and unreliable for identifying a wide range of distinctive
grey literature publications. Using the Advanced Search command in a Google
search will allow you to execute a more targeted search by selecting specific
domains, document types, or year range. Using the Advanced Google Search
command will enable the grey literature results to be more readily identified,
instead of most likely lurking in a far-off page of a standard Google search.

Exclude Search Results from Popular Sites

Also known as the Groucho Marx "I Don't Want to Belong to Any Club That Will Have Me as a Member" search tip. If a Google search for grey literature is retrieving search results from numerous popular non–grey lit sources, consider excluding those sites from your search. This is straightforward—sites can be excluded in the Google Advanced Search screen or by using the "–" command. But be well informed. For example, excluding the term "PubMed" may exclude grey literature publications that list PubMed as a search source, and excluding hits from the specific site http://www.ncbi.nlm.nih.gov/ (National Center for Biotechnology Information) will also exclude search hits from PubMed Commons, PubMed Health, and NCBI Bookshelf.

Have a Plan to Stop Searching

Also known as the "Know Your Limit" search tip. There is a lot in Google and Google Scholar, and there is not an effortless or efficient method to sift through all the search results. The other hurdle is that grey literature documents are similar to coyotes in an urban environment: they are purposefully shy and prefer to remain hidden. The challenge is to find a balance between reviewing a wide range of results and also keeping a Google search manageable. As previously mentioned, there is research suggesting that viewing only the first fifty search results is necessitated, because the most relevant search results will most likely be identified (Hepworth et al., 2011; Bielska, 2009; Hamilton Lopez, Singer Cohen, & Holve, 2012; Kelly et al., 2008).

Decide on Limiting Your Search to Specific Types of Grey Literature Publications

Also known as the "Look for Mr. Right, Not Mr. Right Now" search tip. What types of grey literature do you want to retrieve? If the goal is to identify synthesized sources of information, such as reports from think tanks or NGOs, or if you are searching for grey literature publications such as rapid reviews or evidence briefs, Google searching can be superior to other grey literature search methods. However, if the aim is to identify conference publications, dissertations, or documents from regulatory agencies, then other grey literature sources or search methods may be preferable to Google. For example, if you are searching for conference presentations, searching the websites of specific conferences or databases indexing conference publications may be more efficient than a Google search.

Google Scholar Search Tips

Check for Obvious Grey Lit Content

Otherwise known as "Taking a Test Drive." One way to test the grey litera-ture coverage of Google Scholar is to see if indispensable content is included before you execute a more substantial search. This can be accomplished by searching for a known grey literature publication, such as a specific confer-ence publication or treatment guideline. If the Google Scholar search does not retrieve the publication, then you will know that the Google Scholar grey lit-erature content on that topic or authored by that organization may be lacking.

Check for Recent Content

Otherwise known as the "Time and Tide Wait for No Man (Including Google Scholar)," search tip. Librarians and information professionals are often trusted to direct users to the most current information on a topic. As mentioned earlier in this chapter, Google Scholar's ranking gives preference to older, more frequently cited grey literature publications rather than newly emerging sources. But search results should provide current grey literature publications rather than a retro snapshot of grey literature publications from ten years ago. Confirming the currency of the grey literature content on a specific topic is a crucial search step, otherwise a great deal of relevant con-tent may be missed. For example, if you are familiar with a recently updated guideline from the CDC, see if a Google Scholar search will retrieve that publication.

Have a Narrow Search Strategy

Otherwise known as the Zig Ziglar "If You Aim at Nothing, You Will Hit It Every Time" search tip. Don't have a search strategy that will capture every and any type of search hit—instead, try to take steps to focus your search to retrieve grey literature. Past research has documented that Google Scholar searches retrieve more grey literature publications when the search terms are limited by title (Haddaway et al., 2015). Focusing a Google Scholar search is also a constructive search method for limiting the number of results from the published literature and increasing the retrieval of grey literature hits. A handy Advanced Search command is intitle, which limits search results to common grey literature search terms such as "report" or "white paper."

Google Scholar Is Not the Be All and End All for Grey Lit

Otherwise known as the "Not a One-Size-Fits-All" search tip. While past re-search has documented the benefits of using Google Scholar for identifying grey literature, and Google Scholar does contain far more types of grey literature than other academic databases, the best way to use Google Scholar effectively for searching grey literature is to be wary of its limitations. Since Google Scholar cannot always be used to reliably identify key grey literature sources, other methods should also be used, such as searching the websites of key organizations (Haddaway et al., 2015).

Google Custom Search Tips

Remember That Not All Relevant Results Will Be Displayed

Otherwise known as the "It's Just the Tip of the Iceberg" search tip. A substantial limitation of GCS is that it will only display ten pages of results. Therefore, there should be a plan for further investigating to see if there are more relevant results on your search topic. This can be accomplished either by revising your search terms to see if the number and types of results change, or by searching the individual websites discovered in a GCS for supplementary information.

Remember That Expert Search Commands Can Be Used in a GCS

While Leonardo da Vinci advised that "simplicity is the ultimate sophistication," this may not necessarily be an advisable Googling search tip. Even if searching a GCS can appear deceptively simple, your search results will be of higher quality if you use Advanced Google Search commands. All of Google's Advanced Search commands can be used in a GCS—for example, results from specific sites can be excluded, or you can simply search for results limited to specific file types, such as PDFs, to tease out the grey literature content.

RECOMMENDATIONS BY AGENCIES AND ORGANIZATIONS THAT CREATE KNOWLEDGE SYNTHESIS

Several health care agencies and organizations that support the development of evidence-based practice publications recommend that searches for evidence should include the grey literature. These recommendations are generally included in their publications on information retrieval guidelines. The following is an overview of Google-powered search tools that are recommended by select agencies that produce knowledge synthesis. The available search methodologies are not very detailed, but the available documentation can be used as a starting point.

The Campbell Collaboration

The Campbell Collaboration is an international, not-for-profit, NGO that "aims to help people make well-informed decisions about the effects of interventions in the social, behavioral, and educational arenas" (Campbell Collaboration, "Better Evidence for a Better World," retrieved from https://www.campbellcollaboration.org/). The Campbell Collaboration Information Retrieval Group has published a guide on information retrieval methods for systematic reviews called *Searching for Studies: A Guide to Information Retrieval for Campbell Systematic Reviews*. Section 3.3.3 of the guide recommends that Internet search engines such as Google can be used to identify potential studies, including unpublished studies. Searching the Web is advised toward the end of the search process for a review, in order to identify the most current information. Using Advanced Search commands is recommended for all Internet search engines, along with the inclusion of keywords such as "study," "studies," or "control group" to limit the results to empirical research. While Google Scholar is also listed as a search resource for reviews, it is not specifically recommended for identifying grey literature publications. Use of available topic-specific GCS engines is not listed in the recommendations.

Cochrane

Cochrane (previously the Cochrane Collaboration) is an independent, global, not-for-profit, NGO comprised of Cochrane contributors from over 130 countries. Cochrane's goals include producing up-to-date systematic reviews and other knowledge synthesis, and making that evidence available and accessible to a worldwide population (Cochrane, "About Us," 2017, retrieved from http://www.cochrane.org/about-us). Cochrane produces the *Cochrane Handbook for Systematic Reviews of Interventions* Version 5.1.0, which is a guide on the process of preparing and updating Cochrane systematic reviews. Section 6.2.26 of the handbook states that there is "little empirical evidence as to the value of using general internet search engines such as Google to identify potential studies." Cochrane's search recommendations are based on findings from the study *Evaluation of the Usefulness of Internet Searches to Identify Unpublished Clinical Trials for Systematic Reviews* (Eysenbach, Tuische, & Diepgen, 2001). Google Scholar is listed as a general search engine to use in conjunction with subject-specific databases, although Google Scholar is not specifically recommended for searching grey literature. Use of available topic-specific GCS engines is not listed in the recommendations.

Textbox 9.7. A Decision Aid for Google Search Tools

The following is a proposed decision aid for using Google, Google Scholar, and GCS for a grey literature search:

1. Do you need to identify a specific grey literature publication type?

Just as database searches in Medline or PsycInfo can be limited to review articles, a grey literature search can be restricted to specific grey lit publication types. Google searching for grey literature is an excellent way to identify grey lit documents such as reports or guidelines, but there are far more efficient search methods for locating relevant clinical trials or conference publications. Or if the aim of a grey literature databases is to locate U.S. federal government publications, then the search can be limited to such sources as *Catalog of U.S. Government Publications* or *The NTIS Bibliographic Database*, and the hassle of wading through a sea of Google search results can be avoided.

2. Do you need to identify grey literature publications from specific organizations?

If you know that you want to restrict your grey literature search to target results from specific organizations, such as the Pew Research Center or the RAND Corporation, don't meddle with Google or Google Scholar searching. The best bet is to search the specific websites, as you are less likely to miss relevant publications.

3. Not sure what grey lit is out there?

A structured Google search is a commanding search tool for identifying a wide range of grey literature available from local, national, and international sources. Just be mindful to add specific search restrictions in order to obtain a more manageable number of search results. For example, a clearly defined inclusion criterion such as the origin or the intended audience of the grey literature publication can be handy for narrowing down your search results. Another option is to have set criteria for the number of search results that will be viewed.

4. Looking for grey lit documents that provide instructional or implementation information? Also looking for grey literature publications intended for a specific audience?

Google can be a matchless grey literature search source for identifying publications such as online handbooks, toolkits, checklists, or guidelines for program implementation. It may frequently be simplest to search for such grey literature publications using Google, especially if you are not narrowing your search to results from specific organizations. Additionally, there are numerous grey literature publications intended for specific readers, such as child protection workers, community health workers, nurses, and family physicians. Google is an excellent search tool for identifying such publications.

5. Do you have other options besides Google Scholar?

If you have access to subscription databases for content such as dissertations or conference publications, it may be more efficient to use those sources for a grey literature search than Google Scholar. Additionally, there are a great number of free resources aside from Google Scholar to identify such grey literature publications as dissertations, treatment guidelines, or conference publications.

6. Is there a topic-specific GCS that matches your search topic?

GCS with grey literature content can also be used to identify topic-specific publications. If, for example, a user is hoping to identify grey literature publications on public health–related topics, searching available GCSs can be a quick way to identify grey literature content. There have also been past systematic reviews that used GCS as part of a structured search of grey literature (Godin et al., 2017).

7. Is the search for a systematic review, scoping review, or other type of knowledge synthesis publication?

There are only limited examples of structured Google searches for knowledge synthesis publications. As a result, there are no set or universally accepted standards on how to proceed with structured Google searching for grey literature. Grey literature searches that are part of a larger systematic review or scoping review search may be better served by using other grey literature sources whose use has been more clearly documented in the past. But there are past examples of using Google for systematic review searches, including the Childhood Well-being Research Center working paper "A Rapid Literature Review of Evidence on Child Abuse Linked to Faith or Belief" (Simon et al., 2012), "Considerations When Providing Mental Health First Aid to an LGBTIQ Person: A Delphi Study" (Bond et al.), "Building the Informatics Infrastructure for Comparative Effectiveness Research (CER): A Review of the Grey Literature" (Hamilton Lopez, Singer Cohen, & Holve, 2012), and "Employer Best Practice Guidelines for the Return to Work of Workers on Mental Disorder–Related Disability Leave: A Systematic Review" (Dewa et al., 2016). All of the above-mentioned publications clearly outline the search steps for structured Google searches.

8. Do you need to follow recommended search guidelines?

A librarian or information professional often may use published search guidelines to select search sources. If your overall search plan requires you to follow published search guidelines, you will find that Google searching for grey literature is currently not listed in the recommendations, and there is also limited guidance on using Google Scholar or other Google-powered search tools for identifying grey literature.

The Health and Medicine Division (HMD) of the National Academies of Sciences, Engineering, and Medicine

The HMD of the National Academies of Sciences, Engineering, and Medicine (formerly the Institute of Medicine) is a private U.S. not-for-profit institution with the aim of providing "independent, objective analysis and advice to the nation and conduct[ing] other activities to solve complex problems and inform public policy decisions related to science, technology, and medicine" (National Academies of Sciences, Engineering, and Medicine—HMD, "About HMD," September 2016, retrieved from http://www.nationalacademies.org/hmd/About-HMD.aspx). HMD has published recommended standards for conducting systematic reviews, and its publication *Finding What Works in Health Care: Standards for Systematic Reviews* outlines twenty-one standards for developing high-quality systematic reviews on comparative effectiveness research. Standard 3.2.5, on Web searching, lists that Internet searching is helpful for identifying grey literature publications, but "searching specific websites is more useful than general internet search engines, such as Google. . . . There is little empirical evidence for using general internet search engines, but it might be fruitful." Google Scholar is not listed as a recommended source for grey literature, but it is listed as a free alternative to the subscription databases Web of Science and Scopus. Use of available topic-specific GCS engines is not listed in the recommendations.

The Agency for Health Care Research and Quality (AHRQ)

The AHRQ is a U.S. governmental agency that is part of the U.S. Department of Health and Human Services. AHRQ's mission is "to produce evidence to make health care safer, higher quality, more accessible, equitable, and affordable, and to work within the U.S. Department of Health and Human Services and with other partners to make sure that the evidence is understood and used." The AHRQ Effective Health Care Program has published the *Methods Guide for Effectiveness and Comparative Effectiveness Reviews*, and the chapter "Finding Grey Literature Evidence and Assessing for Outcome and Analysis Reporting Biases When Comparing Medical Interventions: AHRQ and the Effective Health Care Program" does not list using Internet search engines such as Google to identify relevant grey literature on the World Wide Web; instead, searching specific websites such as ClinicalTrials.gov is advised. Additionally, the search guidelines recommend that if the "World Wide Web is used as an information source, the rationale for doing so must be clearly presented, along with the methods for searching." Google Scholar is recommended as a search source in addition to databases such as Web of Science or Scopus, but it is not specifically recommended as a source for grey literature publications. Use of available topic-specific GCS engines is not listed in the recommendations.

National Institute for Health and Care Excellence (NICE)

The NICE is a nondepartmental public body (NDPB) that is accountable to its sponsor department, the Department of Health, United Kingdom. NICE's mission is to improve outcomes for people using the National Health Service and other public health and social services. NICE produces evidence guidance and advice, including NICE guidelines and other evidence summaries. The publication *Developing NICE Guidelines: The Manual* mentions that identifying relevant conference publications may be essential for certain review questions. Appendix G, "Sources for Evidence Reviews," does not include Google searching or other Internet search engines as a source for identifying relevant grey literature publications. Google Scholar is recommended as a source for identifying relevant conference abstracts, but using Google Scholar to locate other types of grey literature is not mentioned. Use of available topic-specific GCS engines is not listed in the recommendations.

CONCLUSION

Google, Google Scholar, and GCS engines can be potent searching tools for locating grey literature, and everyday Google searches can be parlayed into more strategic search strategies. Currently, there is very limited evidence on the use of Google powered search tools in searches for knowledge synthesis; this should not preclude future use of Google powered search tools, as long as searchers are mindful of Google's limitations and biases. The research cited in this chapter may help a searcher decide whether to include Google powered search tools as part of a comprehensive search to identify all relevant grey literature publications or as quick search tool for less complicated requests.

BIBLIOGRAPHY

Antell, K., Strothmann, M., Chen, X., & O'Kelly, K. (2013). Cross-examining Google scholar. *Reference & User Services Quarterly*, *52*(4), 55–61, 279–282.
Bergman, M. K. (2001). White paper: The Deep Web: Surfacing hidden value. *Journal of Electronic Publishing*, *7*(1).

Bielska, I. (2009). *Using Population Health Surveys to Measure the use of Services and the Prevalence of Psychiatric and/or Behavioural Conditions in Individuals with an Intellectual Disability,*

Blackhall, K. (2007). Finding studies for inclusion in systematic reviews of interventions for injury prevention: The importance of grey and unpublished literature. *Injury Prevention: Journal of the International Society for Child and Adolescent Injury Prevention, 13*(5), 359.

Bond, K. S., Jorm, A. F., Kelly, C. M., Kitchener, B. A., Morris, S. L., & Mason, R. J. (2017). Considerations when providing mental health first aid to an LGBTIQ person: a Delphi study. *Advances in Mental Health, 15*(2), 183–197.

Bramer, W. M. (2016). Variation in number of hits for complex searches in Google Scholar. *Journal of the Medical Library Association: JMLA, 104*(2), 143–145.

Capriglione, S., Luvero, D., Plotti, F., Terranova, C., Montera, R., Scaletta, G., . . . & Angioli, R. (2017). Ovarian cancer recurrence and early detection: may HE4 play a key role in this open challenge? A systematic review of literature. *Medical Oncology, 34*(9), 164.

Dewa, C. S., Trojanowski, L., Joosen, M. C., & Bonato, S. (2016). Employer best practice guidelines for the return to work of workers on mental disorder–related disability leave: A systematic review. *The Canadian Journal of Psychiatry, 61*(3), 176–185.

Eliyahu, L., Kirkland, S., Campbell, S., & Rowe, B. H. (2016). The Effectiveness of Early Educational Interventions in the Emergency Department to Reduce Incidence or Severity of Postconcussion Syndrome Following a Concussion: A Systematic Review. *Academic emergency medicine, 23*(5), 531–542.

Eysenbach, J., Tuische, T. L., & Diepgen, G. (2001). Evaluation of the usefulness of internet searches to identify unpublished clinical trials for systematic reviews. *Medical Informatics and the Internet in Medicine, 26*(3), 203–218.

Falagas, M. E., Pitsouni, E. I., Malietzis, G. A., & Pappas, G. (2008). Comparison of PubMed, Scopus, Web of Science, and Google Scholar: Strengths and weaknesses. *FASEB Journal: Official Publication of the Federation of American Societies for Experimental Biology, 22*(2), 338–342.

Gehanno, J., Rollin, L., & Darmoni, S. (2013). Is the coverage of Google Scholar enough to be used alone for systematic reviews? *BMC Medical Informatics and Decision Making, 13*(1), 7.

Giustini, D., & Boulos, M. N. (2013). Google Scholar is not enough to be used alone for systematic reviews. *Online Journal of Public Health Informatics, 5*(2), 214.

Godin, K. M., Kirkpatrick, S. I., Hanning, R. M., Stapleton, J., & Leatherdale, S. T. (2017). Examining guidelines for school-based breakfast programs in Canada: A systematic review of the grey literature. *Canadian Journal of Dietetic Practice and Research, 78*(1), 1–9.

Goodman, M. (2015). *Future crimes: Everything is connected, everyone is vulnerable and what we can do about it.* Anchor.

Haddaway, N. R., Collins, A. M., Coughlin, D., & Kirk, S. (2015). The role of Google Scholar in evidence reviews and its applicability to grey literature searching. *PloS One, 10*(9), e0138237.

Hamilton Lopez, M., Singer Cohen, R., & Holve, E. (2012). Building the informatics infrastructure for comparative effectiveness research (CER): A review of the grey literature.

Hartling, L., Featherstone, R., Nuspl, M., Shave, K., Dryden, D. M., & Vandermeer, B. (2017). Grey literature in systematic reviews: A cross-sectional study of the contribution of non-English reports, unpublished studies and dissertations to the results of meta-analyses in child-relevant reviews. *BMC Medical Research Methodology*, *17*(1), 64.

Hepworth, N., Hooper, V., Hellebrandt, D., & Lankford, B. (2011). *What factors determine the performance of institutional mechanisms for water resources management in developing countries in terms of delivering pro-poor outcomes, and supporting sustainable economic growth? A systematic mapping of literature and evidence. Collaboration for environmental evidence*. Bangor.

Herrera, G. (2011). Google Scholar users and user behaviors: An exploratory study. *College & Research Libraries*, *72*(4), 316–330.

Holve, E., Segal, C., Lopez, M. H., Rein, A., & Johnson, B. H. (2012). The electronic data methods (EDM) forum for comparative effectiveness research (CER). *Medical Care, 50 Suppl*, S7–10.

Hopewell, S., McDonald, S., Clarke, M. J., & Egger, M. (2007). Grey literature in meta-analyses of randomized trials of health care interventions. *Cochrane Database of Systematic Reviews* 2007, Issue 2. Art. No.: MR000010. DOI: 10.1002/14651858. MR000010.pub3.

Jacsó, P. (2005). Google Scholar: The pros and the cons. *Online Information Review*, *29*(2), 208–214.

Junior, O. H., Guijarro-Martínez, R., de Sousa Gil, A. P., da Silva Meirelles, L., de Oliveira, R. B., & Hernández-Alfaro, F. (2017). Stability and surgical complications in segmental Le Fort I osteotomy: a systematic review. *International journal of oral and maxillofacial surgery*, *46*(9), 1071–1087.

Kelly, J., Sadeghieh, T., & Adeli, K. (2014). Peer review in scientific publications: benefits, critiques, & a survival guide. *EJIFCC*, *25*(3), 227.

Kelly, C. M., Jorm, A. F., Kitchener, B. A., & Langlands, R. L. (2008). Development of mental health first aid guidelines for suicidal ideation and behaviour: A delphi study. *BMC Psychiatry*, *8*(1), 17.

Kennedy, S., & Price, G. (2004). Web search—Google big news: "Google Scholar" is born.

Kesselman, M., & Watstein, S. (2005). Google Scholar and libraries: Point/counter-point. *Reference Services Review*, *33*(4), 380–387.

McGowan, J., & Sampson, M. (2005). Systematic reviews need systematic searchers. *Journal of the Medical Library Association: JMLA*, *93*(1), 74–80.

Meireles, C. G., Pereira, S. A., Valadares, L. P., Rêgo, D. F., Simeoni, L. A., Guerra, E. N., & Lofrano-Porto, A. (2017). Effects of metformin on endometrial cancer: Systematic review and meta-analysis. *Gynecologic oncology*, *147*(1), 167–180.

Neuhaus, C., Neuhaus, E., Asher, A., & Wrede, C. (2006). The depth and breadth of Google Scholar: An empirical study. *Portal: Libraries and the Academy, 6*(2), 127–141.

Orduña-Malea, E., Ayllón, J. M., Martín-Martín, A., & López-Cózar, E. D. (2014). About the size of Google Scholar: Playing the numbers. *ArXiv Preprint arXiv:1407.6239.*

Pariser, E. (2011). *The filter bubble: What the internet is hiding from you.* Penguin.

Poladian, C., & Stone, J. (2015, 26 Nov. Web. 7 Feb. 2015). Tour the Deep Web: Illegal marketplaces, book clubs and everything in between. *International Business Times: IBT Pulse.*

Quint, B. (2008). Changes at Google Scholar: A conversation with Anurag Acharya. *Journal of Library Administration, 47*(1–2), 77–79.

Ross, A. M., Kelly, C. M., & Jorm, A. F. (2014). Re-development of mental health first aid guidelines for suicidal ideation and behaviour: A delphi study. *BMC Psychiatry, 14*(1), 241.

Simon, A., Hauari, H., Hollingworth, K., & Vorhaus, J. (2012). *A rapid literature review of evidence on child abuse linked to faith or belief.* Childhood Well-Being Research Center, CWRC Working Paper, 15.

Southern, M. (2016, August 31). Latest Search Market Share Numbers: Google Search Up Across All Devices. [Blog post) Retrieved from https://www.searchenginejournal.com/august-2016-search-market-share/172078/.

Van der Roest, H. G., Wenborn, J., Pastink, C., Dröes, R. M., & Orrell, M. (2017). Assistive technology for memory support in dementia. *The Cochrane Library.*

Van Deursen, A. J., & Van Dijk, J. A. (2009). Using the internet: Skill related problems in users' online behavior. *Interacting with Computers, 21*(5–6), 393–402.

Chapter 10

Developing a Grey Literature Search Plan

Many types of grey literature, along with grey literature search sources, have been discussed in previous chapters. Yet not all grey literature searches are one and the same. Virginia Woolf said, "I am made and remade continually. Different people draw different words from me," and in a similar way, grey literature searches often call for varying search methods. This chapter will discuss doing a needs assessment for grey literature search requests, developing a grey literature search plan, and completing a grey literature search.

LEARNING OUTCOMES

The goal of this chapter is to provide librarians, information professionals, and library students with guidance on the following:

- determining specific questions to ask a patron requesting a grey literature search
- selecting the appropriate search process for a grey literature search
- drafting a search process/search agreement with a patron
- documenting a grey literature search strategy, including
  - tools for keeping track of grey literature search results
  - search filters and exclusion criteria for a grey literature search
  - drafting a methodology for a grey literature search
- sample grey literature searches
- critical appraisal of grey literature documents
- current documented best searching practices for grey literature

FIRST: NEEDS ASSESSMENT

A needs assessment has been defined as a process of acquiring a picture of strengths and weaknesses in order to improve and meet existing challenges (Altschuld & Witkin, 2000). Before beginning a grey literature search, a librarian should first determine what the desired goal of the grey literature search is, as this will help provide a structure for the search. A quick needs assessment is part of the planning process and can assist with making decisions. As discussed in earlier chapters, there is a vast amount of grey literature available, and it is neither feasible nor necessary to include all of this information in a search. The needs assessment process helps to identify which type of approach will be best for the requested grey literature search. This process will aid with making decisions on the following: how to document grey literature search results, what types of search filters to use, and the exclusion criteria that will be used. After conducting a needs assessment, a librarian or information professional will have identified the information that can then be used to commence the grey literature search.

THE REFERENCE INTERVIEW FOR
A GREY LITERATURE SEARCH

As James Thurber wrote, "It's better to know some of the questions than all of the answers." This rings quite true for drafting a grey literature search. The goal is to avoid the *E-trap*: grey lit from *everywhere*, by *everyone*, including *everything*. The basic principles of a tried-and-true reference interview provide much-needed guidance. The reference interview has been defined as a "conversation between a member of the library reference staff and a library user for the purpose of clarifying the user's needs and aiding the user in meeting those needs" (Bopp & Smith, 1995). As research on the reference interview has illustrated, this involves helping the patron formulate a query that clearly identifies what information is needed. There are multifarious components of a reference interview, including gathering general information and getting an overview of the problem, confirming the exact question, and giving information, advice, or instructions. During the reference interview, a librarian should ask the patron questions that will help direct the future grey literature search. At this stage, the librarian has an opportunity to document the patron's questions and potential difficulties with the request, which provides the foundation for the grey literature search planning process.

Moreover, many patrons will request a grey literature search without being familiar with what *actually* constitutes grey literature. If a librarian asks

Textbox 10.1. Scenario #1

Nathan Zuckerman is a research assistant working with a research team that includes an epidemiologist, a health economist, and oncologists. The team is working on a grant proposal to receive funding to perform a systematic review on the burden of cancer among Latino/Hispanic populations. Nathan's supervisors have asked him to provide a grey literature search that will be included in the grant application. Nathan goes to the library and asks the librarian how to limit his Medline search results to grey literature. The grant proposal deadline is in three weeks.

Textbox 10.2. Scenario #2

Dr. Chocho Machine is currently involved with a team that is responsible for researching literature for updating guidelines on the treatment of asthma. Her coauthors want to include both published and unpublished studies on the drug mepolizumab (NUCALA); the drug received FDA approval on November 4, 2015. Dr. Chocho Machine emails the library to ask for a search for unpublished studies on mepolizumab (NUCALA).

Textbox 10.3. Scenario #3

An interprofessional team of nurse mangers—Tigro, Winnifred, and a physician, Dr. Tabitha Monk—are looking for information on best practices on diabetes treatment in comorbid conditions. The team visits the library to ask for a quick literature search, but they also want to include grey literature. They are going to share the search results with their colleagues at their next professional practice departmental meeting, and the research results will be put into use for developing a workplan to guide program development. The interprofessional team requires the search results next week.

several key questions before the search for grey literature begins, potential ambiguities can be clarified, which will help ensure that there will not be significant barriers to overcome during the search process. When the right questions are asked, the search process may take less time and will have a clearly defined scope that can be used as a guide for future grey literature searches; it will also allow for the discovery of key and relevant documents.

The most suitable way to comprehend how vital it is to ask the right questions is to look at the types of requests that are made for a grey literature search. The following scenarios provide some examples.

All of the scenarios listed above provide examples of how there are several types of search requests that require a grey literature search. Regrettably, there is no one-size-fits-all approach for executing a grey literature search—there

---

Textbox 10.4. Scenario #4

Professor Maddie Miller is a health economist and is the project lead for a scoping review on the public health consequences of decriminalizing marijuana. Her team is interested in information from municipal, state/provincial, and federal governments, or reports from think tanks, but the team's preliminary search did not locate much information in journal literature. The research team would like assistance with formulating a plan for locating information from governmental sources and other organizations. Professor Miller's research team is currently in the planning stage for the scoping review and is not yet ready for a detailed search.

---

is not even a one-size-fits-*most* approach. Librarians and other information professionals need to ask definitive questions in order to provide vital guidance. Grey literature requests may not be as daunting after specific issues have been discussed and clarified. As Dorthey Parker said, "It's not the tragedies that kill us; it's the messes." If librarians ask the following ten questions, they will find it less burdensome to decide what type of grey literature search is required. The art of grey literature searching involves imposing (or attempting to impose) order on the disarray of available information—and it guards against a search going sideways.

Let's examine our Top Ten questions in greater detail using our four previously laid-out scenarios.

Textbox 10.5. Top Ten Questions to Ask a Patron

---

1. What types of grey literature would the patron like to include?
2. How much detail is required?
3. Is there a specific geographical focus for the grey literature search?
4. Should the websites of specific organizations be included in the grey literature search?
5. Is this grey literature search request being used to produce a publication or document that is going to be submitted for peer review?
6. Is there a specific year range for the search?
7. Should specific grey literature sources be included in the grey literature search? If so, why should those specific sources be included in the grey literature search?
8. What is the time frame for completing the grey literature search?
9. Should the search be limited to evidence-based practice documents?
10. Are specific search guidelines—such as those outlined in the *Cochrane Handbook for Systematic Reviews of Interventions*—required?

What Types of Grey Literature Would the Patron Like to Include?

Before a grey literature search is commenced, there should be an exceptionally structured and candid discussion with the patron on the types of grey literature that should be included in the search results. Many will often ask for all types of grey literature to be included. The scenarios listed above provide examples of why a search encompassing every and any type of grey literature would *not* be actionable. Also, if a librarian asks a patron what types of grey literature should be included, much can be gleaned about the patron's information needs.

First, the librarian is able to gauge the patron's comprehension of grey literature. For example, in Scenario #1, Nathan Zuckerman may need to have the hidden mysteries of grey literature demystified for him before he receives the search results from the much-needed grey literature search. Otherwise, he will not comprehend what types of grey literature were included in the search results and why. In Scenario #2, Dr. Chocho Machine is specifically requesting information from unpublished studies. This type of grey literature search would be focused on locating completed clinical trials, conference publications, or information from regulatory agencies. Also, if a patron doesn't know what a grey literature search is, perhaps the patron doesn't require a grey literature search immediately—a bit of gentle bibliographic training may be required first.

How Much Detail Is Required?

The level of detail required for a search depends on the reason for the search request. For example, Dr. Chocho Machine is requesting a grey literature search to build upon the evidence base for guideline development. Performing a grey literature search on her topic would require searching all relevant sources, and such a search could potentially retrieve an abundant number of results. Since Nathan Zuckerman is asking for a grey literature search as part of a grant request to complete a proposed systematic review, he may only be in need of (or desperate for) a methodology on how the grey literature search will be conducted. As a result, he does not require detailed search results, but he will still need a search methodology outlining which grey literature sources will be searched. And in Scenario #3, Tigro, Winnifred, and Dr. Tabitha Monk may not want to receive an exhaustive list of search results. Instead, it may be more advisable to provide them with just a select few grey literature search documents that are germane to their reference request.

Is There a Specific Geographical Focus for the Grey Literature Search?

Potential grey literature search sources may be available from a wide range of countries and locations. Asking patrons if they have a specific geographical focus will help narrow down the number of sources that will be searched. For example, in Scenario #2 Dr. Chocho Machine may only be interested in unpublished studies for conference presentations in English or completed clinical trials from the United States or Canada. However, in Scenario #4, the researchers may need information on marijuana decriminalization that includes international sources, perhaps from the Netherlands.

Should the Websites of Specific Organizations Be Included in the Grey Literature Search?

A librarian should always ask patrons if they know of any particular organizations that may be sources of information on their research topic. If patrons provide the names of these organizations, they should be included in the grey literature search by searching the individual websites of each organization. As previously mentioned, there are numerous key search sources, such as databases, web checklists, or topic-specific Google Custom Search engines. For example, if CADTH's *Grey Matters* (see Chapter 8) is used for structuring a search on a topic such as child abuse risk assessment, the librarian should ensure that all the essential sources for grey lit are included on the checklist and determine if supplementary searching is required. In Scenario #4, the researchers want to include search results on the public health consequences of marijuana legalization, but the U.S. Office of National Drug Control Policy is not included on CADTH's *Grey Matters* checklist. This is through no fault of the *Grey Matters* checklist, since the scope of the search source specifically includes health technology and evidence-based practice.

Is This Grey Literature Search Request Being Used to Produce a Publication or Document That Is Going to Be Submitted for Peer Review?

If librarians ask this question in advance, they can avoid many potential bumps in the road ahead. When librarians or information professionals query if the grey literature search request is for a document that is going to be submitted for peer review, they will have much advance warning regarding what level of detail is required, the need to provide potential justification for search terms they will use, and what type of search documentation they will need to record. Even if the grey literature search request is for an internal document, there will be more flexibility in explaining the search methodology and documentation of search results. For example, since Nathan Zuckerman and Dr. Chocho Machine from Scenarios #1 and #2 are working on projects that may be subjected to peer review, there is a chance that the chosen search methodology will be criticized. However, in Scenario #3, Tigro, Winnifred, and Dr. Tabitha Monk only want to include a grey literature search so they can review the research in their professional practice meeting. Although the librarian or information professional should have clearly documented search methods and be able to explain the search process, the level of detail required is not the same.

Is There a Specific Year Range for the Search?

Similar to database searches for relevant published literature, searches on grey literature can also be limited to a specific year range. If librarians ask for guidance regarding year range, they will be able to narrow down search hits to the documents that are most relevant. For example, in Scenario #2, Dr. Chocho Machine may only be interested in unpublished studies from the past ten years.

Should Specific Grey Literature Search Sources Be Included in a Grey Literature Search? If So, Why Should Those Specific Sources Be Included in the Grey Literature Search?

As mentioned earlier, all grey literature search sources and document types have advantages and disadvantages. Patrons may expect to see a specific search source listed in their search methodology, even though the search source may not be relevant. For example, patrons may expect to see Google Scholar listed as grey literature source that was searched. But as mentioned in Chapter 9, Google Scholar is not always an ideal search source for grey literature. If a librarian asks a patron whether specific sources should be searched, there will be an opportunity to tell the patron why a search source should perhaps *not* be included. For example, the researchers in Scenario #4 may not know that Google Scholar will not retrieve information on marijuana decriminalization from many government sources. Or Dr. Chocho Machine may be unaware that Google Scholar is not ideal for locating unpublished studies or other information from regulatory agencies. Providing justifications for search methods before the grey literature search is started is better than explaining an omission afterward.

What Is the Time Frame for Completing the Grey Literature Search?

If patrons have a flexible deadline for receiving grey literature search results, more search sources can be included. If a patron needs a grey literature search quickly, then librarians have the opportunity to narrow the search results to include only the most pertinent sources or the sources that can be searched expediently. For example, in Scenario #3, Tigro, Winnifred, and Dr. Tabitha Monk require search results sooner rather than later, so there is only time to search for a few key sources. However, the research team in Scenario #4 does not have a set deadline, so the search to identify grey literature documents on marijuana decriminalization can be more all-encompassing.

Should the Search Be Limited to Evidence-Based Practice Documents?

A patron may only be interested in grey literature documents that are guidelines or other types of evidence-based practice documents that summarize available information. Not all patrons will want or need to have primary research as part of their grey literature search. For example, in Scenario #3, Tigro, Winnifred, and Dr. Tabitha Monk are not likely to find unpublished studies or dissertations worthwhile for their request. Grey literature documents from such sources as the National Institute for Clinical Effectiveness and the Canadian Diabetes Association would be more beneficial.

Are Specific Search Guidelines Required?

A patron may be required to have a search completed in accordance with specific guidelines, such as the Cochrane guidelines mentioned in previous chapters. Search guidelines that have a list of the types and sources of grey literature that should be included in a search do not rule out additional sources or search methods. For example, a topic-specific Google Custom Search engine could almost be effortlessly added to a search, along with the recommended sources on the list. Following search guidelines ensures that material sources are not neglected and provides sagacious advice on developing a grey literature search plan, but a search can always benefit from the addition of other grey literature sources.

Textbox 10.6. Inclusion/Exclusion

- Geographical location
- Grey literature document types (to select which search methods or sources should be searched)
- Language

TIME TO START THE GREY SEARCH?

Don't put the horse before the cart—grey literature search steps should be followed in a logical, not nonsensical, order. Before a grey literature search is started, the Top Five decisions should be made:

1. Inclusion/exclusion criteria
2. Search filters
3. When to stop searching
4. Tracking search history/search terms
5. Record keeping of results

Decision #1: Inclusion/Exclusion Criteria for a Grey Literature Search

It is best to decide on the inclusion/exclusion criteria before a librarian begins a grey literature search. Inclusion/exclusion criteria are specifications set in advance of a grey literature search, and they enable a librarian to consider what type of grey literature hits will not be relevant before the search begins. A librarian needs to determine what inclusion/exclusion criteria will be used before a search commences, as this will aid with decisions on what types of grey literature sources will be searched. Standards for exclusion criteria in grey literature searches are different from those for Medline searches. A vast array of sources and grey literature document types are available, and it is not feasible to search grey literature and then apply exclusion criteria to the search results. Also, unlike a database search, a grey literature search does not include the option to limit a specific set of search results after a search has been executed. An example of an inclusion criterion is a grey literature search that would only include grey literature documents from U.S. federal government sources and exclude documents from state governments or municipalities. Before the librarian begins searching, the decision is made to only search sources that will identify U.S. federal government publications, such as those on the website for the National Technical Information Service (www.ntis.gov).

Textbox 10.7. Selected Search Filters

Below is a list of search filters that can be used for a grey literature search.

- Types of grey literature documents
  Conference presentations
  Dissertations
  Clinical trials/unpublished research studies
  Guidelines/evidence-based practice documents

- Organization filters
  Documents from specific organizations
  Documents from governmental organizations on the municipal, state/provincial, and federal level
  Documents from non-governmental organizations

Decision #2: Deciding on Search Filters or Search Hedges for a Grey Literature Search

Search filters or hedges are defined as a combination of terms, generally drawing on free-text, controlled vocabulary, and metadata (Wilczynski, McKibbon, & Haynes, 2011). Just as there are search filters to locate specific study types (such as randomized clinical trials) in a database search (Lefebvre, Manheimer, & Glanville, 2011), there are also search filters that can be used for a grey literature search. Our "Top Ten Questions to Ask a Patron" illuminates how various grey literature searches may require search filters. However, unlike search filters for Medline searches, grey literature search filters may need to be selected at the beginning of the search process. Sources and methods for locating grey literature do not have search filters that are as finely tuned as other information sources, such as databases and library catalogs. Search filters can be used in the search process, either by employing specific search commands (such as for structured Google searching) or by restricting the results of a completed search to a specific type of grey literature (such as completed clinical trials).

Decision #3: When to Stop Searching

There isn't a touchstone for benchmarking when a grey literature search is completed—just as there is not a gold standard for executing a grey literature search (Paez, 2017; Conn et al., 2003; Bellefontaine & Lee, 2014; Adams et al., 2016). For quick grey literature searches, it can be fairly painless and uncomplicated to decide when to stop searching, since only a few grey literature hits may be required. For example, a team may simply require a nominal selection of synthesized sources of information, such as guidelines or reports. For more wide-ranging grey literature searches, the process is more labyrinthine, but the best bet is to decide *which* types of grey literature documents are most fitting for the search topic and from *where*. For example, if the intention of a grey literature search is to pinpoint relevant unpublished clinical trials available in English, clinical trial data, or information from regulatory agencies such as the Food and Drug Administration, then a search should retrieve a plentiful range of relevant sources. There has been a limited amount of research of only viewing the first fifty search results from a Google search, because the most relevant search results will most likely be identified (Hepworth et al., 2011; Bielska 2009; Lopez, Cohen, & Holve, 2012; Kelly et al., 2008). But achieving true data saturation may be impractical or futile for grey literature searches, akin to Captain Ahab on his quest for Moby Dick. Instead the aim should be to include a wide range of sources and search methods, so a diverse set of end results will be retrieved. As American singer Bessie Smith said, "It's a long old road, but I know I am gonna find the end"—once you take the multitude of search factors into consideration, the direction is yours to take.

Decision #4: Drafting a Search Agreement and Search Process Plan with a Patron

After a librarian has decided whether to use a detailed grey literature approach or a more focused one, the search process can then be reviewed with the patron. Although writing up a search agreement and a search process may seem like another cumbersome time commitment, it may eventually save time down the road: as noted sixteenth-century Englishman John Heywood wrote, "The more haste, the less speed." A search agreement and a search process plan can be part of a formal search agreement between the librarian and the patron. Ideally it should be drafted *before* the grey literature search begins. Having such a document is useful for both parties because it helps define the expectations of a grey literature search. It is onerous to re-execute a search strategy *with revisions* because it will likely require starting the search over from scratch. If a librarian has determined requisite steps to document the expected needs that a grey literature search will fulfill, then there is less likelihood that search revisions will be required.

Drafting an outline for the search process aids with completing a grey literature search using a predefined search structure. Yet sometimes drafting a detailed search process is not always imperative—it may only be required if the grey literature search is for such outputs as a systematic review, scoping review, or guideline. If required, the draft search process for a detailed grey

---

Textbox 10.8.

A search agreement and search process plan could include the following:

- sources that will be searched
- types of grey literature documents that will be included
- databases that will be searched
- Web checklists that will be used
- key organization websites that will be searched
- search terms that will be used
- how the search strategy and results will be documented
- search filters
- inclusion/exclusion criteria
- timeline for completion

---

literature search can list the sources to be searched, the methods for the search, the search terms to be used, and how the search results will be documented.

Decision #5: Keeping Track of Grey Literature Search Terms and Search Hits

The last decision is how the grey literature search terms and search hits should be recorded. A librarian should retain a record of the search results, methodology, and strategy so that there is archival documentation. There are assorted methods for keeping track of the results from a grey literature search; but the method a librarian selects depends on several factors. For example, the rationale for the search and the types of documents included might be factors that need to be taken into account. As with database searches, it is paramount that there is adequate information so a search can be re-executed. Examples of the types of information that should be recorded include the date a search was completed, the sources searched, the search terms used, and the search results that were retrieved.

Tools for Keeping Track of Grey Literature Search Results

It is imperative to capture both the source *and* the content of the results. Webpage content can be like a great magician—it can be an outstanding disappearing act, and there may be a Houndini-inspired escape act of relevant results if search hits are only documented by links rather than a full text capture. Web pages can transform quickly; it is not rare for a link to a report to be removed or for an organization to merge with another. A librarian should not only keep track of the search terms or search methods used, but should also either print or save the complete record and content of the results. For

---

Textbox 10.9. Sample Search Process for a Grey Literature Search

---

The following is an example of a detailed search process for a grey literature search:

Grey Literature (Websites and Unpublished Documents): The grey literature on prescription monitoring programs will be searched using a search strategy drafted by a librarian. To ensure that grey literature searching is done in a standardized and comprehensive way, the following methods for locating relevant grey literature publications will be used.

Databases: Databases indexing grey literature will be searched for relevant publications, including the Canadian Electric Library, ERIC, OpenSigle, TRIP database, New York Academy of Medicine: Grey Literature Report, and the National Technical Information Service. Databases indexing conference papers (BIOSIS Previews/Conference Papers Index) and dissertations (PyscInfo/ProQuest Dissertations & Theses/Scopus) will also be searched.

Web Checklist: Key organizations publishing in the area of evidence-based practice will be identified by using a peer-reviewed Web check for grey literature searching; the Web checklist to be used is *Grey Matters: A Practical Tool for Searching Health-Related Grey Literature* and is published by CADTH. Using a Web checklist will allow for systematic searching of the listed websites. For more information on CADTH's *Grey Matters*, visit CADTH's website at https://www.cadth.ca/resources/finding-evidence/grey-matters-practical-search-tool-evidence-based-medicine.

Key Organizations: Additional individual websites of known relevant organizations and federal, provincial, and state governments that may be sources of grey literature will be searched, especially organizations publishing grey literature documents related to behavioral health. In particular, the websites for individual prescription monitoring programs worldwide will be searched. In addition, the websites from the following organizations will be searched: Alliance of States with Prescription Monitoring Programs; Prescription Drug Monitoring Program Center of Excellence, Brandeis University; National Association of Boards of Pharmacy; Agency for Healthcare Research and Quality; Best Practices in Mental Health and Addictions BC; Canadian Health Services Research Foundation (CHSRF); Centre for Health Economics and Policy Analysis (CHEPA)—McMaster University; Canadian Evaluation Society—Unpublished Literature Bank; Canadian Institute for Health Information (CIHI); Government of Canada Publications; Health Canada; National Guideline Clearinghouse; National Information Center on Health Services Research and Health Care Technology (NICHSR); National Library of Medicine—HSRProj (Health Services Research in Progress); Ontario Ministry of Health and Long-Term Care; Ontario Prevention Clearinghouse.

Internet Search Engines: Additionally, a structured Google search will be executed for publications that may be available elsewhere and missed by using other search methods. The Google search would be limited to pages from the following countries—United States and Canada. Additionally, CAMH Library Google Custom Search will be searched to identify grey literature documents from over 200 organizations. The Google grey literature search will also be re-executed in the search engine DuckDuckGo, to account for any personalized searching bias from the Google searches.

example, if the abstract of a conference publication is identified as being from the website of the World Heart Conference, the content should be saved rather than just captured with a link. The more detailed the record keeping of information from individual websites, the better. For example, the *Cochrane Handbook for Systematic Review of Interventions* advises printing the content from websites to ensure that access to information is not lost (Lefebvre et al., 2011).

There are many free and widely available tools for keeping track of grey literature search hits.

SELECTING A SEARCH PROCESS THAT IS THE BEST FIT FOR A REQUEST

As our Top Ten questions previously explored, there are various methods for commencing a grey literature search and deciding upon which search sources should be included. Not all grey literature search requests require an overly detailed search process. If the intention of a search is to quickly identify key sources, then librarians and information professionals can select a search process that will only retrieve the most on-topic results. Nonetheless, a librarian would still need to outline what type of search process was used, as this assists with explaining the limitations of the search. For example, if the grey literature search is for a request that is attempting to identify all the available evidence using a systematic approach, then a more detailed search process would be required. If the grey literature search is for a systematic review or a scoping review, then there also needs to be a highly detailed search approach.

Although the appropriate search process was addressed briefly during the discussion of the contrasting search scenarios, a grey literature search may fall into one of many categories.

A Quick Grey Literature Search, with the Goal of Locating Very Few Select Hits

This type of search would provide a general overview of information. Examples of this are searches on how to help firefighters talk to apartment residents about hording issues in units, or the use of the prone position in patient restraints.

Suggested methods:

- Check for available topic-specific Google Custom Search engines
- Structured Google Searching

Textbox 10.10. Tools for Recording Keeping

Ready-Made Web Checklists

Many web checklists provide a set format for tracking search terms and search hits.

- CADTH and Ontario Public Health are easily downloadable documents
- Search steps can be outlined, along with the specific search hits retrieved

MS Office

Tools that are available in MS Office can be easily used to create search logs to keep track of grey literature search results.

- A table can be created in MS Word, and MS Excel spreadsheets can be used for recording relevant information about grey literature search results.
- Examples of select MS Excel fields include:
  date of search
  source/location
  search terms used
  number of results
  grey literature document types identified
  date the source was searched

- The same information can also be captured using MS Word rather than MS Excel.

Google Docs

Google Docs offers a free online version for creating search logs.

- The benefit of creating a Google Doc is that the information can be effortlessly shared online.
- Since Google Docs is conducive for sharing access, a grey literature search can be performed in collaboration with others.

Other Methods

Results of a quick grey literature search can simply be listed in an email.

- Include such information as title, producer, grey literature document type, and a link to the cached page.
- Annotations on the content of the grey literature documents may be helpful.
- Limitations of quick grey literature searches should also be acknowledged—for example, the included results may only represent a proportion of the available material.

Textbox 10.11. Information to Include on Search Logs

- Name of source, including website link and other contact information
- Type of source (e.g., institutional repository, database for dissertations or conference publication, Internet search engine)
- Date of search
- Search terms used
- Number of search hits retrieved
- Number of relevant search hits selected
- Where to access saved search results

- Searching subject-specific databases (such as NIOSH-2 or the SafetyLit database)
- Searching databases for evidence-based practice (such as the National Guidelines Clearinghouse)

A Grey Literature Search for Specific Information from a Predefined List of Organizations

The list of predefined organizations may be sourced from a web checklist such as CADTH's *Grey Matters: A Practical Tool for Searching Health-Related Grey Literature* (see Chapter 8) or from a list of organizations identified by a librarian or patron. The search hits would only include documents from specific organizations, such as the Centers for Disease Control and Prevention (CDC) and the World Health Organization (WHO). An example of this search is lifestyle interventions for diabetes.

Suggested methods:

- Check for available topic-specific Google Custom Search engines
- Use a web checklist (such as *Gray Matters: A Practical Search Tool for Searching Health-Related Grey Literature*)
- Identify relevant organizations using a directory (such as the National Directory of Non-Profit Organizations)

A Grey Literature Search That Focuses on Only Locating Specific Types of Grey Literature Publications

This type of grey literature search would concentrate on completing a search where the goal is to locate specific types of *documents*, instead of limiting the search to results from specific *organizations*. This type of search uses multiple search sources to locate specific document types. Examples include a search to find unpublished clinical trial results on brain cancer and immunotherapy. This search would focus on finding results from databases indexing conference presentations, dissertations, and websites such as ClinicalTrials. gov.

Suggested methods:

- Search specific websites (such as ClinicalTrials.gov for completed clinical trials)
- Search specific databases indexing conference publications (such as PapersFirst)
- Search specific databases indexing dissertations (such as ProQuest Dissertations and Thesis
- Search the websites of relevant conferences

A Grey Literature Search That Intends to Identify a Great Number of Results, Even When Potential Sources May Be Unknown

In this type of grey literature search, the librarian may wish to identify new sources of information. This may be the case if the subject area is exceptionally broad and diffusely defined. The librarian might approach this search using a multitude of search methods, such as grey literature search databases, web checklists, searching specific websites, and web searching. This type of search has an extremely detailed approach to investigating and identifying the wide range of information available. Examples of this type of search include identifying key grey literature publications on providing health services to homeless populations, or strategies to improve maternal and infant health care.

Suggested methods:

- Use a web checklist (such as CADTH's *Grey Matters: A Practical Tool for Searching Health-Related Grey Literature* or the Ontario Public Health Libraries Association's *Public Health Grey Literature Sources*)
- Search a wide range of sources for specific grey literature types (for example, reports from think tanks such as the RAND Corporation, government publications, and unpublished research from clinical trials or other research studies)
- Identify relevant organizations using a directory (such as NIRA'S International Think Tank Directory) and search the websites of individual organizations (such as the National Coalition for the Homeless)
- Search subject-specific grey literature databases (such as POPLINE)
- Structured Google searching

- Search alternatives to Google, such as Million Short
- Check for available topic-specific Google Custom Searches
- Search select institutional repositories (if an institution is noted for its research in a particular area).

A Quick Grey Literature Search to Prepare for a More Detailed Grey Literature Search in the Future

This may sound contradictory—after all, what is the rationale of doing a grey literature search that is not complete? The reason a librarian would do this type of grey literature search is to aid with drafting the needed scope of a future grey literature search. The approach of this type of search is exploratory and could be utilized to draft the grey literature search methodology required for a grant proposal. The aim is to undertake a quick environmental scan of the types of grey literature publications that are available rather than identifying *all* the relevant results. The librarian may not have decided what types of grey literature documents should be included, what sources should be searched, or if a web checklist including specific organizations should be used. The intention of this type of search is not to identify specific grey literature documents; rather, it is to identify *sources* that will be searched for grey literature documents. However, a librarian must be familiar with where the relevant documents would be published, which is why this is only an exploratory search. An example of this type of search is one that would identify potential sources of grey literature that provide information on improving care for patients with metastatic breast cancer.

Recommended search methods:

- A quick, structured Google search to see the range of grey literature publications available
- Check for available topic-specific (no need to search) Google Custom Search engines
- A quick Google Scholar search to see the range of both national and international grey literature documents
- Identify topic-specific databases (such as the TRIP Database or the National Guideline Clearinghouse)
- Identify sources for specific grey literature publications (such as unpublished clinical trials or dissertations)

A Grey Literature Search for a Systematic Review

Grey literature can play a key role in a systematic review since its inclusion broadens the available evidence base (Benzies et al., 2006; Blackhall,

2007; Hammerstrøm, Wade & Jørgenson; Hopewell et al., 2007; McAuley, Tugwell, & Mohen, 2000; Rothstein & Hopewell, 2009), and those involved with searching and conducting systematic reviews should include unpublished research to guard against bias (Blackhall & Ker, 2007). Past research analyzing a sample of Cochrane systematic reviews documented that the majority included unpublished research (Hartling et al., 2017), but other research has documented that numerous meta-analyses from other sources did not include unpublished data in the pool of studies analyzed (Cook et al., 1993). There is a deficit of uniform standards or explicit directions on how to search for relevant grey literature documents for inclusion in a review (Goden et al., 2015; Mahood, Van Eerd, & Irwin, 2013; Paez, 2017; Adam, Smart, & Huff, 2016), as there is no gold standard for grey literature searching (Paez, 2017; Conn et al., 2003; Bellefontaine & Lee, 2014; Adams et al., 2016). But since a systematic review's aim is to synthesize the results of several individual studies, and those studies would likely be ones containing original reports of research findings, a grey literature search would most likely concentrate on locating original research that has not been published rather than secondary sources of information. Examples of primary unpublished research would be completed clinical trials, clinical trial data, dissertations, conference publications, information from regulatory agencies, unpublished empirical research, and other unpublished data. Systematic reviews require systematic searching (McGowan & Sampson, 2005), and while it's a trial to execute a systematic search of grey literature, a methodical approach can still be utilized.

A grey literature search for a systematic review can include a diverse range of sources and methods to identify unpublished research, just as a systematic review search often includes a multitude of searches in multiple databases. Examples would be a search on the potential adverse effects of the drug indomethacin for halting premature labor, or prevalence of HIV testing in minority populations.

Suggested methods:

- Search specific websites containing unpublished research (such as ICTRP Search Portal for completed clinical trials; the YODA Project or HSRProj for unpublished research studies)
- Search specific websites of relevant conferences
- Search specific databases indexing conference publications (such as BIOSIS Previews)
- Search specific databases indexing dissertations (such as Canadian Thesis Portal)
- Search institutional repositories for unpublished original research

- Search sources to locate unpublished epidemiological data, including governmental agencies (such as the Centers for Disease Control and Prevention)
- Google Scholar (since it is increasingly being listed as a grey literature source in systematic reviews)
- Search databases including grey literature (such as PsycExtra or Wonder)
- Search for regulatory documents from the FDA or the European Medicines Agency
- Ask the research team if other grey literature publications should be included and search additional sources for that information

VERY LAST SEARCH STEPS

If a grey literature search has been completed for a manuscript being sub-mitted for publication and there has been a significant delay between the completion of the grey literature search and the data extraction, a quick search update should be attempted. Updating a grey literature search may not be as simple as rerunning a saved PubMed search, but most grey litera-ture search sources allow a search to be limited to a specific year range. Key organizations or known authors with relevant research output can also be contacted individually to check for additional information.

You Have the Search Results: Now What?

As discussed in Chapter 2, it is a misconception that grey literature documents are low-quality and inferior to peer-reviewed published literature. Woefully, too often grey literature documents are not included in a search because of the possible lack of peer review. Research has documented that a substan-tial percentage of grey literature publications are indeed peer-reviewed—for example, dissertations and organizational reports have been subject to some level of peer review.

Grey literature documents can also be appraised in a manner similar to the appraisal of the methodological quality of a systematic review or a clinical trial. Specific quality checklists—comparable to such tools as the *Cochrane Risk of Bias Assessment Tool* or the *JBI Critical Appraisal Checklist for Case Control Studies*—are available for grey literature. Although librarians and information professionals are not often involved with the data extraction or evaluation of results, they can provide suggestions on methods for deter-mining the quality of grey literature documents.

The first quality checklist is the exceptionally tried-and-true C.R.A.P. Test for evaluating resources. The C.R.A.P. Test was developed by Molly

Beestrum and Kenneth Orenic, and had been adapted by several libraries to help guide the evaluation of online information. Four major elements of a source are assessed: Currency, Reliability, Authority, and Purpose/Point of view. The C.R.A.P. Test can be used to evaluate grey literature documents and is especially well suited to assessing grey literature documents to be included in a quick grey literature search. The C.R.A.P. Test is also especially practical for appraising grey literature documents from think tanks with political affiliations, such as the Hoover Institution or the Rosa Luxemburg Foundation. The C.R.A.P. Test is widely available online.

Another source for evaluating grey literature documents is the AACODS checklist, developed by Jess Tyndall. The AACODS is somewhat comparable to the C.R.A.P. Test, but it is more suited specifically for a comprehensive evaluation of grey literature documents. The AACODS checklist evaluates for the following six criteria: Authority, Accuracy, Coverage, Objectivity, Date, and Significance. The checklist has been adapted by NICE to assess grey literature documents for inclusion in reviews. The AACODS is available at https://dspace.flinders.edu.au/jspui/bitstream/2328/3326/4/AACODS_Checklist.pdf.

WRITING UP A GREY LITERATURE
SEARCH METHODOLOGY

The approach for writing up a grey literature search methodology depends on the purpose for the initial grey literature search. Certain types of grey literature searches will require a more detailed search methodology write-up—examples would be searches for systematic reviews, scoping reviews, and guidelines. Quick grey literature searches may not require a detailed search methodology write-up. Generally, the search methodology of a grey literature search will be included in the search methodology that also addresses the database searches. Unfortunately, it is acutely common for authors to simply *mention* that a grey literature search was completed, without providing any supplementary information.

Guidelines on how to write up a search methodology can be reviewed from such sources as *Developing NICE Guidelines: The Manual*, which NICE has adapted for writing up a grey literature search methodology. If an appendix can be included with the submitted manuscript, then there will be opportunity to provide details on how the grey literature search was completed.

Textbox 10.12. Selected Steps for Writing Up a Grey Literature Search Methodology

---

- List the search terms used
- Provide details on the development of the search strategy
- Indicate what types of grey literature documents were included
- List search sources used, such as databases or web searches
- Indicate whether the search results were limited to specific grey literature document types
- List any search filters for the search results
- List any inclusion/exclusion criteria for the search results
- List any language or year limits

EXAMPLES OF GREY LITERATURE SEARCHES

The following publications also provide noteworthy examples of completed grey literature searches and include thorough details on the search methods employed. Ralph Waldo Emerson said, "Do not go where the path may lead, go instead where there is no path and leave a trail"—in this spirit, many of the following citations provide examples of varying and newly emerging methodologies for searching grey literature.

- **Source**: Elliott, M. J., Gil, S., Hemmelgarn, B. R., Manns, B. J., Tonelli, M., Jun, M., & Donald, M. (2017). A scoping review of adult chronic kidney disease clinical pathways for primary care. *Nephrology Dialysis Transplantation, 32*(5), 838–846.
  Access: https://academic.oup.com/ndt/article-lookup/doi/10.1093/ndt/gfw208
  Grey Literature Search Methods: Targeted searching of specific websites, web checklist *Grey Matters: A Practical Tool for Searching Health-Related Grey Literature*, and Google searching limiting to specific countries (such as Australia).
- **Source**: Canadian Institute of Health Information. (2011). Urban physical environments and health inequalities. *Literature Search Methodology Paper*.
  Access: https://www.cihi.ca/en/cphi_upe_litsearch_method_en.pdf
  Grey Literature Search Methods: Targeted searching of specific websites. Includes an extensive write-up of search methods and screening of research for inclusion. The article sorting form may be especially useful.
- **Source**: Toppenberg-Pejcic, D., Noyes, J., Allen, T., Alexander, N., Vanderford, M., and Gamhewage, G. (2017). Rapid grey literature evidence review to support the guideline on emergency risk communication. *WHO Guidelines on Emergency Risk Communication.*

Access: http://www.who.int/risk-communication/guidance/process/Final-Report-Rapid-Grey-Lit-Review.pdf?ua=1

Grey Literature Search Methods: Databases searched and targeted searching of websites. WHO experts also were queried for grey literature document suggestions. This report also provides a great example of setting an inclusion/exclusion criterion, data extraction, critical appraisal of sources, and analysis of results. Appendix 1 provides an outline of the grey literature search strategy and list of sources searched.

- **Source**: Enticott, J., Buck, K., & Shawyer, F. (2017). Finding "hard to find" literature on hard to find groups: A novel technique to search grey literature on refugees and asylum seekers. *International Journal of Methods in Psychiatric Research*.

  Access: https://www.ncbi.nlm.nih.gov/pubmed/?term=Finding+%E2%80%9Chard+to+find%E2%80%9D+literature+on+hard+to+find+groups%3A+A

  Grey Literature Search Methods: Targeted website searching, Google searching, and Google Scholar searches. This article discusses limiting the search time to manage the scope of a systematic grey literature search. The article also provides highly detailed examples of selecting inclusion/exclusion criteria, prioritizing sources of grey literature, and critical appraisal of grey literature documents.

- **Source**: Avery, J. C., Bowden, J. A., Dono, J., Gibson, O. R., Brownbill, A., Keech, W., Roder, D., & Miller, C. L. (2017). Sugar-sweetened beverage consumption, correlates and interventions among Australian Aboriginal and Torres Strait Islander communities: A scoping review protocol. *BMJ Open*, *7*(7), e016431.

  Access: http://bmjopen.bmj.com/content/7/7/e016431.long

  Grey Literature Search Methods: Outlines the process that will be used for searching Google and relevant databases. This article provides an example of a protocol for a future grey literature search.

- **Source**: Wilson, D., Gill, C., Olaghere, A., & McClure, D. (2016). Juvenile curfew effects on criminal behavior and victimization: A systematic review. *Campbell Systematic Reviews*, *12*(3).

  Access: https://campbellcollaboration.org/media/k2/attachments/Wilson_Review_Curfew_1.pdf

  Grey Literature Search Methods: Includes targeted searching of specific websites and database searches. See the search notes for detailed information on sources searched and record keeping for search strategy.

- **Source**: Adams, J., Hillier-Brown, F. C., Moore, H. J., Lake, A. A., Araujo-Soares, V., White, M., & Summerbell, C. (2016). Searching and synthesising "grey literature" and "grey information" in public health: Critical reflections on three case studies. *Systematic reviews*, *5*(1), 164.

Access: https://www.ncbi.nlm.nih.gov/pmc/articles/PMC5041336/

Grey Literature Search Methods: This article discusses the benefits and drawbacks of various search approaches, including database searching and using Internet search engines. Search reproducibility, data management, and extraction are also addressed.

- **Source**: Rosella, L., Bowman, C., Pach, B., Morgan, S., Fitzpatrick, T., & Goel, V. (2016). The development and validation of a meta-tool for quality appraisal of public health evidence: Meta Quality Appraisal Tool (MetaQAT). *Public Health*, *136*, 57–65.

  Access: http://www.sciencedirect.com/science/article/pii/S00333 50615004370?via%3Dihub

  Grey Literature Search Methods: Targeted searching of specific websites such as the National Institute for Health and Clinical Excellence (NICE) and the European Centre for Disease Prevention and Control (ECDC). Select institutional repositories were also searched.

- **Source**: Briscoe, S. (2015). Web searching for systematic reviews: A case study of reporting standards in the UK Health Technology Assessment programme. *BMC Research Notes*, *8*(1), 153.

  Access: https://www.ncbi.nlm.nih.gov/pmc/articles/PMC4406036/

  Grey literature Search Methods: This study outlines the Web searching methods used to identify grey literature sources. It includes a discussion about Google searches and targeted searching of specific websites, along with a discussion of search transparency and reproducibility.

- **Source**: Godin, K., Stapleton, J., Kirkpatrick, S. I., Hanning, R. M., & Leatherdale, S. T. (2015). Applying systematic review search methods to the grey literature: A case study examining guidelines for school-based breakfast programs in Canada. *Systematic Reviews*, *4*(1), 138.

  Access: https://www.ncbi.nlm.nih.gov/pmc/articles/PMC4619264/

  Grey Literature Search Methods: Utilizes databases, topic-specific Google Custom Search engines, targeted searching of specific websites, and contacting individuals. This study also provides impressive examples of setting inclusion/exclusion criteria and a template for conducting future grey literature searches.

- **Source**: Mahood, Q., Van Eerd, D., & Irvin, E. (2014). Searching for grey literature for systematic reviews: Challenges and benefits. *Research Synthesis Methods* *5*(3), 221–234.

  Access: http://onlinelibrary.wiley.com/doi/10.1002/jrsm.1106/abstract

  Grey Literature Search Methods: Search methods include database searching, Web search engines, and hand searching. This article also provides much insight on the process of a detailed grey literature search on participatory ergonomics.

- **Source**: Bradley, L. A., Palomaki, G., Gutman, S., Samson, D. J., & Aronson, N. (2013). PCA3 testing for the diagnosis and management of prostate cancer. *Agency for Healthcare Research and Quality: Comparative Effectiveness Reviews 98*. Report No. 13-EHC030-E.

  Access: https://www.ncbi.nlm.nih.gov/books/NBK132752/?report=reader

  Grey Literature Search Methods: Clinical trial registries, conference publications, organizations publishing guidance/review documents, and government documents. See Appendix C for detailed information on sources searched and record keeping for search strategy.

- **Source**: Hamilton Lopez, M., Singer Cohen, R., & Holve, E. (December 2012). Building the informatics infrastructure for comparative effectiveness research (CER): A review of the grey literature. *EDM Forum, Academy Health.*

  Access: http://www.academyhealth.org/publications/2012-12/building-informatics-infrastructure-comparative-effectiveness-research-cer

  Grey Literature Search Methods: Outlines a detailed search process for Google searching for grey literature and targeted searching of specific websites. Also addresses refining database search strategies for grey literature.

BEST PRACTICES FOR GREY LITERATURE SEARCHING

As discussed in previous chapters, grey literature search guidelines from knowledge exchange organizations such as Cochrane and the Campbell Collaboration can vary. Past research has also documented the lack of specific guidance for grey literature searching—there is currently no gold standard for grey literature searching (Conn, 2003; Bellefontaine, 2014; Guistini, 2006). But grey literature's paramount contribution to the evidence base is becoming more frequently acknowledged (Pisa Declaration on Policy Development for Grey Literature Resources Statement of Intent, 2014). As mentioned, an increasing array of methods are being used to locate relevant grey lit documents, but these methods have not been standardized. As time passes, hopefully more validated grey literature search methods will be published. What we have now is a bit reminiscent of Inspector Clouseau in the movie *A Shot in the Dark*: "I believe everything and I believe nothing. I suspect everyone and I suspect no one." A patchwork quilt of recommended search processes and standards *is* available, but the information is too fragmentary to draw a decisive conclusion on what works best.

CONCLUSION

Before a grey literature search is underway, there are varying reasons to develop an outline of the goal of the search. Both the librarian and the patron need to take the time to answer a copious number of questions so the right decisions can be made about conducting the search strategy. As the American poet Henry Wadsworth said, "Great is the art of beginning, but greater is the art of *ending*." A grey literature search needs to be structured properly from the very beginning, and the results must be recorded appropriately in order to reach a triumphant conclusion.

APPENDIX

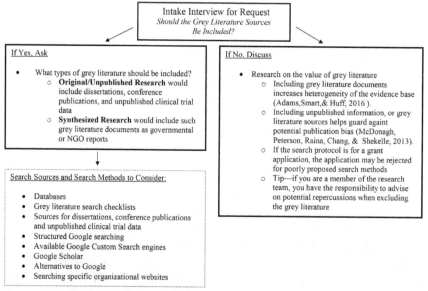

Figure 10.1   Decision Aid for Inclusion of Grey Literature for Inclusion as Part of a Search Protocol. *Figure created by author.*

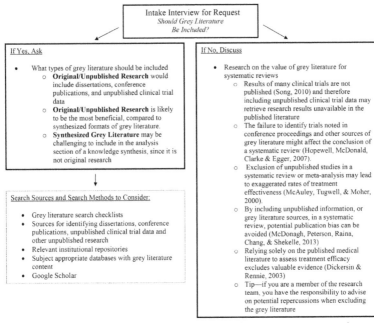

Figure 10.2 Decision Aid for Inclusion of Grey Literature to Systematic Reviews, Scoping Reviews and Other Knowledge Synthesis. *Figure created by author.*

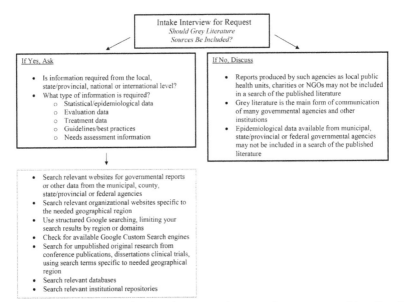

Figure 10.3 Decision Aid for locating Grey Literature for Requests with a Specific Regional or National Focus. *Figure created by author.*

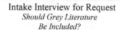

Figure 10.4   **Decision Aid for Inclusion of Grey Literature for Quick Requests.** *Figure created by author.*

BIBLIOGRAPHY

Adams, R. J., Smart, P., & Huff, A. S. (2017). Shades of grey: guidelines for working with the grey literature in systematic reviews for management and organizational studies. *International Journal of Management Reviews, 19*(4), 432–454.

Altschuld, J. W., & Witkin, B. R. (2000). *From needs assessment to action: Transforming needs into solution strategies.* Sage.

Bellefontaine, S. P., & Lee, C. M. (2014). Between black and white: Examining grey literature in meta-analyses of psychological research. *Journal of Child and Family Studies, 23*(8), 1378–1388.

Benzies, K. M., Premji, S., Hayden, K. A., & Serrett, K. (2006). State-of-the-evidence reviews: Advantages and challenges of including grey literature. *Worldviews on Evidence-Based Nursing, 3*(2), 55–61.

Bielska, I. (2009). *Using Population Health Surveys to Measure the use of Services and the Prevalence of Psychiatric and/or Behavioural Conditions in Individuals with an Intellectual Disability,*

Blackhall, K., & Kerr, K. (2007). Finding studies for inclusion in systematic reviews of interventions for injury prevention the importance of grey and unpublished literature. *Injury Prevention: Journal of the International Society for Child and Adolescent Injury Prevention, 13*(5), 359.

Bopp, R. E., & Smith, L. C. (Eds.). (2011). *Reference and Information Services: An Introduction: An Introduction.* ABC-CLIO.

Conn, V. S., Valentine, J. C., Cooper, H. M., & Rantz, M. J. (2003). Grey literature in meta-analyses. *Nursing Research, 52*(4), 256–261.

Cook, D. J., Guyatt, G. H., Ryan, G., Clifton, J., Buckingham, L., Willan, A., et al. (1993). Should unpublished data be included in meta-analyses?: Current convictions and controversies. *JAMA, 269*(21), 2749–2753.

Discussion Papers. (2013). In *Collins.com*. Retrieved from https://www. collinsdictionary.com/dictionary/english/discussion-paper.

Gehanno, J., Rollin, L., & Darmoni, S. (2013). Is the coverage of Google Scholar enough to be used alone for systematic reviews. *BMC Medical Informatics and Decision Making, 13*(1), 7.

Giustini, D. (2006). Finding the hard to finds. [PowerPoint Slides] Retrieved from https://www.slideshare.net/giustinid/ finding-the-hard-to-finds-searching-for-grey-gray-literature-2006.

Goodman, M. (2015). *Future crimes: Everything is connected, everyone is vulnerable and what we can do about it.* Anchor.

Hammerstrøm, K., Wade, A., Jørgensen, A. K., & Hammerstrøm, K. (2010). Searching for studies. *Education, 54*, 11.3.

Hartling, L., Featherstone, R., Nuspl, M., Shave, K., Dryden, D. M., & Vandermeer, B. (2017). Grey literature in systematic reviews: A cross-sectional study of the contribution of non-English reports, unpublished studies and dissertations to the results of meta-analyses in child-relevant reviews. *BMC Medical Research Methodology, 17*(1), 64.

Hopewell, S., McDonald, S., Clarke, M. J., & Egger, M. (2007). Grey literature in meta-analyses of randomized trials of health care interventions. Cochrane Database of Systematic Reviews 2007, Issue 2. Art. No.: MR000010. DOI: 10.1002/14651858. MR000010.pub3.

Lefebvre, C., Manheimer, E., & Glanville, J. (2011). Cochrane handbook for systematic reviews of interventions version 5.1. 0 [updated March 2011].

McAuley, L., Tugwell, P., & Moher, D. (2000). Does the inclusion of grey literature influence estimates of intervention effectiveness reported in meta-analyses? *Lancet, 356*(9237), 1228–1231.

McGowan, J., & Sampson, M. (2005). Systematic reviews need systematic searchers. *Journal of the Medical Library Association: JMLA, 93*(1), 74–80.

Orenic, K., & Beestrum, M. (2008). *The CRAP Test.*

Paez, A. (2017). Gray literature: An important resource in systematic reviews. *Journal of evidence-based medicine, 10*(3), 233–240.

Pariser, E. (2011). *The filter bubble: What the internet is hiding from you.* Penguin UK.

Pisa Declaration on Policy Development for Grey Literature Resources Statement of Intent, April 7, 2014.

Poladian, C., & Stone, J. (2015, 26 Nov. Web. 7 Feb. 2015). "Tour the Deep Web: Illegal marketplaces, book clubs and Everything in between." *International Business Times: IBT Pulse.*

Rothstein, H. R., Hopewell, S., Cooper, H., Hedges, L. V., & Valentine, J. C. (2009). The handbook of research synthesis and meta-analysis. *New York: Russell Sage Foundation.*

Sullivan, S. M., Coyle, D., & Wells, G. (2014). What guidance are researchers given on how to present network meta-analyses to end-users such as policymakers and clinicians? A systematic review. *PloS One, 9*(12), e113277.

Tyndall, J. (2008). How low can you go? Towards a hierarchy of grey literature. Retrieved from https://dspace.flinders.edu.au/xmlui/handle/2328/3326.

Wilczynski, N. L., McKibbon, K. A., & Haynes, R. B. (2011). Sensitive Clinical Queries retrieved relevant systematic reviews as well as primary studies: an analytic survey. *Journal of clinical epidemiology, 64*(12), 1341–1349.

Chapter 11

Grey Literature

Keeping Current with Emerging Trends and Suggested Learning Tools

Grey literature is not a static form of publication. There have been agreed-upon definitions of "white literature" for a long time. What constitutes an academic journal article or novel is *generally* agreed upon. In comparison, grey literature is transforming constantly (Schmidmaier, 1983), and "grey literature" in and of itself is indeed a bit of a catchall term. Grey literature can be applied to multitudinous formats and types of documents, and newly created types of grey lit can often be added to the already elephantine wellspring of "grey" information. This book has attempted to capture the present state of grey literature and the current relevant sources for searching grey literature. But the hazard is that once this book has gone to press, new types and sources of grey literature will belatedly emerge. And sadly, some invaluable sources currently listed in this book for searching grey literature may become unavailable. As James Thurber said, "The past is an old armchair in the attic, the present an ominous ticking sound, and the *future* is anybody's guess." But hopefully the following resources listed below will be a bellwether keeping updating on future directions in grey literature.

CONFERENCE ON GREY LITERATURE AND REPOSITORIES

- **National Repository of Grey Literature**
  Access: https://nrgl.techlib.cz/conference/
  About: Hosted by the Czech National Library, the goal of this conference is knowledge dissemination of grey literature from an international perspective, with a focus on grey literature and digital repositories.

255

- **GreyNet International**

  Access: http://www.greynet.org/

  About: Also known as the Grey Literature Network Service. This is the go-to source for keeping up with trends in grey literature, especially from a global perspective. GreyNet International is a premier source for information on open access, publication, education and raising public awareness of grey literature, and innovative research on grey literature. GreyNet is also a point of access for grey literature resources such as:
  - The International Directory for Organizations in Grey Literature
  - The Grey Journal
  - The Grey Guide: Repository and Guide to Good Practices and Resources in the Grey Literature
  - GreySource Index
  - The GreyNet Newsletter

  If you want to add just one source for keeping current on developments, educational opportunities, and newly emerging sources such as repositories for grey literature, look no further, as this is it!

- **Grey Literature Strategies**

  Access: http://greylitstrategies.info/

  About: Funded by the Australian Research Council, Grey Literature Strategies is a source for keeping current on the latest trends in grey literature and best practices regarding its management and production. It is also a prime resource for keeping current on grey literature trends across the Pacific.

- **Grey Literature**

  Access: http://hlwiki.slais.ubc.ca/index.php/Grey_literature

  About: Produced by HLWIKI Canada, this resource is matchless for keeping current on state-of-the-art sources for searching grey literature. It includes information on the various definitions of grey literature, grey literature search methods, and other learning resources, such as posted presentations and handouts. It is also a prime source for Canadian resources on grey literature.

- **GL Conference Proceedings**

  Access: http://www.textrelease.com/publications/proceedings.html

  About: Also known as the International Conference on Grey Literature, the GL Conference Proceedings are an unmatched source for keeping up to date on the "new wave" in grey literature, including the dynamic changes in the typology of grey literature. Papers presented at past conferences can be browsed online, but a subscription is required.

- **OpenGrey**

  Access: http://www.opengrey.eu

About: OpenGrey focuses on European grey literature. While OpenGrey is a source for identifying European grey literature publications (see Chapter 2), it is also an excellent resource for keeping current on the latest grey literature trends from a European Perspective.

ADDITIONAL LEARNING TOOLS

- **LibGuides**
  About: There are LibGuides galore on grey literature. Good old Google is best for locating LibGuides on grey literature—simply Google "LibGuides" and "grey literature" or "gray literature." The advantage of LibGuides is that individual guides will often focus on searching for grey literature in specific disciplines, such as nursing or public policy.
- **LISA: Library and Information Science Abstracts**
  Access: http://www.proquest.com/products-services/lisa-set-c.html
  About: LISA indexes more than 440 library and information studies–related periodicals from 68 countries and is essential for searching the scholarly research on grey literature. Setting up search alerts is an easy way to track new academic research on grey literature.
- **PubMed**
  Access: https://www.ncbi.nlm.nih.gov/pubmed/
  About: The PubMed database is the go-to source for accessing research on life sciences and biomedical topics. But PubMed can also be used to identify grey literature search methods—simply search for "grey literature" or "gray literature" in the Title or Abstract fields. A PubMed search alert is also one of the easiest ways to keep up-to-date with current and new search methods for locating grey literature publications in the life sciences and medicine. If you are interested in tracking documented research methods for locating grey literature, setting up an alert with the phrase "grey literature/gray literature" in the Title or Abstract is the best bet.
- **Google Scholar**
  Access: https://scholar.google.com/
  About: Google Scholar is a free search engine for searching multidisciplinary academic research. Like PubMed, Google Scholar can also be used to research grey literature search methods, and Google Scholar alerts with "grey/gray literature" as a search term can be used to track new multidisciplinary publications that mention searching grey literature sources. In order to receive the most on-topic results, it is best to limit your search to the term "grey literature" or "gray literature" in the Title or Abstract fields.

ADDITIONAL RECOMMENDATIONS

Keeping informed on the latest in grey literature may seem like a formid-able task, particularly as the landscape of grey literature does not possess a definitive form and is relevant to an abundant number of disciplines. Many conferences and events hosted by such organizations as the Medical Library Association and the Special Library Association may provide opportunities to attend presentations or continuing education courses on grey literature. But the foremost takeaway is that grey literature is an indispensable and enduring source of information, and it will most definitely continue to transform itself over the coming years. It can be demanding to keep current with grey litera-ture, but in the spirit of Emily Dickinson, "You can stay young as long as you learn."

BIBLIOGRAPHY

Schmidmaier, D. (1983). *Serials and "Grey Literature."* Proceedings of the IATUL Conferences, Purdue University, Paper 16, retrieved from http://docs.lib.purdue.edu/iatul/1983/papers/16.

Index

About the Author

Sarah Bonato is a reference/research librarian at the Centre for Addiction and Mental Health (CAMH) in Toronto, Ontario. She is a graduate of the MIS program at the University of Toronto and has a BA in Sociology from Kalamazoo College. At the CAMH Library, she is the team leader for reference, research, and user services. Her other work activities include research, systematic-review/scoping-review searching, instruction, search coaching, supervising library students on special projects, and writing for the CAMH Library blog. She has also been listed as the coauthor of systematic reviews/guidelines in the subject area of behavioral health. Like many a librarian, she has cats and scads of books.